"THE MOST IMPORTANT BOOK OF THE DECADE!"
—Jim C. Cates
Director of the University of Texas
Adult Performance Level Project

"HE WRITES WITH SO MUCH PASSION AND GRACE, like a wrathful angel set loose upon the world with words. . . . If it is a sin to read with pleasure about other people's illiteracy, then Kozol makes us deeply guilty." —Barbara Ehrenreich, in *Mother Jones*

"COMPELLING . . . GRIPPING STORIES MAKE A BOLD AND IMPASSIONED STATEMENT about a subject we can no longer afford to overlook. It is a message worth reading and heeding."
—*Dallas Times Herald*

"AN ANGRY BOOK AND AN IMPORTANT ONE. . . . Its anger is legitimate; it rightfully accuses us of ignoring our illiterates. Then it goes on to suggest remedies we can't afford to ignore."
—Harold Howe II, former U.S.
Commissioner of Education

"KOZOL HAS FASHIONED A JEWEL OF A BOOK, ONE THAT EVERY AMERICAN SHOULD BE ABLE TO READ."—*Newsday*

(For more acclaim, please turn page. . . .)

Jonathan Kozol is the author of *Death at an Early Age* (winner of the National Book Award), *The Night Is Dark, Free Schools,* and other books. He has received awards from the Guggenheim, Ford, and Rockefeller Foundations and has taught at Yale University and, most recently, at South Boston High School.

Jonathan Kozol

ILLITERATE AMERICA

A PLUME BOOK

NEW AMERICAN LIBRARY

NEW YORK AND SCARBOROUGH, ONTARIO

This is an authorized reprint of a hardcover edition
published by Anchor Press/Doubleday & Company, Inc.

 PLUME TRADEMARK REG. U.S. PAT. OFF. AND FOREIGN COUNTRIES
REG. TRADEMARK—MARCA REGISTRADA
HECHO EN HARRISONBURG, VA., U.S.A.

SIGNET, SIGNET CLASSIC, MENTOR, PLUME,
MERIDIAN and NAL BOOKS are published *in the United
States* by New American Library, 1633 Broadway, New
York, New York 10019, *in Canada* by The New American
Library of Canada Limited, 81 Mack Avenue, Scarborough,
Ontario M1L 1M8

Library of Congress Cataloging-in-Publication Data

Kozol, Jonathan.
    Illiterate America.

    1. Literacy—United States. I. Title.
LC151.K68   1985b   370′.973   85-29742
ISBN 0-452-25807-3

First Plume Printing, March, 1986

1 2 3 4 5 6 7 8 9

PRINTED IN THE UNITED STATES OF AMERICA

For my mother and my father

This book evolved out of a year of study made possible by a fellowship granted to the author by the Humanities Division of The Rockefeller Foundation. I am deeply grateful to Alberta Arthurs, Steven Lavine, and the Trustees of the Foundation for their generous support.

The final writing of this book was completed under a fellowship from the John Simon Guggenheim Memorial Foundation. I would like to thank the Trustees of the Foundation and, in particular, Gordon Ray and Stephen Schlesinger for a vote of confidence which allowed me both the time and the reflection to deepen and rethink a work which has, in a real sense, been germinating now for almost eighteen years.

CONTENTS

PART THREE
Beyond Utility

I can't help thinking of the Venetian Republic in their last half-century. Like us, they had once been fabulously lucky. They had become rich, as we did, by accident. They had acquired immense political skill, just as we have. A good many of them were tough-minded, realistic, patriotic men. They knew, just as clearly as we know, that the current of history had begun to flow against them. Many of them gave their minds to working out ways to keep going. It would have meant breaking the pattern into which they had crystallised. They were fond of the pattern, just as we are fond of ours. They never found the will to break it.

–C. P. Snow

AUTHOR'S INTRODUCTION

It was in autumn 1964, fresh from Harvard College, from a term at Oxford, and from the indulgence of three years as an expatriate and social dropout on the fringes of the literary life on the Left Bank of Paris, that I returned to the United States and chose, for reasons which I do not wholly understand, to find a job within a fourth grade classroom of the Boston Public Schools. I had never read the works of Gunnar Myrdal, Michael Harrington, or Robert Coles. But it was in that year in Boston that I saw before my eyes a world of suffering, of hopelessness and fear, that I could never have imagined in the privileged and insulated decades of my childhood and schooling.

Up until 1964 I had been to Roxbury on very few occasions. Sometimes, on a Wednesday night, I had accompanied my father as we drove into the city to drop off the live-in maid who cleaned our house and cooked my meals and cared for me and for my sister six days out of seven. Thursday was the maid's day off. I used to wonder what she did, whether she had children and a household of her own, whether she suffered for the time in which she could not see them, how they could manage with no mother in their home. I knew that she was both a competent and gentle-hearted woman. She could clean and she could cook and she could offer love unstinted. I knew she couldn't read or write. That didn't seem to count. She did not need to read in order to perform the work of polishing the silverware and scrubbing kitchen floors.

When I asked her one day whether she had children, she replied that she had three. They lived in Roxbury with their grandmother. I worried about this sometimes, but not often. Not by the intention of my mother and my father, but by the enormous distance that divided my suburban life from anything that happened on that distant street of darkened houses where we dropped her off on Wednesday nights, I was inoculated against pangs of conscience. My curiosity about her children and about their lives was rapidly dissolved as I proceeded to evolve the plans for my career.

In 1964 I learned at last, and with a wave of shame and fear that turned before long into an unbounded and compensatory rage, that the children of our colored maid had been denied the childhood and happiness and care that had been given to me by their mother. I knew now that these children had been robbed of childhood. I had not robbed them: I had been recipient of stolen goods. What had been stolen from them seemed unspeakable: a crime, an evil past imagination.

Few of the children that I met in 1964 knew how to read and write. In the springtime of their fourth grade year, most of those kids were lucky to be reading at the level of the second grade. As I came to know their families and friends I realized that their situation was the norm, not the exception. Their parents were not all domestic maids. A few had better jobs; a larger number had no jobs at all. A few could read and write and help their children to make up for what they lost within that medieval school; most of their parents could not read beyond a very limited degree. Many could not read at all.

In 1965 I rented an apartment in their neighborhood. I lived in that neighborhood, then in others not far off, for eighteen years. The children that I came to know during that year in Boston are no longer children now. They will not be given any second chance to live those years of their imperfect childhood again. Even in the richest, most developed and advanced society, you do not get to live your childhood twice.

People who read *Death at an Early Age* when it was published in the 1960s meet me today and ask me sometimes whether I know what happened to the children I described. "What happened to Stephen? Angelina? Frederick? Did they somehow manage to survive?"

Stephen called me from prison this winter. That is one answer to the question.

Frederick is not yet in prison. He is a successful pimp. He tells me that he deals in drugs. He cannot read. He is not married. He has several children he has never seen.

That is another answer.

Angelina has three children, lives on welfare in the neighborhood where I first met her as an eight-year-old. She cannot read the Boston *Globe*, advertisements for jobs, or welfare forms. She cannot read the homework papers of her children. She will not read this book.

That is another answer.

The senior editor of one of New York's largest publishers discussed with me the terms on which he would accept this book for publication. He did it in person, in his office, in a calm and reasonable voice. "A book on ethics will not sell in 1985. If you could somehow give it a more hard-nosed focus—something like 'The Billion Dollar Error'—something like that would hit the reader in the pocketbook . . . I would like to do it . . . Let me know . . ."

That is another answer.

In one of his greatest and most tortured works, William Faulkner told the story of a slaveowner named Sutpen. After certain years of muscular and ardent desperation, Sutpen won his stake of land and employed a team of "wild" slaves to make the black soil prosper. Sutpen's sin was that he was unable to acknowledge his mulatto son. His fate was that of other men and nations that disown their young. The refusal to acknowledge those who are our sons or daughters, brothers, sisters, neighbors, fellow citizens, or former students, but whom we have relegated to statistical oblivion, holds some dangers that a sane society would not ignore. Societal denial of the crime by which it lives demonstrates political ineptitude and ethical betrayal; but it also tells us of that civic pride that goes before a fall.

My feelings on this subject are too strong to be contained within an understated work. Certain scholars will be forced to view the consequences with distaste; others, I think, will understand that any other tone, for someone who has seen the demolition of these children, would be less than human.

These are some reasons why I have the obligation to create this book.

PART ONE

*Invisible Minority:
The Growing Crisis
of Illiterate America*

1

A Third of the Nation Cannot Read These Words

> You have to be careful not to get into situations where it would leak
> out . . . If somebody gives you something to read, you make believe
> you read it . . .*

He is meticulous and well-defended.

He gets up in the morning, showers, shaves, and dresses in a dark gray business suit, then goes downstairs and buys a New York *Times* from the small newsstand on the corner of his street. Folding it neatly, he goes into the subway and arrives at work at 9 A.M.

He places the folded New York *Times* next to the briefcase on his desk and sets to work on graphic illustrations for the advertising copy that is handed to him by the editor who is his boss.

"Run over this with me. Just make sure I get the gist of what you really want."

The editor, unsuspecting, takes this as a reasonable request. In the process of expanding on his copy, he recites the language of the text: a language that is instantly imprinted on the illustrator's mind.

At lunch he grabs the folded copy of the New York *Times*, carries it with him to a coffee shop, places it beside his plate, eats a sandwich, drinks a beer, and soon heads back to work.

* For this and all other items of quotation, documentation, or public record, see Notes beginning on page 225.

At 5 p.m., he takes his briefcase and his New York *Times*, waits for the elevator, walks two blocks to catch an uptown bus, stops at a corner store to buy some groceries, then goes upstairs. He carefully unfolds his New York *Times*. He places it with mechanical precision on a pile of several other recent copies of the New York *Times*. There they will remain until, when two or three more copies have been added, he will take all but the one most recent and consign them to the trash that goes into a plastic bag that will be left for pickup by the truck that comes around during the night and, with a groaning roar, collects and crushes and compresses all the garbage of the occupants of this and other residential buildings of New York.

Then he returns upstairs. He opens the refrigerator, snaps the top from a cold can of Miller's beer, and turns on the TV.

Next day, trimly dressed and cleanly shaven, he will buy another New York *Times*, fold it neatly, and proceed to work. He is a rather solitary man. People in his office view him with respect as someone who is self-contained and does not choose to join in casual conversation. If somebody should mention something that is in the news, he will give a dry, sardonic answer based upon the information he has garnered from TV.

He is protected against the outside world. Someday he will probably be trapped. It has happened before; so he can guess that it will happen again. Defended for now against humiliation, he is not defended against fear. He tells me that he has recurrent dreams.

"Somebody says: WHAT DOES THIS MEAN? I stare at the page. A thousand copies of the New York *Times* run past me on a giant screen. Even before I am awake, I start to scream."

If it is of any comfort to this man, he should know that he is not alone. Twenty-five million American adults cannot read the poison warnings on a can of pesticide, a letter from their child's teacher, or the front page of a daily paper. An additional 35 million read only at a level which is less than equal to the full survival needs of our society.

Together, these 60 million people represent more than one third of the entire adult population.

The largest numbers of illiterate adults are white, native-born Americans. In proportion to population, however, the figures are higher for blacks and Hispanics than for whites. Sixteen percent of white adults, 44 percent of blacks, and 56 percent of Hispanic citizens are functional or marginal illiterates. Figures for the younger generation of black adults are increasing. Forty-seven percent of all black seventeen-year-olds are functionally illiterate. That figure is expected to climb to 50 percent by 1990.

Fifteen percent of recent graduates of urban high schools read at less than sixth grade level. One million teenage children between twelve and seventeen cannot read above the third grade level. Eighty-five percent of juveniles who come before the courts are functionally illiterate. Half the heads of households classified below the poverty line by federal standards cannot read an eighth grade book. Over one third of mothers who receive support from welfare are functionally illiterate. Of 8 million unemployed adults, 4 to 6 million lack the skills to be retrained for hi-tech jobs.

The United States ranks forty-ninth among 158 member nations of the U.N. in its literacy levels.

In Prince George's County, Maryland, 30,000 adults cannot read above a fourth grade level. The largest literacy program in this county reaches one hundred people yearly.

In Boston, Massachusetts, 40 percent of the adult population is illiterate. The largest organization that provides funds to the literacy programs of the city reaches 700 to 1,000 people.

In San Antonio, Texas, 152,000 adults have been documented as illiterate. In a single municipal district of San Antonio, over half the adult population is illiterate in English. Sixty percent of the same population sample is illiterate in Spanish. Three percent of adults in this district are at present being served.

In the State of Utah, which ranks number one in the United States in the percent of total budget allocated to the education sector, 200,000 adults lack the basic skills for employment. Less than 5 percent of Utah's population is black or Hispanic.

Together, all federal, state, municipal, and private literacy programs in the nation reach a maximum of 4 percent of the illiterate population. The federal government spends $100 million yearly to address the needs of 60 million people. The President has asked that this sum be reduced to $50 million. Even at the present level, direct federal allocations represent about $1.65 per year for each illiterate.

In 1982 the Executive Director of the National Advisory Council on Adult Education estimated that the government would need to spend about $5 billion to eradicate or seriously reduce the problem. The commission he served was subsequently dismissed by presidential order.

Fourteen years ago, in his inaugural address as governor of Georgia, a future President of the United States proclaimed his dedication to the crisis of Illiterate America. "Our people are our most precious possession . . . Every adult illiterate . . . is an indictment of us all . . . If Switzerland and Israel and other people can end illiteracy, then so can we. The responsibility is our own and our government's. I will not shirk this responsibility."

Today the number of identified nonreaders is three times greater than the number Jimmy Carter had in mind when he described this challenge and defined it as an obligation that he would not shirk.

On April 26, 1983, pointing to the literacy crisis and to a collapse in standards at the secondary and the college levels, the National Commission on Excellence in Education warned: "Our Nation is at risk."

2

Matters of Equivocation: Dangers of the Numbers Game

> Donny wanted me to read to him. I told Donny: "I can't read." He
> said: "Mommy, you sit down. I'll read it to you." I tried it one day,
> reading from the pictures. Donny looked at me. He said, "Mommy,
> that's not right." He's only five. He knew I couldn't read . . . Oh, it
> matters. You *believe* it matters!

One of the classic methods of equivocation, in literacy as in every other area
where social justice is at stake, is to adhere to endless, self-repeating statements
that "we don't yet know enough," "we need more research," "we are just not
sure." A certain degree of caution is essential in an area of human misery that,
by its very nature, challenges detection and fends off enumeration. A false
humility, on the other hand—what certain activists have aptly called "Fake
Humblehood"—can also be self-serving. Politicians can exploit a laborious sequence of reiterated doubts to postpone action even in those areas of which they
are quite certain. Intellectuals can underwrite their income while purporting to
be doing "the essential groundwork" that has already been done ten years before.

Dozens of studies of this subject have been conducted since the early
1970s. Many of them advance the ritual of recondite complexification to the
point at which the reader's main reaction is exhaustion in the face of numbers
and capitulation in the face of doubts as to "the proper definition" of the very
words we use and "the criteria" by which we speak of an illiterate man or
woman "in the context of American society." Fifteen years later, the same

debates take place; and some of those who were contributors to the debates of
1970 are telling us once more that we may not yet have at hand "sufficient
information" to be sure of "where we go from here . . ."

Taking action even in the context of a limited confusion ought to be one
obligation of a conscientious scholar; but the confusion in this instance is compounded by the contradictory information that emerges from a multitude of
government reports.

The U.S. Department of Education tells us (1983) that 23 million American adults are totally or functionally illiterate. An additional 23 million function
at a level which is marginal at best.

In a separate statement, the Office of Vocational and Adult Education
states that "74 million Americans . . . function at a marginal level or less."

A third release, distributed by the White House on September 7, 1983,
states that "26 million Americans are functionally illiterate . . . An additional
46 million Americans may be considered marginally functional, for a total of 72
million Americans who function at a marginal level or below."

In another statement, the Director of the National Institute of Education
tells us (January 1984) that an estimated 23 million adults are functionally
illiterate while, six months later, *Newsweek* reports that 26 million are functionally illiterate. *Newsweek* adds that this is one fifth of the adult population, a
calculation which diminishes the adult population of the nation by 40 million
people.

The Bureau of the Census meanwhile states that "virtually 100 percent" of
"the general population" are literate but that the figure is "about 96 percent"
for "members of minority groups." The Bureau drew most of its figures from a
written answer to a printed form.

A natural reaction to this arithmetic saga might be the unfortunate
humility that paralyzes action on the pretext that "nobody knows." In actual
fact, we do know now a great deal more than when the numbers game began.
Some of the most compelling evidence has been assembled in a Ford Foundation study carried out by David Harman and Carman St. John Hunter and
published in 1979. More recent data gathered in the six years since provides us
with a realistic picture of the crisis we confront.

In 1973, the Adult Performance Level (APL), a study carried out at the
University of Texas under the direction of Dr. Norvell Northcutt, employed a
list of sixty-five "objectives"—areas of competence which were associated with
Northcutt's definition of "adult success"—in order to identify how many adults
were unable to cope with the responsibilities of everyday life. Previous efforts
had done little more than to establish "simple literacy" and did so purely on the
basis of the years of school a person had completed. Literacy, by this standard,
indicated little more than the capacity to sign one's name and perhaps to under-

stand a handful of three-letter words. The Texas study therefore represented an important breakthrough in the effort to describe American realities in 1973.

The U.S. Office of Education, applying the standards of the APL, calculated that, during the early 1970s, 57 million Americans did not have the skills required to perform most basic tasks. Of that number, almost 23 million lacked the competencies necessary to function. The remaining 34 million were able to function, "but not proficiently."

Looking at a different body of criteria, Hunter and Harman reported that a maximum of 64 million persons sixteen and over had not completed high school (and were not presently in school) in 1979. While rejecting grade-completion levels as reliable determinants of literacy levels, Hunter and Harman drew attention to the fact that numbers drawn from two entirely different sources (grade completion and the APL) appeared to be so close. Hunter believes that a figure in excess of 60 million is a realistic estimate for 1984.

Calculations from other groups and other scholars indicate that even this is a conservative projection. Harvard professor Jeanne Chall, while understandably impatient with the numbers game, states that total estimates of 75 to 78 million seem to have some merit.

Most important in untangling these numbers, the authors of the APL have made their own updated calculations. They have done so in a manner that can render the statistics less abstract:

Given a paycheck and the stub that lists the usual deductions, 26 percent of adult Americans cannot determine if their paycheck is correct. Thirty-six percent, given a W-4 form, cannot enter the right number of exemptions in the proper places on the form. Forty-four percent, when given a series of "help-wanted" ads, cannot match their qualifications to the job requirements. Twenty-two percent cannot address a letter well enough to guarantee that it will reach its destination. Twenty-four percent cannot add their own correct return address to the same envelope. Twenty percent cannot understand an "equal opportunity" announcement. Over 60 percent, given a series of "for sale" advertisements for products new and used, cannot calculate the difference between prices for a new and used appliance. Over 20 percent cannot write a check that will be processed by their bank—or will be processed in the right amount. Over 40 percent are unable to determine the correct amount of change they should receive, given a cash register receipt and the denomination of the bill used for payment.

From these and other forms of evidence, the APL concludes that 30 million men and women are now "functionally incompetent." Another 54 million "just get by." This total of 84 million far exceeds all other estimates that we have seen.

Rather than throwing up our hands once more, we should recognize some explanations for these latest areas of disagreement. Some of the figures refer to

1973 compilations. Others represent an effort to update these figures, but all methods of updating cannot be identical. No one can be certain which of several methods is the best. Other differences depend on where we draw the line between the categories "functional" and "marginal." Again, this is a somewhat random matter and it simply isn't possible, or worth our time, to try to legislate an arbitrary line. The points that matter, in my own opinion, are the following: Nobody's updated figure for the "functional" and "marginal" together is less than 60 million. The total present adult population (1984) is 174 million. By even the most conservative calculations, then, we are speaking here of well above one third of all American adults.

In recent discussions with Hunter and with the directors of the Texas APL, I have proposed the following minimal estimates for 1984: 25 million reading either not at all or at less than fifth grade level; 35 million additional persons reading at less than ninth grade level. Note that, in both cases, I am speaking of performance, not of years of school attendance.

It requires ninth grade competence to understand the antidote instructions on a bottle of corrosive kitchen lye, tenth grade competence to understand instructions on a federal income tax return, twelfth grade competence to read a life insurance form. Employment qualifications for all but a handful of domestic jobs begin at ninth grade level. I have argued, therefore, that all of these 60 million people should be called "illiterate in terms of U.S. print communication at the present time." Both Hunter and the APL agree that these are cautious figures. These, then, are the figures I have used within this book.

In this discussion I have been obliged to use grade levels as the benchmarks of desirable but unattained proficiency. The need to do this is a function of the need to offer standards that may have some meaning for those citizens whose only reference points are those which are familiar from their years in public school.

Nonetheless, a certain caveat is called for. Grade equivalents have little meaning in an era in which grade completion has, at best, occasional connection with the levels of proficiency that numbers of this sort suggest. Wherever grade levels do appear, it will be helpful to remember that I do not have in mind the level of a person who has "sat it out" in school for three or five or seven or twelve years. I am speaking of a person who can do what those who master the objectives of specific grades in excellent and successful schools can do: not what they are "certified to have attempted."

In this chapter I have also been obliged to make use of the category "functionally illiterate" in order to refer to studies that have been conducted in the past. I do not like this term. Its connotations are all wrong and will be studied later. Wherever possible, I will attempt to use instead two terms of my own choice: "illiterate" in order to refer to those who scarcely read at all; "semiliterate" in order to refer to those whose reading levels are unequal to societal demands. At some moments, for the sake of unencumbered prose, I will combine both categories in the single phrase "Illiterate America." This does not indicate a loss of recognition of the spectrum that extends from marginal ability to none at all. What it does imply is that all 60 million are substantially excluded from the democratic process and the ordinary commerce of a print society. The distinctions are important for the organization of a plan of action; it is the totality, however, which defines a crisis we have yet to meet head-on.

One troublesome objection rears its head whenever we address this situation. Literacy, certain people say, is "an elitist concept," a residue of our excessive education, a "hang-up" from our years at Harvard or Ann Arbor. The ordinary person, whether literate or not, "can do a lot of things that are beyond our own hypertrophied imaginations," possesses simple virtues that elude us, demonstrates an ingenuity and basic hardihood that render us incompetent by contrast, and may only be endangered by our overeager plans. "People like that do very well without us. Why should we encumber them with cultural constraints they do not need? Why burden them with middle class ambitions which they may do very well without? Is literacy going to make someone *happy?*"

The simplest answer is provided by Jeanne Chall: "Does literacy make men happy? Only highly literate people seem to ask [this] question. And only the well-educated seem to say that it does not. They are like the rich who doubt that money makes one happy. Significantly, such doubts come only after they have accumulated enough money and do not have to worry . . . And so with the highly literate. They doubt that literacy will contribute to the happiness of those who are not yet literate only because they themselves use it so well and easily in living, working, playing, and in making choices . . ." So well, indeed, that they are unaware of the advantages and options it affords.

The idealization of "the simple and unlettered human being," unencumbered by our burden of self-serving and at times destructive words, might have some meaning for a people who were not surrounded and conditioned by the print reality from which they are excluded but whose skilled practitioners control the chief determinants of their existence. No community in the United States today, not even one that dwells apart in the most isolated village, is exempt from these determinants.

This, then, is an issue we should put to rest. No matter how decent and how earnest in their views, those who raise such arguments in printed prose deserve at most a swift riposte. Soon enough, they will return to their typewriters.

This much we know, and this much we should have the confidence to state in clean and unencumbered words: Whatever the "right number" and whatever the "right definition," we are speaking of at least one third of all adults who live in the United States in 1984. The cost to our economy, as we shall see, is very great. The cost to our presumptions and our credibility as a democracy is greater still. The cost in needless human pain may be the greatest price of all.

"At this point," wrote Michael Harrington, "I would beg the reader to forget the numbers game. Whatever the precise calibrations, it is obvious that these statistics represent an enormous, an unconscionable amount of human suffering . . . They should be read with a sense of outrage."

Harrington wrote these words in 1962. We have been entangled in the numbers game too long. It is unlikely that we shall escape these rituals with any greater ease today than when those words were written. The only hope, in my belief, lies in that "sense of outrage" which, with few exceptions, has been absent from the academic discourse on this subject for ten years.

In this book I will describe the problem and delineate a plan of action. Finally, I will do my best to shape a vision and refine a definition of that universal humane literacy which has eluded us so long but which represents a sane, essential, and realistic goal for a society that hopes to govern not by the mechanical and docile acquiescence of the governed but by the informed consent of those who are empowered to participate within the act of governance itself. I am speaking, then, not of a single tour de force, a pedagogic space shot or a technological quick fix. I am speaking of a humanistic longing to embark upon a voyage that will take more than a single decade or a single year: a voyage which, in the most capacious sense, will last as long as our adherence to American democracy prevails.

3

The Price We Pay

In 1975, a herd of prime beef cattle was destroyed by accident in Chicago. A feedlot worker could not read the labels on the bags that he found piled in the warehouse and fed poison to the cattle by mistake. He thought that he was adding a nutrition supplement to their feed basins . . .

–story reported in the New York Times

What does illiteracy cost America in dollars?

The Senate Select Committee on Equal Educational Opportunity estimated a figure of $237 billion in unrealized lifetime earnings forfeited by men twenty-five to thirty-four years old who have less than high school level skills. That estimate, made in February 1972, requires serious updating.

Direct costs to business and taxpayers are approximately $20 billion.

Six billion dollars yearly (estimate: mid-1970s) go to child welfare costs and unemployment compensation caused directly by the numbers of illiterate adults unable to perform at standards necessary for available employment.

$6.6 billion yearly (estimate of 1983) is the minimal cost of prison maintenance for an estimated 260,000 inmates—out of a total state and federal prison population of about 440,000—whose imprisonment has been directly linked to functional illiteracy. The prison population represents the single highest concentration of adult illiterates. While criminal conviction of illiterate men and women cannot be identified exclusively with inability to read and write, the fact that 60 percent of prison inmates cannot read above the grade school level surely provides some indication of one major reason for their criminal activity.

Swollen court costs, law-enforcement budgets in those urban areas in which two fifths of all adults are unemployable for lack of literacy skills, not even to speak of the high cost of crime to those who are its victims, cannot be guessed but must be many times the price of prison maintenance.

Several billion dollars go to workers' compensation, damage to industrial equipment, and industrial insurance costs directly caused by on-site accidents related to the inability of workers to read safety warnings, chemical-content designations, and instructions for the operation of complex machines.

While there is no way to prove direct causation in all cases, and while substantial unemployment would exist in any case among some sectors of the population—whether people were illiterate or not—it is reasonable to believe, based only on an update of the isolated items listed here, that we now incur a minimal annual loss of $20 billion in direct industrial and tax expenditures.

Health expenditures necessitated by the inability of the illiterate adult to use preventive health care measures are not documented. We cannot guess the vast expense required for obstetric or abortion services to women whose un-wanted pregnancies are often linked to lack of information caused by inability to read. So too with the cost of mental health care and of rehabilitation programs for drug users and for alcoholics. Emotional stress and frequently uninterrupted desperation are familiar patterns in the life of an illiterate adult. If there is no way to calculate these costs, we can believe that they run into many billions.

Business interests suffer in at least two ways.

In a decade of high unemployment, hundreds of thousands of entry-level and even middle-level jobs remain unfilled for lack of applicants with competence equivalent to need. The *Wall Street Journal* documents, across the nation, "localized difficulties in finding clerical workers, bank tellers, nurses, para-legals . . ." One of the nation's largest job-referral agencies reports that it is now impossible to find the personnel to meet employment orders.

A New York insurance firm reports that 70 percent of its dictated corre-spondence must be retyped "at least once" because secretaries working from recorders do not know how to spell and punctuate correctly. Another insurance firm reports that one illiterate employee mailed out a check for $2,200 in settle-ment of a dental claim. Payment of $22.00 had been authorized.

Less easily documented, but possibly a great deal more important than the problems of the work force, is the loss of contact between business and its clientele. An incorrectly comprehended mailing from a polling agency or from a market research firm is surely more misleading to the agency than one that is not understood at all. Marketing firms spend millions of dollars in the effort to find out what customers exist for planned or present services and products.

Millions of people can't be reached. Millions more will offer useless or misleading answers.

Billing, banking, public disclosure information, customers' rights (above all, the right to be informed of what those "rights" might be) depend upon communication through the mails. Yet even notices of undelivered letters left in the mailbox by the postal service will be read only with difficulty by a minimum of 35 million people. They will not be read at all by 25 million more.

Certified mail, registered letters, items that call for signature (sometimes for payment) on receipt—all depend upon a superstructure of assumptions that can bear no relevance to millions of adult Americans. Most of us already find ourselves perplexed by complicated mailings that purport to tell us why electric service rises in expense each year, stipulate what portion of the bill is due to fuel expense, what portion represents a state or local tax, and advise us that electric power cannot be cut off to those who are "the elderly, infirm, or parents of small children." How many of those who need this information most can read it? What right has any business firm to call for payment from a customer who did not understand the prior basis of agreement? Legalities aside, the loss of any certitude that real communication has transpired represents a cost-deficient nightmare.

Virtually any financial item on the reader's desk—a checkbook or bank statement or a summary of salary deductions—will suggest the endless acreage of governmental and commercial chaos that underlies the seemingly efficient surface of American communication. Illiterates too frequently have no idea if the deductions from their paychecks are correct. Too often they are not. We shall see the bitterness and justified suspicion this creates among those many millions who will have no way to know if they were cheated.

If business does not know its clientele, neither does government know its population. We have seen already the spectacular miscalculations of the Bureau of the Census. A nation that does not know itself is no less subject to the consequences of occluded vision than the blind protagonist of classic tragedy. Oedipus tearing at his eyes, Lear in his demented eloquence upon the moors, Gloucester weeping from those "empty orbs"—these are the metaphors of cultural self-mutilation in a stumbling colossus. Eyeless at Gaza, Samson struggled to regain the power to pull down the pillars that destroyed him and his enemies together. The U.S. Bureau of the Census meanwhile sends out printed forms to ask illiterate Americans to indicate their reading levels.

"Know thyself" is an injunction that applies to the United States today at least as much as to the body politic or to the separate citizens of Periclean Greece. "Who am I?" This is a question that cannot be answered even in the most mechanical and trivializing sense by an illiterate democracy that governs nonetheless by a persistent faith in written words.

Whatever was meant by John Locke's social contract or by Rousseau's general will is rendered meaningless within a context of denied participation. The governor does not know the governed. The census cannot total up its own demography. The candidate cannot fathom—even where he cares to ascertain —the needs or the beliefs of the electorate. The postman rings twice, leaves his little piece of incoherence in the hollow box, and those who patiently attend upon the answer will be waiting many years to understand why there is no response.

"Divestiture!"

I have this notification on my desk. It came in the same envelope that brings the bill each month from the phone company. "To comply with new mandated calling areas, we have asked the Department of Public Utilities (DPU) for permission to modify our optional calling plans. These modifications redefine the service areas . . . Customers affected by this change are being notified by letter of their service options . . . The FCC had ordered local companies to begin to bill you for an access charge to offset the loss of subsidy formerly provided . . . This has changed. The change will amount to $2.00 monthly on your lines . . . WHAT'S NEXT? Starting in late 1984, other elements of long-distance calling will begin to change . . . You'll be notified of all these changes well before they occur . . ."

What's next?

Who will be notified? Who will be affected? How? By what? By whom?

Many of us find it hard to navigate this jargon. Most at least can isolate the crucial words—"$2.00 monthly"—and take proper warning. Illiterates have no hope at all of calculating the expense of local service, let alone long-distance calls.

There is, of course, one possible alternative: Damn the rules. Tear up the bill. Call anyone you love or hate. Talk for an hour. Call collect. Call someone in Bolivia, Brazil, Vancouver, or Afghanistan. Nobody will collect the bill. Instead, you will receive another letter.

Newspapers are folding. Paper costs are high, but loss of literate readers is much higher. Forty-five percent of adult citizens do not read newspapers. Only 10 percent abstain by choice. The rest have been excluded by their inability to read. Even the most undistinguished daily papers are now written at an estimated tenth grade level. Magazines such as *The Nation, The New Republic, Time, Newsweek,* and *The National Review* are written at a minimum of twelfth grade level. Circulation battles represent a competition for the largest piece of a diminished pie. Enlargement of that pie does not yet seem to have occurred to those who enter these increasingly unhappy competitions. The only successful major paper to be launched in the last decade, *USA Today,* relies on a simplistic lexicon, large headlines, color photographs, and fanciful weather maps that seek to duplicate the instant entertainment of TV.

One might have thought that editors and writers, more than any other group in the commercial world, would have demonstrated more alacrity in learning why their clientele has been reduced. Those who live by the word, in this case, now are dying by the intellectual asphyxiation of a populace to whom the word has been denied.

Booksellers and publishers of books are feeling the results of mass illiteracy too. According to a spokesman for McGraw-Hill, there was a steady decline throughout the 1970s in the sale and publication of hardcover books. While certain reports suggest that book sales have increased in recent years, they also demonstrate that only the more privileged sector of the population buys them. Growth in sales is caused by greater use of books by only one third of the population. Thirty-seven percent of adults under twenty-one do not read books at all. The United States ranks twenty-fourth in the world in terms of books produced per capita.

The legal system flounders in its own morass of indefensible defendants, incoherent witnesses, and injudicious jurists. It was first held in 1582 in England, and subsequently respected in the United States in 1930, that "a deed executed by an illiterate person does not bind him" if its terms have not been read to him correctly. This precedent, if strictly honored in 1984, would throw the legal system into chaos.

More disturbing questions have to do with those who serve on juries. High levels of literacy are not demanded by the courts as a prerequisite to jury service, but those who read at only marginal levels are reduced to passive roles in the deliberation of the jury. Lawyers frequently make use of print displays to explicate the details of a complicated case. Once sequestered, juries often study written documents and, sometimes, transcripts of the testimony heard some weeks or even months before. In arduous debate, the semiliterate or illiterate juror is too readily won over by the selectivity of a persuasive reader.

If the high rate of convictions for illiterate defendants had not been so solidly established, none of this might represent a prejudicial aspect of the jury system. But trial by a jury of one's peers does, at the minimum, require a fair representation of poor persons. The number of illiterates among the poor and the nonwhite forces a choice that few defense attorneys would regard as any choice at all. Either they must look for jurors who are competent to judge and understand all written data but are of a different class and race than the defendant; or they must attempt to find more sympathetic jurors who may not be able to read documents which other members of the jury will interpret for them. Since interpretation is too seldom neutral, and can never be entirely neutral, the jury process cannot represent a genuine judgment by one's peers.

Even one of the most common forms of litigation, that which arises from contract law, is undermined by the pervasive lack of literacy skills. Contracts, according to a treatise published first in 1844, were regarded as non-binding if "an intelligent understanding of [their] terms" was not established. If this view still holds in the United States today, the problem for the courts will be enormous. An obvious example was reported recently in Tennessee. Contracts for the residents of housing projects were examined by some reading specialists and lawyers and were found to have been written well above a college level. Knowing the way most housing agencies are run, we cannot believe that anyone has read these contracts to the tenants; yet it is for breach of terms within such documents that people are evicted.

The social ideology of the United States and of Great Britain has been built on contract law. If this form of law cannot survive the test of reading competence within the population, the contract system and the social edifice that it supports will be no better able to sustain themselves than any other aspect of American society described above.

The U.S. military pays a high price too. Thirty percent of naval recruits were recently termed "a danger to themselves and to costly naval equipment" because of inability to read and understand instructions.

The Navy reports that one recruit caused $250,000 in damage to delicate equipment "because he could not read a repair manual." The young recruit had tried to hide his inability to read by using common sense and following the pictures that accompanied the text. "He tried [but] failed to follow the illustrations . . ." How many more illiterates are now responsible for lower-level but essential safety checks that are required in the handling of missiles or the operation of a nuclear reactor?

Some of the means used by the military to explain mechanical procedures are devastating in their banal degradation. Books resembling comics are one of the common methods of instruction. A five-page picture book is needed to explain the steps required to release and lift the hood of army vehicles. How long are the comics needed to explain the operation of those vehicles, to tell the semiliterate soldier where to drive and whom he is to rescue, kill, or capture when he gets there?

Illiteracy poses greater military risks than this. One that is potentially explosive is the disproportionate number of both poor and nonwhite men who are assigned the most subordinate positions and who therefore represent a disproportionate percentage of the frontline soldiers and of battle casualties in time of war. We have seen some instances of shipboard mutiny in recent years; one such instance was explicitly connected to the point established here. We can expect to see more frightening rebellions of this sort during the years ahead.

There are other military dangers. Many citizens will view with grave alarm the passive and noncritical status of uneducated soldiers trained at best to a mechanical efficiency in areas too tightly circumscribed to offer any vision of the moral or immoral consequences of their actions. Whether from the point of view of the most jingoistic citizen, therefore, or from that of the most ardent pacifist, the present situation holds intolerable dangers. On this, if nothing else, both left and right can certainly agree.

What is the cost to universities and public schools?

Affluent people tend to look upon illiteracy with comfortable detachment. Their sole concern is that their children may be cheated of an opportunity for college preparation by "adulterated" courses and by "lowered" standards, both of which they have associated with the more inclusive policies of public schools and, in particular, with race desegregation. Many imagine they can isolate their children from these problems: a few by application to exclusive prep schools, the rest by tougher discipline and more remorseless tracking systems in the public schools. Sophisticated parents, on the other hand, have started to perceive that isolation of this sort is seldom possible today and that, where it still seems possible, the price that they will later pay for such shortsighted selfishness is greater than the short-term gain.

Excellence at the top, in short, is intimately tied to the collapse of literacy levels at the bottom. Even in the richest suburbs there are well-concealed but frequently extensive neighborhoods inhabited by poor people. Children from those neighborhoods attend the same schools as the children of the rich. More to the point, the line that separates the inner cities from the suburbs will increasingly be broken down in years ahead. Present patterns of resegregation may appease the fearful; legal actions, even if they take another decade, will not leave these stark inequities unchanged. As school desegregation is more fully implemented, only the most isolated suburbs will remain exempt.

Tracking schemes, at present in resurgent fashion, will be recognized for what they are: archaic pedagogy and divisive social policy. Legal actions will be launched to fight the obvious denial of a child's civil rights which is inherent in the self-fulfilling prophecy of rigid track separations.

To state it bluntly: There will at length be no more places for all but the very privileged to hide.

Even for those who may contrive to isolate their kids during the years preceding college, higher academic life will be affected by the growing presence of the poorly educated and the semiliterate. Ethnic tensions consequent from this are seen already both in public institutions like the City University of New York and in private institutions such as Boston University. Even at graduate schools like Harvard Law we have seen a rapid growth of interethnic acrimony in the past five years. Nonwhite students with marginal entrance scores remain close to the bottom of the class; few are admitted to the prestigious *Law Review*. Recent policies that have facilitated their admission have been met with strong resistance from those students who have seen "their" place assumed by someone who, according to the test scores, is less qualified than they.

Virulent graffiti on the redbrick walls and Georgian porticoes of Harvard

University remind us that the price of excellence for very few in early years of public school, if it is an excellence achieved by separation from the children of poor people, is an ethical contamination that even the most honored law school in the nation cannot manage to escape.

If conscience cannot turn the tide, perhaps it is the panic of self-interest which will finally do the job. Panic may not be a noble motive for redress of social wrongs; but there are sufficient grounds for panic, and perhaps the only reason that there is not more alarm among the population is the fact that most of us have never stopped to recognize the perils that surround us.

Imagine a familiar situation: The traveller walks into an airport lobby to obtain the ticket for a flight which has already been reserved. The well-dressed woman at the ticket desk projects a confident smile as she taps the buttons on a modern console, asks our seating preference, and hands over a computer-printed boarding pass. We never get to meet the men and women in their oil-coated overalls or jeans who do the more important work of checking out the plane we are about to board. Some of us might be alarmed if we should ever wander through the wrong door by mistake and watch the semieducated persons who attempt to figure out the charts and other manuals that instruct them in the safety details that the government requires: details most of us will never find the time to think about until it is too late.

Without warning, on May 5, 1983, an Eastern Airlines jumbo jet en route to Nassau from Miami, crowded with passengers enjoying their first cocktail and perusing their newspapers, dropped three miles in the sky. Three engines had gone dead. By luck one engine came to life just as the pilot had prepared the passengers to ditch. The cause of engine failure was at length discovered. Nothing was wrong with the mechanical equipment. Two members of a ground crew had neglected to insert three tiny oil seals described as "O" rings into the fuel line during the routine check that took place prior to departure. The lives of several hundred people came within three minutes of extinction. The maintenance men, it was reported, "hadn't read" the manual of instructions that the airline had prepared. Eastern Airlines never reported, and perhaps has never learned, whether the maintenance men had failed to look at the instructions or whether they had been unable to decipher them.

Failure to follow maintenance instructions led another man, in March of 1979, to leave unsecured the open valves that were a major reason for the near-catastrophe at Three Mile Island: a catastrophe which, had it taken place, would have spread its radiation far beyond the precincts of a single neighborhood in Pennsylvania and might have endangered lives as far away as in New Jersey and New York.

Neither of these two events can be identified with evidence of inability to read. Nonetheless, the presence of so many millions of unrecognized illiterates in the work force guarantees that hundreds of mistakes, with consequences we may never know, must take place daily. Many more will take place in the years ahead.

The Secretary of Education is correct. The nation is at risk. He very likely does not understand the nature of the risk that he describes. We are all held hostage to each other in this nation. There are no citizens, no matter how wealthy, no matter how removed they may believe themselves to be, who will not be forced to pay a formidable price. The items I have summarized above may prove to be among the least important of these costs, but these matters in themselves are great enough to mandate a dramatic, urgent, and immediate political response.

4

The Human Cost
of an Illiterate Society

PRECAUTIONS. READ BEFORE USING.
Poison: Contains sodium hydroxide (caustic soda-lye).
Corrosive: Causes severe eye and skin damage, may cause blindness.
Harmful or fatal if swallowed.
If swallowed, give large quantities of milk or water.
Do not induce vomiting.
Important: Keep water out of can at all times to
prevent contents from violently erupting . . .

—warning on a can of Drano

We are speaking here no longer of the dangers faced by passengers on Eastern Airlines or the dollar costs incurred by U.S. corporations and taxpayers. We are speaking now of human suffering and of the ethical dilemmas that are faced by a society that looks upon such suffering with qualified concern but does not take those actions which its wealth and ingenuity would seemingly demand.

Questions of literacy, in Socrates' belief, must at length be judged as matters of morality. Socrates could not have had in mind the moral compromise peculiar to a nation like our own. Some of our Founding Fathers did, however, have this question in their minds. One of the wisest of those Founding Fathers (one who may not have been most compassionate but surely was more prescient than some of his peers) recognized the special dangers that illiteracy would pose to basic equity in the political construction that he helped to shape.

"A people who mean to be their own governors," James Madison wrote, "must arm themselves with the power knowledge gives. A popular government without popular information or the means of acquiring it, is but a prologue to a farce or a tragedy, or perhaps both."

Tragedy looms larger than farce in the United States today. Illiterate citizens seldom vote. Those who do are forced to cast a vote of questionable worth. They cannot make informed decisions based on serious print information. Sometimes they can be alerted to their interests by aggressive voter education. More frequently, they vote for a face, a smile, or a style, not for a mind or character or body of beliefs.

The number of illiterate adults exceeds by 16 million the entire vote cast for the winner in the 1980 presidential contest. If even one third of all illiterates could vote, and read enough and do sufficient math to vote in their self-interest, Ronald Reagan would not likely have been chosen president. There is, of course, no way to know for sure. We do know this: Democracy is a mendacious term when used by those who are prepared to countenance the forced exclusion of one third of our electorate. So long as 60 million people are denied significant participation, the government is neither of, nor for, nor by, the people. It is a government, at best, of those two thirds whose wealth, skin color, or parental privilege allows them opportunity to profit from the provocation and instruction of the written word.

The undermining of democracy in the United States is one "expense" that sensitive Americans can easily deplore because it represents a contradiction that endangers citizens of all political positions. The human price is not so obvious at first.

Since I first immersed myself within this work I have often had the following dream: I find that I am in a railroad station or a large department store within a city that is utterly unknown to me and where I cannot understand the printed words. None of the signs or symbols is familiar. Everything looks strange: like mirror writing of some kind. Gradually I understand that I am in the Soviet Union. All the letters on the walls around me are Cyrillic. I look for my pocket dictionary but I find that it has been mislaid. Where have I left it? Then I recall that I forgot to bring it with me when I packed my bags in Boston. I struggle to remember the name of my hotel. I try to ask somebody for directions. One person stops and looks at me in a peculiar way. I lose the nerve to ask. At last I reach into my wallet for an ID card. The card is missing. Have I lost it? Then I remember that my card was confiscated for some reason, many years before. Around this point, I wake up in a panic.

This panic is not so different from the misery that millions of adult illiterates experience each day within the course of their routine existence in the U.S.A.

Illiterates cannot read the menu in a restaurant.

They cannot read the cost of items on the menu in the *window* of the restaurant before they enter.

Illiterates cannot read the letters that their children bring home from their teachers. They cannot study school department circulars that tell them of the courses that their children must be taking if they hope to pass the SAT exams. They cannot help with homework. They cannot write a letter to the teacher. They are afraid to visit in the classroom. They do not want to humiliate their child or themselves.

Illiterates cannot read instructions on a bottle of prescription medicine. They cannot find out when a medicine is past the year of safe consumption; nor can they read of allergenic risks, warnings to diabetics, or the potential sedative effect of certain kinds of nonprescription pills. They cannot observe preventive health care admonitions. They cannot read about "the seven warning signs of cancer" or the indications of blood-sugar fluctuations or the risks of eating certain foods that aggravate the likelihood of cardiac arrest.

Illiterates live, in more than literal ways, an uninsured existence. They cannot understand the written details on a health insurance form. They cannot read the waivers that they sign preceding surgical procedures. Several women I have known in Boston have entered a slum hospital with the intention of obtaining a tubal ligation and have emerged a few days later after having been subjected to a hysterectomy. Unaware of their rights, incognizant of jargon, intimidated by the unfamiliar air of fear and atmosphere of ether that so many of us find oppressive in the confines even of the most attractive and expensive medical facilities, they have signed their names to documents they could not read and which nobody, in the hectic situation that prevails so often in those overcrowded hospitals that serve the urban poor, had even bothered to explain.

Childbirth might seem to be the last inalienable right of any female citizen within a civilized society. Illiterate mothers, as we shall see, already have been cheated of the power to protect their progeny against the likelihood of demolition in deficient public schools and, as a result, against the verbal servitude within which they themselves exist. Surgical denial of the right to bear that child in the first place represents an ultimate denial, an unspeakable metaphor, a final darkness that denies even the twilight gleamings of our own humanity. What greater violation of our biological, our biblical, our spiritual humanity could possibly exist than that which takes place nightly, perhaps hourly these days, within such overburdened and benighted institutions as the Boston City Hospital? Illiteracy has many costs; few are so irreversible as this.

Even the roof above one's head, the gas or other fuel for heating that protects the residents of northern city slums against the threat of illness in the winter months become uncertain guarantees. Illiterates cannot read the lease that they must sign to live in an apartment which, too often, they cannot afford. They cannot manage check accounts and therefore seldom pay for anything by mail. Hours and entire days of difficult travel (and the cost of bus or other public transit) must be added to the real cost of whatever they consume. Loss of interest on the check accounts they do not have, and could not manage if they did, must be regarded as another of the excess costs paid by the citizen who is excluded from the common instruments of commerce in a numerate society.

"I couldn't understand the bills," a woman in Washington, D.C., reports, "and then I couldn't write the checks to pay them. We signed things we didn't know what they were."

Illiterates cannot read the notices that they receive from welfare offices or from the IRS. They must depend on word-of-mouth instruction from the welfare worker—or from other persons whom they have good reason to mistrust. They do not know what rights they have, what deadlines and requirements they face, what options they might choose to exercise. They are half-citizens. Their rights exist in print but not in fact.

Illiterates cannot look up numbers in a telephone directory. Even if they can find the names of friends, few possess the sorting skills to make use of the yellow pages; categories are bewildering and trade names are beyond decoding capabilities for millions of nonreaders. Even the emergency numbers listed on the first page of the phone book—"Ambulance," "Police," and "Fire"—are too frequently beyond the recognition of nonreaders.

Many illiterates cannot read the admonition on a pack of cigarettes. Neither the Surgeon General's warning nor its reproduction on the package can alert them to the risks. Although most people learn by word of mouth that smoking is related to a number of grave physical disorders, they do not get the chance to read the detailed stories which can document this danger with the vividness that turns concern into determination to resist. They can see the handsome cowboy or the slim Virginia lady lighting up a filter cigarette; they cannot heed the words that tell them that this product is (not "may be") dangerous to their health. Sixty million men and women are condemned to be the unalerted, high-risk candidates for cancer.

Illiterates do not buy "no-name" products in the supermarkets. They must depend on photographs or the familiar logos that are printed on the packages of brand-name groceries. The poorest people, therefore, are denied the benefits of the least costly products.

Illiterates depend almost entirely upon label recognition. Many labels, however, are not easy to distinguish. Dozens of different kinds of Campbell's soup appear identical to the nonreader. The purchaser who cannot read and does not dare to ask for help, out of the fear of being stigmatized (a fear which is unfortunately realistic), frequently comes home with something which she never wanted and her family never tasted.

Illiterates cannot read instructions on a pack of frozen food. Packages sometimes provide an illustration to explain the cooking preparations; but illus-

trations are of little help to someone who must "boil water, drop the food—
within its plastic wrapper—in the boiling water, wait for it to simmer, instantly
remove."

Even when labels are seemingly clear, they may be easily mistaken. A
woman in Detroit brought home a gallon of Crisco for her children's dinner.
She thought that she had bought the chicken that was pictured on the label.
She had enough Crisco now to last a year—but no more money to go back and
buy the food for dinner.

Recipes provided on the packages of certain staples sometimes tempt a
semiliterate person to prepare a meal her children have not tasted. The longing
to vary the uniform and often starchy content of low-budget meals provided to
the family that relies on food stamps commonly leads to ruinous results. Scarce
funds have been wasted and the food must be thrown out. The same applies to
distribution of food-surplus produce in emergency conditions. Government inducements to poor people to "explore the ways" by which to make a tasty meal
from tasteless noodles, surplus cheese, and powdered milk are useless to
nonreaders. Intended as benevolent advice, such recommendations mock reality
and foster deeper feelings of resentment and of inability to cope. (Those, on the
other hand, who cautiously refrain from "innovative" recipes in preparation of
their children's meals must suffer the opprobrium of "laziness," "lack of imagination . . .")

Illiterates cannot travel freely. When they attempt to do so, they encounter
risks that few of us can dream of. They cannot read traffic signs and, while they
often learn to recognize and to decipher symbols, they cannot manage street
names which they haven't seen before. The same is true for bus and subway
stops. While ingenuity can sometimes help a man or woman to discern directions from familiar landmarks, buildings, cemeteries, churches, and the like,
most illiterates are virtually immobilized. They seldom wander past the streets
and neighborhoods they know. Geographical paralysis becomes a bitter metaphor for their entire existence. They are immobilized in almost every sense we
can imagine. They can't move up. They can't move out. They cannot see
beyond. Illiterates may take an oral test for drivers' permits in most sections of
America. It is a questionable concession. Where will they go? How will they get
there? How will they get home? Could it be that some of us might like it better
if they stayed where they belong?

Travel is only one of many instances of circumscribed existence. Choice, in
almost all its facets, is diminished in the life of an illiterate adult. Even the
printed TV schedule, which provides most people with the luxury of preselec-
tion, does not belong within the arsenal of options in illiterate existence. One
consequence is that the viewer watches only what appears at moments when he
happens to have time to turn the switch. Another consequence, a lot more
common, is that the TV set remains in operation night and day. Whatever the

program offered at the hour when he walks into the room will be the nutriment that he accepts and swallows. Thus, to passivity, is added frequency—indeed, almost uninterrupted continuity. Freedom to select is no more possible here than in the choice of home or surgery or food.

"You don't choose," said one illiterate woman. "You take your wishes from somebody else." Whether in perusal of a menu, selection of highways, purchase of groceries, or determination of affordable enjoyment, illiterate Americans must trust somebody else: a friend, a relative, a stranger on the street, a grocery clerk, a TV copywriter.

"All of our mail we get, it's hard for her to read. Settin' down and writing a letter, she can't do it. Like if we get a bill . . . we take it over to my sister-in-law . . . My sister-in-law reads it."

Billing agencies harass poor people for the payment of the bills for purchases that might have taken place six months before. Utility companies offer an agreement for a staggered payment schedule on a bill past due. "You have to trust them," one man said. Precisely for this reason, you end up by trusting no one and suspecting everyone of possible deceit. A submerged sense of distrust becomes the corollary to a constant need to trust. "They are cheating me . . . I have been tricked . . . I do not know . . ."

Not knowing: This is a familiar theme. Not knowing the right word for the right thing at the right time is one form of subjugation. Not knowing the world that lies concealed behind those words is a more terrifying feeling. The longitude and latitude of one's existence are beyond all easy apprehension. Even the hard, cold stars within the firmament above one's head begin to mock the possibilities for self-location. Where am I? Where did I come from? Where will I go?

"I've lost a lot of jobs," one man explains. "Today, even if you're a janitor, there's still reading and writing . . . They leave a note saying, 'Go to room so-and-so . . .' You can't do it. You can't read it. You don't know."

"The hardest thing about it is that I've been places where I didn't know where I was. You don't know where you are . . . You're lost."

"Like I said: I have two kids. What do I do if one of my kids starts choking? I go running to the phone . . . I can't look up the hospital phone number. That's if we're at home. Out on the street, I can't read the sign. I get to a pay phone. 'Okay, tell us where you are. We'll send an ambulance.' I look at the street sign. Right there, I can't tell you what it says. I'd have to spell it out, letter for letter. By that time, one of my kids would be dead . . . These are the kinds of fears you go with, every single day . . ."

"Reading directions, I suffer with. I work with chemicals . . . That's scary to begin with . . ."

"You sit down. They throw the menu in front of you. Where do you go from there? Nine times out of ten you say, 'Go ahead. Pick out something for the both of us.' I've eaten some weird things, let me tell you!"

Menus. Chemicals. A child choking while his mother searches for a word she does not know to find assistance that will come too late. Another mother speaks about the inability to help her kids to read: "I can't read to them. Of course that's leaving them out of something they should have. Oh, it matters. You *believe* it matters! I ordered all these books. The kids belong to a book club. Donny wanted me to read a book to him. I told Donny: 'I can't read.' He said: 'Mommy, you sit down. I'll read it to you.' I tried it one day, reading from the pictures. Donny looked at me. He said, 'Mommy, that's not right.' He's only five. He knew I couldn't read . . ."

A landlord tells a woman that her lease allows him to evict her if her baby cries and causes inconvenience to her neighbors. The consequence of challenging his words conveys a danger which appears, unlikely as it seems, even more alarming than the danger of eviction. Once she admits that she can't read, in the desire to maneuver for the time in which to call a friend, she will have defined herself in terms of an explicit impotence that she cannot endure. Capitulation in this case is preferable to self-humiliation. Resisting the definition of oneself in terms of what one cannot do, what others take for granted, represents a need so great that other imperatives (even one so urgent as the need to keep one's home in winter's cold) evaporate and fall away in face of fear. Even the loss of home and shelter, in this case, is not so terrifying as the loss of self.

"I come out of school. I was sixteen. They had their meetings. The directors meet. They said that I was wasting their school paper. I was wasting pencils . . ."

Another illiterate, looking back, believes she was not worthy of her teacher's time. She believes that it was wrong of her to take up space within her school. She believes that it was right to leave in order that somebody more deserving could receive her place.

Children choke. Their mother chokes another way: on more than chicken bones.

People eat what others order, know what others tell them, struggle not to see themselves as they believe the world perceives them. A man in California speaks about his own loss of identity, of self-location, definition:

"I stood at the bottom of the ramp. My car had broke down on the freeway. There was a phone. I asked for the police. They was nice. They said to tell them where I was. I looked up at the signs. There was one that I had seen before. I read it to them: ONE WAY STREET. They thought it was a joke. I told them I couldn't read. There was other signs above the ramp. They told me to try. I looked around for somebody to help. All the cars was going by real fast. I couldn't make them understand that I was lost. The cop was nice. He told me: 'Try once more.' I did my best. I couldn't read. I only knew the sign above my head. The cop was trying to be nice. He knew that I was trapped. 'I can't send out a car to you if you can't tell me where you are.' I felt afraid. I nearly cried. I'm forty-eight years old. I only said: 'I'm on a one-way street . . .' "

The legal problems and the courtroom complications that confront illiterate adults have been discussed above. The anguish that may underlie such matters was brought home to me this year while I was working on this book. I have spoken, in the introduction, of a sudden phone call from one of my former students, now in prison for a criminal offense. Stephen is not a boy today. He is twenty-eight years old. He called to ask me to assist him in his trial, which comes up next fall. He will be on trial for murder. He has just knifed and killed a man who first enticed him to his home, then cheated him, and then insulted him—as "an illiterate subhuman."

Stephen now faces twenty years to life. Stephen's mother was illiterate. His grandparents were illiterate as well. What parental curse did not destroy was killed off finally by the schools. Silent violence is repaid with interest. It will cost us $25,000 yearly to maintain this broken soul in prison. But what is the price that has been paid by Stephen's victim? What is the price that will be paid by Stephen?

Perhaps we might slow down a moment here and look at the realities described above. This is the nation that we live in. This is a society that most of us did not create but which our President and other leaders have been willing to sustain by virtue of malign neglect. Do we possess the character and courage to address a problem which so many nations, poorer than our own, have found it natural to correct?

The answers to these questions represent a reasonable test of our belief in the democracy to which we have been asked in public school to swear allegiance.

5

The Disenfranchised:
Silent and Unseen

Im 33 now and finly made a go. But the walls are up agent. and this
time I don't think I can go around them. What Im I to do. I still have
some engeny left. But running out. Im afraide to run out. I don't
know if I can settle for noting.

—letter to the author, 1983

It is difficult for most Americans to place full credence in the facts described
above.

If we did, we would be forced to choose between enormous guilt and
efficacious action. The willingness of decent people to withhold belief or to
anaesthetize their capability for credence represents the hardest problem that
we need to overcome in dealing with the dangers that we know in abstract ways
but somehow cannot concretize in ways that force us to take action.

One reason for the nation's incredulity, of course, is the deceptive impact
of the U.S. census figures. Until recent years, these figures have been taken as
authoritative indices of national reality. While it has been recognized for decades that the nonwhite population has been underrepresented in the census, it
may be that it is not black people but illiterate adults who represent, in categori-
cal terms, the largest sector of invisible Americans. Many blacks and other
minorities decline, for fear of government intrusion, to respond to written
forms. Illiterates do not "decline"; they cannot read the forms at all.

This, however, is not the only explanation. Illiterates find it painful to
identify themselves. In a print society, enormous stigma is attached to the adult

nonreader. Early in the game we see the evolution of a whole line of defensive strategies against discovery by others. "Lying low" and watching out for "traps" become a pattern of existence.

An illiterate young man, nineteen years of age, sits beside me in a restaurant and quietly surveys the menu. After a time he looks at the waitress, hesitates as if uncertain of his preference, then tells her: "Well, I guess I'll have a hamburger—with french fries." When she asks what he would like to drink, he pauses again, then states with some conviction: "Well, I guess I'd like a Coke."

It took me several months, although I was this young man's neighbor, to discover that he could not read a word. He had learned to order those three items which he felt assured of finding in all restaurants. He had had a lot of hamburg and french fries in nineteen years.

Peter had been victimized initially by some incredibly incompetent officials in the Boston schools. He could not look for backup to his family. His father could not read. His mother had died when he was very young. This was a one-parent family which, unlike the stereotype that is accepted as the norm, was headed not by an unmarried woman but by an undereducated and religious man. But Peter had been victimized a final time by some of those (myself included) who were living in his neighborhood and who ought to have perceived that he was literally frozen in the presence of the written word.

Being ingenious and sophisticated far beyond his years, he was able to disguise his fear of words to a degree that totally deceived me. I might never have identified his inability to read if it had not been for an entirely social happenstance. One day, driving by the ocean north of Boston, I stopped to take him to a seafood restaurant in Gloucester. He broke into a sweat, began to tremble, and then asked if we could leave. He asked me, suddenly, if we could go to Howard Johnson's.

This, I discovered, was the one escape hatch he had managed to contrive. Howard Johnson's, unattractive as it may appear in contrast to a lobster restaurant beside the sea, provided Peter with his only opportunity for culinary options. Here, because of the array of color photographs attached in celluloid containers to each item on the menu, he was able to branch out a bit and treat himself to ice cream sodas and fried clams. Howard Johnson's, knowingly or not, has held for many years a captive clientele of many millions of illiterate adults.

Today, the other fast-food chains provide the pictures too. Certain corporations, going even further in the wish to give employment to illiterate teenagers, now are speaking of a plan to make use of cash registers whose keys are marked with product symbols in the place of numbers. The illiterate employee merely needs to punch the key that shows "two burgers" or one "Whopper." It is a good device for giving jobs to print (and numerate) nonreaders. Obviating errors and perhaps some personal embarrassment, it pacifies the anguish of illiterates but it does not give them motivation to escape the trap which leaves them powerless to find more interesting employment. Illiterates, in this way, come to be both captive customers and captive counter workers for such corporations.

An illiterate cattle farmer in Vermont describes the strategies that he employs to hide his inability to read. "You have to be careful," he explains, "not to get into situations where it would leak out . . . You always try to act intelligent . . . If somebody gives you something to read, you make believe you read it."

Sooner or later, the strategies run out. A man who has been able to obtain a good job in a laboratory testing dairy products for impurities survives by memorizing crystals and their various reactions. Offered promotion, he is told that he will be obliged to take a brief exam. He brings home the books that have been given to him by his boss for preparation. Knowing the examination is a written one, he loses heart. He never shows up at his job again. His boss perhaps will spend some hours wondering why.

Husbands and wives can sometimes cover for each other. Illiterates may bring home applications, written forms of various kinds, and ask their spouse or children to fill in the answers. When this stratagem no longer works (when they are asked, for instance, to check out a voucher or a bill of lading on the job) the game is up, the worker disappears.

Once we get to know someone like Peter, we can understand the courage that it takes for an illiterate adult to break down the defenses and to ask for help. Our government's refusal to provide an answer for the millions who have found the nerve to ask seems all the more heartbreaking for this reason. One hundred forty thousand men and women in the State of Illinois alone have asked for literacy help from local agencies which have been forced to turn them down for lack of federal funds. They have been consigned to waiting lists. How many of these people, having asked and been refused, will find the courage to apply for help again?

On the streets of New York City or Chicago, one out of every three or four adults we pass is a nonreader. Unlike the stranger who does not speak English, or whose skin is brown or black, the person who is illiterate can "pass." By virtue of those strategies that guard them from humiliation, illiterates have also managed to remain unseen.

Political impotence may represent an even larger obstacle to recognition than the fear of personal humiliation.

Others who have been victimized at least are able to form lobbies, organize agendas, issue press releases, write to politicians, and, if they do not receive responsive answers, form a voting bloc to drive those politicians out of office. Illiterates have no access to such methods of political redress.

We are told in school that, when we have a problem or complaint, we should write a letter "to our representative at City Hall" or to an elected politician in the nation's capital. Politicians do not answer letters that illiterates can't write. The leverage of political negotiation that we take for granted and assign such hopeful designations as "the Jeffersonian ideal" is denied the man or woman who cannot participate in print society. Neither the press release nor the handwritten flier that can draw a crowd into a protest meeting at a local church lies within the reach of the nonreader. Victims exist, but not constituencies. Democracy is posited on efficacious actions that require print initiative. Even the most highly motivated persons, if they do not read and write, cannot lobby for their own essential needs. They can speak (and now and then a journalist may hear) but genuine autonomy is far beyond them.

Illiterates may carry picket signs but cannot write them and, in any case, can seldom read them. Even the rock-bottom levels of political communication —the spray paint and graffiti that adorn the walls of subways and deserted buildings in impoverished neighborhoods—are instruments of discourse which are far beyond the range of the illiterate American. Walking in a ghetto neighborhood or in a poor white area of Boston, we see the sprawl of giant letters that decry the plight of black, Hispanic, women, gay, or other persecuted groups. We read no cogent outcries from illiterates.

The forfeiture of self-created lobbies is perhaps the major reason for political inaction. Those who might speak, however, on behalf of the illiterate— neighborhood organizers, for example, or the multitude of private literacy groups—tend to default on an apparent obligation. For this, there seems to be at least one obvious explanation.

Community leaders—black leaders in particular—have been reluctant to direct the focus of attention to the crisis of adult illiteracy within the lowest economic levels of the population. Their reticence is based upon misguided fear. In pointing to the 44 percent of black adults who cannot read or write at levels needed for participation in American society, they are afraid that they may offer ammunition to those racist and reactionary persons who are often eager to attribute failure to innate inadequacy or who, while they may refrain from stating this, will nonetheless believe it. Naming the victim should not be equated with the age-old inclination to place blame upon the victim. Indeed, it tends to work the other way around. Refusal to name a victim and, still more, to offer details as to how that victimization is perpetuated and passed on is a fairly certain guarantee that people in pain will not be seen and that their victimization will not be addressed. Well-intentioned white allies of black political groups are even more susceptible to this mistake than most black leaders.*

Sensible organizers understand that silence on this subject is a no-win strategy. If people are injured, injury must be described. If they have not been injured—as the silence of some partisans dogmatically implies—then they have no claim upon compassion and no right to seek corrective measures. Blaming

* For an important exception, see description of the black-run organization "Assault on Illiteracy," cited in Notes.

the victim is vindictive. Naming the victim is the first step in a struggle to remove the chains.

If understandable, this hesitation on the part of many leaders is politically unsound. They lose the massive voting bloc which otherwise might double and, in certain urban areas, quadruple their constituencies. Black citizens, illiterate or not, may vote in overwhelming numbers for black candidates. When, as in some recent mayoral elections and in the campaign of Jesse Jackson in the presidential primaries of 1984, the options are a single black and one or more white candidates, the voting power of black people is self-evident. But when, in the more common situation, the choices are among a number of white candidates of widely differing positions (or, for that matter, a number of black candidates of widely differing degrees of merit), a black electorate which is substantially excluded from print access cannot make discerning or autonomous decisions. A physically attractive demagogue who knows the way to key his language to immediate and short-term interests of poor people may win himself a large part of the vote from those for whom his long-term bias and his past performance ought to constitute a solemn admonition.

Illiterate voters, cut off from the most effective means of repossession of the past, denied the right to learn from recent history because they are denied all access to the written record of the candidate (or to the editorial reminders of that record which most newspapers supply), are locked into the present and enslaved by the encapsulated moment which is symbolized by the sixty-second newsclip on TV or the thirty-second paid advertisement that candidates employ in order to exploit the well-organized amnesia of Americans.

Illiterate Americans, denied almost all contact with the print-recorded past, cannot effectively address the present nor anticipate the future. They cannot learn from Santayana's warning. They have never heard of Santayana.

Exclusion from the printed word renders one third of America the ideal supine population for the "total state" that Auden feared and Orwell prophesied: undefended against doublespeak, unarmed against the orchestrated domination of their minds. Choice demands reflection and decision. Readers of the press at least can stand back and react; they can also find dissenting sources of opinion. The speed and power of electric media allow no time for qualified reflection. The TV viewer, whether literate or not, is temporarily a passive object: a receptacle for someone else's views. While all of us have proven vulnerable to this effect, it is the illiterate who has been rendered most susceptible to that entire domination which depends upon denial of the full continuum of time and its causations.

There is some danger of implicit overstatement here. Illiterate people do not represent a single body of undifferentiated human beings. Most illiterates do not remain all day in front of the TV, silent and entranced, to "drink it in." Many, moreover, draw upon their own experience to discount or refute nine tenths of what they see before them on TV. Others can draw on oral history, the stories they hear, the anecdotes they have been told by parents or by older friends. Injustice itself is a profound instructor. Intuitive recognition of a fraud —a politician or a product—can empower many people to resist the absoluteness of control which television otherwise might exercise upon their wishes or convictions.

Nonetheless it is the truth that many illiterates, deeply depressed and socially withdrawn, do not venture far from home and, out of the sheer longing for escape and for the simulation of "communication," do become for hours and weeks the passive addicts of the worst of what is offered on TV. Their lives and even eating schedules have been parcelled out to match the thirty-minute packages of cultural domestication and the sixty-second units of purported information which present the news in isolation from the history that shaped it or the future that it threatens to extinguish.

Many of these people would not choose to undermine or to refute a form of entertainment which has come to take a permanent place within their home —their one fast-talking friend. Many more have been so long indoctrinated to indict themselves, and not society, for their impoverished and illiterate condition that there is no chance of taking lessons from injustice. They cannot denounce what seems to them to be the normal world of those who have the "know-how" to enjoy it. Nor can they profit from the learnings of an older family member who is frequently too weary and depressed to speak at length about a lifetime (or a recent history) which he or she may not desire to remember and may have been led to view not as a blessing to pass on but as a curse to be denied or wished away.

For people like these (and there are many millions, I believe) the following is true: They live in a truncated present tense. The future seems hopeless. The past remains unknown. The amputated present tense, encapsulated by the TV moment, seems to constitute the end and the beginning of cognition.

Many black children, when they speak about their lives, do not seem to differentiate between the present, past, and future. "I be doing good today." "Last year I be with my family in Alabama." "Someday I be somebody important." In the year that I began to teach, knowing little about sociology and less about linguistics, I perceived this first as inability, then as unwillingness, to conjugate. I summarized my explanation of the matter in somewhat these terms: People who are robbed of history, whether by slavery or by the inability to read, do not have much reason to distinguish between past and present. Those who have been robbed of opportunity to shape a future different from the ones their parents and grandparents knew do not have much reason to distinguish between now and never.

I was equally perplexed by something else about the patterns of my students' speech. Even the continuous present tense that seemed to me to be the common usage of these kids was not expressed in present indicative but in a form that seemed to hold subjunctive implications. The children did not say: "I am." They said: "I be." This too appeared to me to carry metaphoric meaning. Existence itself, I felt, had been grammatically reduced to a subjunctive possibility.

Now it turns out that all of this is true except the starting point, which is entirely incorrect and which derives from my lack of awareness of some basic points of history and speech. Many scholars I have studied since have made it clear that nonwhite children "conjugate" as well as anybody else, that what I heard was not exactly what the children really said, that I was missing out on words as well as intonations that conveyed a sense of tense and mode to anyone (all of their friends, for instance) who shared in a knowledge of the language which they chose to use and one that had a logic and consistency that I could not perceive. It is not "a failure to differentiate" which was at stake. The differentiation was effected, rather, by a different body of linguistic rules.

Metaphors have a curious way of living beyond the point at which the evidence from which they grew has been discarded. It is now quite obvious to me that nonwhite children, whatever the thefts they have incurred, distinguish very well between the past and present. No matter how grim the future may appear, they also distinguish clearly between "now" and "never." The fact that they can do so, and persist in doing so, may be regarded as a tribute to their courage and indomitable refusal to accede before appalling odds. The metaphor, born of my first encounter with their pain and with a world I did not understand, remains to haunt me.

Whatever the language children use, the fact that matters here may be established in few words: Illiterate adults have been substantially excluded from political effectiveness by lack of access to the written word. Political impotence, in turn, diminishes the visibility of those in greatest verbal subjugation and makes it all the harder for the rest of us to recognize the full dimensions of their need.

It is argued by some cynical observers that elected leaders are politically astute to follow policies which keep out of the voting booth those who, reinforced by substantive decision-making data, could not quite so easily be led to vote for those who do not serve their needs. I suspect that such observers have attributed a little too much shrewdness and a great deal too much keen farsightedness to those whose actions seem more often motivated by a nineteenth century myopia than by a sinister anticipation of the future.

Enlightened politicians, if they wish to win at once political success and moral credibility, soon may demonstrate the acumen of picking up an issue which can hardly fail to better their position. Few of the votes of those who have been viewed for so long as expendable are likely to be cast for politicians who have done their best to cut off aid to programs that have given even fleeting glints of hope to those who cannot read and write.

This is the point at which to take a second look at the miscalculations of the census.

For one hundred years, starting in 1840, the census posed the question of the population's literacy level in its ten-year compilations. The government removed this question from its survey in the 1940 census. The reason, according to a U.S. Census Bureau publication, was a general conviction that "most people [by this time] could read and write . . ."

In 1970, pressured by the military, the Bureau of the Census agreed to reinstate the literacy question. Even then, instead of posing questions about actual skills, the census simply asked adults how many years of school they had attended. More than 5 percent of those the census reached replied that they had had less than a fifth grade education. For no known reason, the government assumed that four fifths of these people probably could read and, on this dangerous assumption, it was publicly announced that 99 percent of all American adults could read and write. These are the figures which the U.S. government passed on to the United Nations for the purposes of worldwide compilations and comparisons.

The numbers in the 1980 census improved a bit on those of 1970. This time it was found that 99.5 percent of all American adults could read and write.

It will help us to assess the value of the U.S. census figures if we understand the methods used in 1980. First, as we have seen, the census mailed out printed forms and based most of its calculations upon written answers in response to questions about grade-completion levels. A second source of information was provided by a subdivision of the Bureau of the Census known as "Current Population Surveys." This information, based on only a small sample, was obtained by telephone interviews or home visits. In all cases the person was asked how many years of school he (she) had completed. If the answer was less than five, the person was asked if he or she could read. This was the full extent of the investigation.

It is self-evident that this is a process guaranteed to give a worthless data base. First, it is apparent that illiterates will not have much success in giving written answers to a printed questionnaire. The census believed that someone in the home or neighborhood—a child or a relative perhaps—could read enough to interview those who could not and that that person would complete the forms. This belief runs counter both to demographics and to the demands of human dignity. Illiterate people tend to live in neighborhoods of high illiteracy. In the home itself, it is repeatedly the case that mother, father, grandparent, and child are illiterate. Parents, moreover, try very hard to hide their lack of competence from their children and indeed, as we have seen, develop complicated masking skills precisely to defend themselves against humiliation. The first assumption of the Census Bureau, therefore, must be viewed as fatuous at worst, naive at best.

Illiterates, being the poorest of our citizens, are far less likely to have telephones than others in the population. Those who do are likely to experience repeated cutoffs for nonpayment. Anyone who organizes in a poverty community takes it as a rule of thumb that mail and telephone contacts are the worst of ways to find out anything about the population. Experienced organizers also understand quite well that doorway interviews are almost certain to be unsuccessful if the occupant does not know or trust the person who is knocking at the door. Decades of well-justified distrust have led poor men and women to regard the stranger with his questionnaire and clipboard as the agent of a system which appears infrequently and almost never for a purpose which does not portend substantial danger. Bill collector, welfare worker, court investigator, census taker, or encyclopedia salesman—all will be received with the same reticence and stealth. If the census taker should elicit any facts at all, there is a good chance that they will be facts contrived to fence him out, not to enlighten him as to the actualities of anyone's existence.

In the case of illiterates, moreover, living already with the stigma of a disability that is regarded as an indication of inherent deficit, there is an even stronger inclination to refuse collaboration with the government's investigator. Many will profess a competence which they do not possess.

Finally, there is a problem with the question that the census seeks to pose. The fact that someone has attended school through fifth grade cannot be accepted as an indication that that person reads at fifth grade level. People who are doing well in school are likely to continue. Those who drop out are almost always people who already find themselves two years or more behind the class and see no realistic hope of catching up. With the sole exception of those children who (as in the migrant streams) drop out of school because their families need another pair of hands to add a tiny increment of income, those who leave the schools in elementary years are those who have already failed—or who have *been* failed by the system. The census, therefore, in asking people how long they have sat it out in public school, is engaging in a bit of foolishness which cannot easily be justified by ignorance or generosity. At best, by asking questions keyed not to attainment but to acquisition of grade numbers, the Bureau of the Census might be learning something vague about the numbers of adults who read at any point from first to third grade level. As we have seen, however, even this much information is unlikely to be gleaned by methods flawed so badly and so stubbornly maintained.

A census, of course, may have more than one purpose in a modern nation. Certain information is desired for enlightened national self-interest. Other forms of information are required for the purposes of international prestige. Literacy statistics are one of the universal indices of national well-being. The first statistics listed in the "nation profiles" that are used for international comparisons include illiteracy, infant mortality, per capita income, life expectancy. It can be argued, from the point of view of chauvinistic pride, that it is in the short-term interest of an unwise nation to report the lowest possible statistics for illiterates. In a curious respect, therefore, the motives of the Census Bureau coincide with those of the distrustful or humiliated adult who is frightened to concede a problem that is viewed as evidence of human failing. A calamitous collusion is the obvious result: The nation wants to guard its pride. The illiterate needs to salvage self-respect. The former wants to hide its secret from the world; the latter wants to hide it from the nation. It is easy to understand, in light of all of the above, why a nation within which 60 million people cannot even read the 1980 census should offer census figures to UNESCO that announce our status as a land of universal literacy.

In the preface to a 1969 edition of *The Other America,* Michael Harrington pointed to "the famous census undercount" of 1960. "Almost six million Americans, mainly black adults living in Northern cities, were not enumerated. Their lives were so marginal—no permanent address, no mail, no phone number, no regular job—that they did not even achieve the dignity of being a statistic."

The same may be said in 1985 for the much larger number—not 6 million this time, but some tens of millions—who do not exist within the inventories of the Bureau of the Census. The census tabulations would be less alarming if at least the nation's scholars would agree to disavow them. Instead, too many scholars take these figures with a certain skepticism but proceed to rescue them from condemnation by allowing that they hold at least one particle of truth. Their resolution of the conflict works somewhat like this: They interpret the census as an accurate indication that there are "no absolute nonreaders" in the nation. They then go on to indicate that—on a higher level, and by using definitions more appropriate to a developed nation—we are doing much less than we can. The second of these two points is correct. The first one is not.

The census itself, though unintentionally, suggests that 5 percent (over 8 million adults) read at third grade level or below. If we make some rough adjustments for the recent immigrants and the undocumented residents, but especially for all those the census doesn't reach and those who claim that they can read to get the census taker off their back, we can bet that well above 10 million adult residents of the United States are absolute or nearly absolute illiterates. The government, as we have seen, has now conceded an enormous crisis constituted by the "functionally illiterate" in our society; but it has attempted to convey the somewhat reassuring thought that none of these people are "nonreaders" in the sense that word would hold for Third World nations. In all likelihood, almost one third of those defined as "functional" nonreaders would be judged illiterate by any standard and in any social system.

It was Michael Harrington who spoke of "an underdeveloped nation" living within the borders of America. This is an accurate description. There is a Third World hidden in the First World; because its occupants must live surrounded by the constant, visible, and unavoidable reminders of the comforts and the opportunities of which they are denied, their suffering may very well be greater than that which is undergone by those who live with none of those reminders in a nation where illiterate existence is accepted as the norm.

Even for those who read at fifth or sixth grade levels in this nation, the suffering, by reason of the visible rewards identified with verbal and with arithmetic competence around them, must be very, very great. "The American poor," wrote Michael Harrington, "are not poor in Hong Kong or in the sixteenth century; they are poor here and now in the United States. They are dispossessed in terms of what the rest of the nation enjoys, in terms of what the society could provide if it had the will. They live on the fringe, the margin . . . They are internal exiles."

We know enough by now to treat the census figures with the skepticism and the indignation they deserve. History will not be generous with those who have compounded suffering by arrogant concealment. Sooner or later, the world will find us out. Neither our reputation nor our capability for self-correction can fail to suffer deeply from the propagation of these lies.

6

What Is Now Being Done?

But, though our perception be dim, it isn't dim enough to obscure one truth: that one mustn't despise the elemental needs, when one has been granted them and others have not. To do so is not to display one's superior spirituality. It is simply to be inhuman, or more exactly anti-human.

–C. P. Snow

Scholars have identified by now the full dimensions of this crisis. Why is it that we have, as yet, achieved so little?

Four major national literacy efforts now exist. One is the government's official program, Adult Basic Education. A second is the U.S. military's program of remediation for its own recruits. Together, these two efforts claim to reach between 2 and 3 million people. The military, however, seldom accepts a person reading at below the fifth grade level. Adult Basic Education is not legally restricted from admitting persons reading at the lowest levels; but the traditional modes of ABE discourage their participation. Its methods of recruitment, its institutional setting, its replication of a school-like situation, its physical distance from the neighborhoods in which the poorest and least literate people live, as well as the mechanistic nature of the methods it employs, have virtually assured that few of those who read beneath the fifth grade level will begin, complete, or ever have a chance to hear about its programs.

For those who do participate, the figures for "separation" (i.e., incompletion) are disastrous. Forty percent of those who enter ABE are "separated."

Only thirty percent of those who leave these programs prior to completion do so because they have achieved their goals. Other reasons given in a recent poll are these: inconvenient scheduling of classes, physical distance causing transportation problems, change of address, conflicts with employers, lack of interest . . . All, with the possible exception of employer conflicts, apply with equal force to dropout rates from public schools. Those who failed in public school are those, too frequently, who will be failed by ABE as well.

The other two programs are both privately supported. Laubach Literacy serves fifty thousand people. Literacy Volunteers of America (LVA) serves twenty thousand. These and several church-run programs do effective work with those they reach; but those they reach, as we shall see, are very few.*

The same is true of the municipal and state-run programs. One of the largest urban efforts, recently begun in Boston, allocates $1 million for a population that contains about 200,000 semiliterate or illiterate adults: $5.00 yearly per nonreader. The California Literacy Campaign—one of the most impressive of the statewide programs—allocates $2.5 million for a nonreading population of at least 5 million. Funding for this program, undertaken with a federal grant, now depends precariously on state support.

Corporations such as Citibank provide in-service literacy help for some of their employees. Since many corporations turn to groups like LVA to operate their programs, numbers are deceiving. Those they serve, moreover, are employable already. What they learn is only what they need to function more effectively in areas specific to the profits of the corporations. Only 1 percent of all funds spent for training of employees by American corporations has gone to basic math and reading/writing skills as opposed to skills required to perform a narrow task.

If we speak of education, then, as something separate from mechanical job training, and if we describe not those who "enter" but those who complete what they have set out to achieve, total figures for all programs in the nation do not much exceed 2 million. Even this is probably exaggeration. Government and corporations are not known for understatement of results. We can believe that far fewer than 2 million people are now being reached and also learning anything of substance.

Adult Basic Education is by far the largest program in existence. Federal funding for this program, after sixteen years of incremental growth, has been frozen at existing levels for the past four years and therefore, in constant dollars, has diminished. The $100 million budget now assigned to ABE needs to be viewed once more in context of the annual cost of $20 billion to taxpayers.

Many imaginative people are involved in Adult Basic Education. Most are

---

* I have not included here those very small community-based programs I admire most. Several of these will be examined later.

cognizant of its shortcomings. Many would like to introduce the relevant materials, decentralized learning centers, and the neighborhood involvement which might reduce the staggering dropout figures. Few serious people involved in ABE can feel much satisfaction in a program that purports to serve 2 million men and women but loses four in ten of those it reaches and which has been holding several hundred thousand people on its waiting lists for months and often years. Nor can many of these leaders feel rewarded by the consequences for those few who *have* been reached and who have *not* dropped out. Only 8.5 percent of those who go through Adult Basic Education programs have been able to get jobs, or better jobs, as a result of ABE. Fewer than 2 percent of those who have completed ABE report that they have voted for the first time as a consequence of the instruction they received. We can understand why ABE has won so little popular support.

Those who work in programs where the chances for success have been so badly compromised from the beginning cannot long sustain an activist mentality. The sense of failure and the arid and despondent atmosphere that gradually set in create a fatalistic mood, a sense of apathy, and finally an acquiescence in the bureaucratic status quo.

We need to ask another question too: not only how many people are now being served, but also who those people are.

People served, with very few exceptions, are those already on the edge of functional effectiveness or those who, literate in another language, do not suffer from a sense of broken hopes engendered by societal injustice. Those who read and write already in another language come out of one realm of confidence into a new arena of potential opportunities: one they are prepared to enter and within which they predictably do well.

Political refugees, many whose origins were middle class and most of whom were brought to the United States because of sympathies which correspond to U.S. interests—refugees from Laos and Cambodia, for instance—tend to be reached with relative ease. These are the "best examples" offered up to visiting journalists and scholars in the course of on-site visits. Marginal Americans who still can buy in on the promise of American prosperity and have reason to accept the myth of equal access (since, for these people, access is in fact imaginable) constitute almost the full remaining complement of those who now are given literacy help in the United States.

Those who are in the greatest need, who live in the most painful situations, whose friends and neighbors are most often burdened with the same or comparable dilemmas and can therefore offer least by way of intervention and support, those in the urban barrios and ghettos of Miami, New York City, Cleveland, Houston, San Antonio, Los Angeles, Atlanta, Boston, and Chicago, and those in the isolated rural areas of Alabama, Georgia, Mississippi, northern Maine, New Hampshire, West Virginia, and the Carolinas—those in short who constitute the major body of Illiterate America, the truly oppressed, the generational victims—these are the people who have not been served at all.

"How do we find them?"

This is a dishonest question that is heard too often among literacy groups. Having first created programs which, by reason of their setting, timing, and dispassionate condition, cannot provide the context for a moral struggle that transcends the atmosphere of public school in which adult illiterates have failed already, literacy experts turn the tables on the clientele they have not won and ask each other "where the people are" and "why they don't respond . . ."

Numerous surveys have been carried out to pose these questions. "Student recruitment is [the] number one problem," one group is reported to have found. The Contact Literacy Center tells us that an organization based in Chattanooga with the ultimate in low-key designations, CALM (Chattanooga Area Literacy Movement), finds "that the ghetto area prospects do not respond." Among the methods they have tried, but find most ineffective, are the following: door-to-door solicitation; "skits" and "plays" concerning literacy; "placards" in all city buses; printed flyers mailed to social agencies, clinics, hospital emergency rooms, and laundromats; recruitment through low-income churches . . .

Looking at this list of methods which do not work for the "ghetto area prospects," we are forced to wonder why the two approaches to a liberating struggle that have always worked so well in grass-roots organizing efforts— knocking on doors and working through the churches—do not seem to work for groups with names and attitudes like CALM. I have seen hundreds of people respond when, in the company of five or ten dynamic neighborhood residents and with a handful of effective organizers from outside the neighborhood, I have walked for days from door to door, signing up black and poor white people to attend the organizing session for a literacy center which was designated as a Freedom School. (We called it that, not "CALM," because we were not calm; nor were the crowds that packed the basements of the churches where we met and where our classes subsequently would be conducted.) Churches, if the ministers or members had been asked to join our earliest discussions, proved to be the settings for intensely moving rallies. It was out of one such meeting that a gentle and articulate young mother rose to ask me if I needed an assistant. Offering her help for free, she soon became the link to several dozen other neighborhood leaders and, still more important, to a total of 400 children and adults who soon signed up and regularly appeared for six or seven hours of instruction weekly. Within four months that woman had replaced me in my organizing role.

During those hectic and exciting months in which at least 200 persons nightly filled the basement of our church and overflowed into a network of apartments that we rented in the many semivacant buildings of the neighborhood in which we worked, most of us (teachers and learners both) were also taking action on the words we learned and on the world of anguish and injustice which those words revealed. Literacy sessions that evolved around such words as "tenant," "landlord," "lease," "eviction," "rat," and "roach" led to one of the first rent strikes in our city. Words, connected to the world, led—not in years but in a matter of days—to the reward of a repainted building, the replacement of illegal exits which could be opened only from outside the building, and the reconstruction of a fire escape that served the tenants of a building of five stories but could not be used because it had been rotted into empty air above the second floor. Success so vivid and concrete, within the troubled streets beyond the little rooms in which we worked, became the basis for additional recruitments.

Other groups which I have visited in San Francisco, Washington, New York have met with similar results from similarly comprehensive efforts to recruit (and to retain) illiterate adults by building, not a mechanistic replication of the public school, but something which at length is nothing less than a collective action-center structured upon words that can denounce the world in which the learners live and leading to events which, even by extremely modest stages, start the transformation of that world in ways that cannot fail to justify the classroom hours that have been expended.

None of the adults with whom I worked during those years was ever willing to settle for "the functional abilities" of bottom-level job slots in available custodial positions. Dozens, however, soon became effective leaders in the struggle to desegregate the Boston schools. Two are now community advisers to desegregated schools. Several run neighborhood social service centers. Three (although they lacked a college education) received degrees from Harvard's Graduate School of Education and returned to work within the neighborhoods in which we met. The woman who stood up in church to volunteer to be my "aide" is now a mortgage officer in Boston's largest bank.

Success of this exceptional degree could not be universal. Often we failed. We did not state it otherwise. We did not say our students failed. We knew that we had not been wise enough to meet their needs. Frequently, the damage done already in the public schools, as well as the entire syndrome of substandard housing, illness, and depression that our students knew, proved far beyond our powers to reverse. Of one thing, however, I am certain. Recruitment, no matter how difficult it appears, is never the real problem. It masks some deeper questions which too many of these passionless and top-down programs do not choose to pose: (1) Who is it who is doing the recruiting? (2) What is it, in effect, they are recruiting for? If the work is done exclusively by middle class outsiders, if it is done in ways that bear the marks of a school venture, and if the goals and the rewards that have been offered are domesticating in their nature and subordinating in their tone, recruitment will forever seem to be the problem while the real one will not ever be acknowledged.

All of this omits the obvious absurdity of other methods which, as CALM reports, do not appear to work. It is hardly surprising that "skits" and "plays," so redolent of juvenile activities identified with first or second grade, do not stir the exaltations of the adult victims of those dreary rituals of public school. Nor is it surprising that the placards posted in the laundromats or city buses do not draw a swift response from those who cannot read them.

"Illiterate? Sign up for classes on November 25, two blocks east of Kennedy, one block south of Main."

Beneath the irony, some cruelty remains. The pretense of "a problem in recruitment" in this situation is reminiscent of the ways that government officials speak of those who are reported to be hungry but who, as the experts tell us, do not take advantage of the food stamps and the surplus foods which are presumably "there for the asking."

"If they are hungry, it must be that they have chosen not to eat. All the needed services are now in place."

These words are hardly more benighted than the language that we heard during the record cold and hunger that afflicted many sections of the nation in the winter months of 1983 and '84. If the government is failing at all, its representatives concede, it may be at worst a case of failing to make known the largesse which is presently available. This statement is made despite the documented fact of government reductions of the food stamp programs and even in the face of many documented incidents of near-starvation on the part of families that have run through all their food supplies and funds. Whether in literacy or in nutrition, both the problem and the answers are the same: There isn't enough. What little there is offends both by the way that it is offered and by the multiple humiliations which the applicant is forced to undergo. Answer: "We've got to do a better job of making known available facilities . . . Next, we've got to motivate the starving, the illiterate, to ride the bus and stand in line for what they may or may not find in stock when they arrive."

Whether the offering is weary words or surplus cheese, those who line up are waiting still; and those who have grown weary of that wait are scarcely likely to respond to middle class inducements to "apply" once more. Hunger— whether cognitive or nutritive—will not be relieved by methods such as these. Meanwhile CALM persists in finding more inventive ways by which to win "the ghetto prospects" to the recognition that it might be wise for them to learn to overcome their inhibitions and to join the barren table for a nonexistent feast.

One bitter instance of "a problem in recruitment" comes from literacy experts in the State of Florida. A poster developed in 1979 by the Florida State Department of Education for recruitment of illiterate adults is carefully designed to simulate the "Ten Most Wanted" criminal posters in the lobbies of the U.S. postal service.

WANTED

White female between the ages of 16 and 44, currently unemployed and receiving public assistance. Must be lacking in basic reading and writing skills, and be willing to spend a few hours per week to improve literacy ability to a minimum of 5th grade. Call your local ABE for further information.

It is the stark photograph beside the text which makes the connotation unmistakable. If the goal here is to draw attention, it is certainly successful. If the goal is to attract adult nonreaders into literacy programs, we may wonder what results can be expected.

If this poster should succeed at all, we may suspect that its most damaging success is to instill the lowest possible self-image in potential learners. Those who are not already drawn to criminal careers might have been given a good push in that direction by the anger which this poster, where it can be comprehended, might well be expected to incite. The dreadful format is, however, not the most degrading aspect of this poster. Conscious or not, the wording that is used (the reference to "white female") represents a not-so-subtle slur. It summons up the far more common phrase ("black male") which is familiar from the bulletins and the alerts so often issued by police. Precisely by selecting the exact reverse, the poster resurrects the image of the stereotype ("black public menace") which it then seems to deny. An arduous and awkward effort to avoid the racial stereotype manages, in a shocking way, to place racism foremost in our fears.

Finally, we need to ask to whom the writing is addressed. Not to the illiterate white woman who can read at best at fourth grade level. The vocabulary chosen is far too complex. The intended reader then must be somebody else: someone who can read the words and recognize the culprit's face. "Wanted" posters are not addressed to those the FBI would like to find. They are addressed to law enforcement officers, to civic-minded citizens, and those of vigilante disposition who might like to share in the excitement of the chase. This then is recruitment in the mode of the dogcatcher or the lynch mob. Few inducements to the world of printed words could be less tempting or more reminiscent of the worst traditions of the posse and the hunt. The poster was conceived, no doubt, with good intentions. Cruel assumptions nonetheless explode out of its mode of presentation. Who are we after? What is it our aspiration to achieve? Is this divine arrest or liberation?

It remains to emphasize, despite all the above, that neither recruitment nor accessibility represents the greatest reason for the failure of existing literacy efforts. Even if the programs that exist today were made available in every neighborhood of every city and in every rural slum, and even if recruitment were enlightened and facilities immeasurably improved, they would make little difference. The ultimate obstacle is not one of technique but of political and ethical constraint.

People who suffer in a thousand ways apart from inability to read and write cannot be expected to achieve substantial gains in literacy skills if those skills are not directly linked to other areas of need and if those links do not consist of energizing words that can legitimize an often unacknowledged sense of rage. No program in existence on a national or statewide scale has ever dared to speak in terms like these.

Effectuated rage is a forbidden concept in the politics of adult education. It does not even need to be forbidden; the people who run these programs are not angry. They cannot elicit or respond to an emotion they do not experience. Neutralized by the advantages that they possess, anaesthetized by the credentializing process they have undergone, tailored by their lifelong training to an understated mode of temperate articulation, they do not feel—and, if they ever felt, would rapidly suppress—the sense of indignation which defines illiteracy not as a technical mistake, an error or an aberration in an otherwise just and equitable nation, but rather as one vivid symptom of societal oppression. The word "oppression" does not appear in government reports nor in the voices of the people who control the major literacy programs of this nation. They have no inclination to make use of angry language of this kind. If they did, they would think twice before acceding to such inclinations. They are afraid (and properly so) that they would lose their governmental funds or forfeit the philanthropy that they depend on.

Even the best of programs that exist today are crippled by such feelings of dependence. Where government affiliations aren't at stake, it is the good will of the corporations and foundations that constrains them. University affiliations are at times still more restrictive. The research interests of the universities take precedence almost always over concrete actions, and such actions as may be permitted are repeatedly immobilized by academic language that intimidates by raising questions about "insufficient knowledge" or "potentially disruptive consequences."

I was asked in 1979 to set up a "National Literacy Center" at one of the major schools of education. Optimistic and somewhat naive, I set about the task of raising funds and organizing operations. Within one month I was accused of compromising academic interests by my failure to assign the first funds raised to salaries for doctoral assistants. By the second month I was attacked for failing to respect the primacy of research goals. "We need to know a great deal more about the problem," I was told. "Psycholinguistics ought to be included. We have some doctoral candidates who could be employed for that component . . ." By the end of six months I was locked into an alphabetic labyrinth of professional subdivisions, no one of which could be excluded from the planning stage for fear of injuring their fragile dignity. Threatened interests bristle at the first sign that they might be superseded; rituals of pacification must be undertaken.

Drowning in neutral language, I discovered with a sense of shock that I had invested half a year in every possible aspect of adult illiteracy except adult illiterates. Despite the backing of a loyal and enlightened dean, I resigned abruptly and returned to literacy work within illiterate communities. "Too bad," a university administrator told me. "You could have run a million-dollar program."

It is too bad. A million dollars was available for research while not $100 was available for taking action on the things that we already know.

Research, however, is not the primary obstacle to passionate endeavor. Encrusted and competitive hegemonies represent the most immobilizing force. Each group already in existence, even the most progressive of these groups, seems to view the possible expansion of the literacy struggle with a thinly veiled alarm. Everyone wants more money and support, but no group wants to see that money go to someone else—or something new. They compete with each other; but the deeper competition is with any unknown future venture that might render them tangential or eclipse them altogether by success. Anything that reaches 25 to 60 million people would inevitably eclipse all programs in existence. Any struggle rooted in politicized and grass-roots mobilization is bound to overshadow even the most earnest efforts of politically inhibited endeavors.

While lobbying for funds, therefore, such groups are cautious to ensure that any funds which come available will be assigned to programs like their own. The motives of individuals may be benign, but the function of their organizations is regressive. They speak of wishing to affect (not to transform) the future; but, most of all, they want to supervise that future. They claim an ideological neutrality, but this is not an honest claim. Their ideology is self-perpetuation. The consequence, in terms of dry and jargon-ridden verbiage, is worse than mere futility. It is a decorated impotence that chokes off all imaginative fury, all bravado, and all sense of an imperative to strong mandated deeds.

The teachers' unions suffer from another inhibition. If they concede the true size of the problem, how can they avoid the risk that this may be imputed to their failure? Hence the tendency to speak of "problems" or "dilemmas," not of "victims," of "exclusion," of "oppression." To speak of those who are "oppressed" is to suggest that there must be "oppressors." Words like these are interdicted by the pretense of political neutrality. Political passion does not grow from seeds as dry as these.

In response to a recent wave of national concern and to some belated media attention, literacy groups have now begun to coalesce in networks, coalitions, and the like. Some of these networks are better than others; one in particular holds out the promise of attracting powerful allies in the ranks of the booksellers and some other corporate groups whose resources may enable us to draw attention to the needs of people who, up to this time, have never found the vocal advocates that they require.

The necessary question, nonetheless, must be addressed: What is it that these networks are connecting? We cannot build a network out of fragmentized defeat. Ivan Illich once observed that, as societies lose faith in God, they build more intricate cathedrals. As literacy proprietors awaken to the failure of their dreams and the aridity of their ideals, they join in coalitions. What do these networks literally do? They network nothingness. They form a coalition of historic losers. They "keep in touch"—or so they claim. With what? With one another's failure. Unless there is a sweeping transformation of the ways in which the current crisis is defined, and in the nature of the goals that we pursue, universal adult literacy in the United States will not find its genesis in groups like these.

Two recent, highly publicized events have helped to bring the literacy crisis to the national attention. One is of governmental origin. The other is a private venture.

The government's action, sponsored by the White House, is by far the less impressive of the two. The federal Adult Literacy Initiative, announced by Secretary of Education Terrel Bell in early fall of 1983, included a total of eight items, only three of which proposed an effort that did not exist already and only one of which involved an allocation of new funding. Five of the proposals were for insubstantial gestures such as "cooperation with the private sector," counsel (but not financial help) to literacy groups already in existence, encouragement of "liaison" with those programs that depend on volunteers, "encouragement" of state and local literacy councils—and, alas, "networking." Two of the three more substantive proposals were to promote the use of college credit to encourage literacy volunteers (neither a new idea nor one the government could possibly enforce) and an emphasis on literacy work by federal government employees.

The one proposal that involved a bit of money for instruction was the one-time allocation of $360,000 for a pilot program using students on work-study grants for literacy action. The White House urged the colleges to view this as a model to become involved in literacy work in future years. No funding was proposed to make this possible. The White House, moreover, went out of its way to emphasize that only "existing money"—i.e., no new funds—would be available. The point was promptly made that colleges and universities, relying as they do upon work-study funds for the employment of their students in the ordinary jobs (in cafeterias and dormitories, for example) which are needed for the maintenance of their institutions, could not be expected to assign more than a small part of these funds to programs that were taking place off-campus and did not provide a subsidy for academic operations.

The government's "initiative," therefore, was even more deficient than that timid word implied. It wasn't a struggle. It wasn't a campaign. Above all, it was not a demonstration that the federal government had finally perceived its own responsibility to sponsor and directly fund an all-out answer to a crisis which it had defined as being national in scope and danger.

The White House initiative did perhaps have one real and unfortunate result. By offering to the press and public the illusion of a genuine commitment, the government managed to sedate some people with the notion that "something important" was now going to be done. Those who accepted this idea were, to the degree that they had been persuaded, granted the self-exempting sense that it did not depend on them to launch this battle. "Somebody else is doing something now. We can remove this issue, therefore, from our own front burner. If it is on the government's agenda, then it need not be on ours." The White House initiative functioned in this way not as a mandate but as a disincentive.

The same had been true a decade before when President Nixon launched a similarly empty program known as "Right to Read." Six years later, the program was downgraded after being termed a failure by its own director. Reiteration of a decade-old deception could not fail to foster an enhanced sense of futility. Rituals of guaranteed or, at least, predictable defeat do something worse than disappoint. They also teach us to regard such disappointment as inevitable. To the degree that we accept such rituals without denunciation, we are colluding in the further subjugation of illiterate adults.

The other publicized event of 1983, the forming of an operational alliance among a number of previously isolated and too frequently competitive private groups, offered better grounds for optimism than the government's promotional endeavor. By pulling together both the major volunteer groups (LVA and Laubach), as well as Adult Basic Education and two of the largest scholarly organizations now involved in the teaching of reading and in the teaching of adults, and by combining them in a working coalition with the American Library Association and the nation's largest bookseller, B. Dalton, the private alliance offered hope of a reduction in the turf mentality I have described above. More important, the leadership role assumed by the booksellers and the library profession served to inject into the literacy debate an element that had been absent from all government reports and, indeed, from almost all discussion of the issue up to now. The problem had always been addressed in terms of dollar costs, employment, signs, instructions, menus, manuals, and the military needs, but never with reference to the use of reading skills *in order to read books*. Strange as it appears in retrospect, such an omission was probably an inevitable result of the demeaning mechanistic thrust of government concern. The role of the ALA and of B. Dalton might serve henceforth as a clear reminder of the one historic and surpassing reason for the growth of literacy 400 years before and, a century later, here in the New England colonies: not to read booklets of mechanical instruction but in order to gain access to the spiritual endowment of a sacred book and, subsequently, to secular words—to poetry, to literature, to history, as well.

My reservations in regard to coalitions nonetheless remain. Even with an open-minded willingness to find our allies where they may appear, we should recognize the fragile nature of such coalitions, as well as their susceptibility to government cooption fostered in part by niceties of sociable behavior which the established nature of this sort of coalition can too easily enforce as the accepted level of debate. In any event, whatever our longing to suspend our disbelief and to be grateful for all blessings, the minuscule impact of all public and nonpublic efforts undertaken up to now must force us to look first into our hearts—not to another coalition—for the answers.

Case Study: Beyond Statistics

Statistics have a dangerous capacity to undermine the vividness of many of these issues. Beyond the talk of coalitions, alphabetic organizations, and the like, there are at length real people. A recent incident reminds me of the terrible frustration that is undergone by those who keep on working day by day, and year by year, to lessen the anguish of the people in the neighborhoods they serve and to persist, with spirits high, despite the paltry and insulting levels of assistance they receive.

In December 1983, I am invited to an adult literacy center, not far from my home in Massachusetts. A single overheated room within the local "Y" provides the setting for a program that employs three teachers to provide instruction to 400 adult pupils. A total of $60,000 yearly pays for rent ($8,000), salaries (the three instructors plus one woman who is secretary and coordinator of the center), all materials, recruitment, publications, phone expenses, and insurance.

"The students are here before I open up the door each morning," says one teacher. "Even in the coldest weather, they are waiting on the street. Many of these people need to take two buses and walk several blocks. They have to leave their home by 7:30 to be here at 9:00 . . ."

Half the money for this center comes from federal funds; the other half is raised through municipal sources and by begging to the local corporations and foundations. One of their staff, a gifted woman who might otherwise increase the teaching force to four, has to devote her time to raising funds. Even with her best efforts they can allocate only $150 to each learner.

"Often we have twenty people sitting in this room at once. We can work with maybe six or seven at a time. The rest just wait. They sit and wait for any one of us to give them help. Sometimes we have twelve or fifteen people here, just waiting. Some of those people don't come back. Problems come up. The kids get sick, the husband's out of work, the phone bill's due, the heating gets cut off . . . Maybe they're just tired of waiting."

This is the only adult literacy center in an impoverished mill town which is home to 80,000 people. Over 10 percent of adults in this town are unemployed. Many are third generation French Canadians, Italian, Irish, Greek. A smaller number come from Haiti, the Dominican Republic, the Far East.

"After teachers, the biggest problem is the shortage of supplies. Then the kinds of materials we get. Then the distance people have to travel just to be here . . ."

There is only one copy of a workbook and one low-vocabulary reader in the center. Both are the outdated products of a firm that publishes "adult materials for the adult nonreader."

This is a gun.
It is Mr. Hill's gun.
It is his big gun.

"Forty-year-old women can't connect with stuff like this," the teacher says. "Easy? Yes. It's at the lowest level, like they say. But who is going to get energized with sentences like these? Isn't there something better?"

This is the Smith family.
The Smith family lives in the city.
That man is Jack Black.
Jack Black lives in the valley.
Jack is visiting the Smith family.

The point of the lesson is to emphasize short *a*. Along with Jack and Black, valley and family, these words are listed on the previous page: bag, basket, happy, marry, carry . . . "Why not angry? Angry is as short an *a* as happy, carry, marry! Most of the women who come through those doors aren't happy! They are angry—and a lot more angry than they ever could be happy at the load of shit they have to carry with a guy they wish to God they didn't marry!"

I ask: "Why don't you use that sentence? That sounds like a lot of energetic *a*'s."

"Energetic wouldn't do in Adult Basic Education," she replies.

The teacher who is speaking is a forty-year-old Irish woman, once a reading teacher in the local public schools but recently laid off after a cut in funds. She has the steel blue eyes and weathered skin of someone who has worked hard all her life and has emerged from many sufferings, of which she is too proud to speak, with an unbroken spirit and a toughened decency that give to her bleached hair and bargain-basement clothes, her raw thick hands and sharp-edged jaw, a saving grace of dignity and strength that utterly transform the dreary space in which we sit and speak. I am reminded of a hundred other people like this, in a dozen other bootstrap operations of this kind, who have trusted me with their too-vulnerable toughness on a hundred other days in San Antonio and San Francisco and New York.

"This is the Smith family! That man is Jack Black! I don't know of anybody named Jack Black. No one by the name of Smith came in this room last year. Lots of Angelos, Morenos, some O'Dougalls, maybe an O'Neill . . . Who is America made of? Who thinks up these little books? I'd like to turn this page someday and find somebody with a name like Goldberg! Someone you could really meet. Someone whose name comes out of the real world. But this is the kind of books we get. And, as it is, we only got one copy."

The learners come from all over the city; over half come from the project which is just across the street. "If we had the money to set up some satellites, one in each of seven projects in this city, then to staff them, then to get some extra staff to teach, then to go to neighborhood meetings now and then and see what folks are saying and to pick up their ideas, we could reach 4,000 people in this city. As it is, we reach 400—and just barely. How many other folks are out there we will never see? How would they get here? What would it take for them to come? So many other things in life are wrong at the same time. I know what it's like. My job was cut. My husband worked for General Electric. He was laid off too. We got no warning. I've been through it all. I've lined up for food stamps, seen the way they treat you when you show up fifteen minutes late. You know what happens? They tell you that you have to make a new appointment. Then you got to sit at home and add up all of your receipts and bills, your phone bill and your gas bill and the money that you spent on food. Anything you did for fun, you got to show that too. Add it up. List anything you earned. Show them your checkbook. Tell them if you've got a car . . . How do you think somebody does this? You sit up with your husband and you try to find all of the papers and receipts. You read the rules. You try to add it up. Now how would you do this if you couldn't read? How do you do it if you can't do math? Where do you find all of those little bits of paper? How do you make sure that you get to the right office on the right day at the right street, at the time that you're assigned? You spend an hour waiting in line. Then they say: 'You're fifteen minutes late! You got to make a new appointment!' Nobody needs to tell me what it's like for them. I know it. I've been there."

She describes the cycle of depression that surrounds the lives of people she has tried to teach. "First they need to find a baby-sitter so that they can come. If she can't she brings the baby with her. The baby screams. We don't have the funds to rent another room and hire someone else for day care. She goes to welfare and she asks for money for a baby-sitter. She doesn't qualify for money if she hasn't been here. She can't hire the baby-sitter if she doesn't qualify. One woman, if her food stamps are late, she couldn't eat. She was so weak she couldn't come. But she wouldn't get the money if she couldn't prove that she had come.

"This woman comes in. She's bitter. Bitter at us. Bitter at everything. She brings her grocery receipt. She thinks that she's been cheated. She asks me to add it up. There are only three items. I add it up. She's right. She *has* been cheated. Not by any corner grocer—by the A&P! So then I understand why she's so bitter. She's right to be bitter. Why shouldn't she be bitter? Who can she trust? Then how can she trust me?

"Another woman. She can read but she cannot do math. Her mother lives in Los Angeles. Her mother cannot read. She works for Perdue, the chicken man. She thinks that she's been cheated on her pay. She sends her pay stubs to her daughter. The daughter brings them in for class. She asks me if her mother's being cheated. I figure it out. The woman is right. She's cheated on withholding. I help her write a letter to her mother. She comes in to this little shabby place in Massachusetts to ask us to tell her if her mother has been cheated in L.A.! So we help her write an answer to her mother. Right there you have two very angry women. Add me—you've got three. Why don't they use *angry* in this primer?"

I ask her what would be ideal conditions for the program.

"More money. More staff. More materials. Different materials. Three or four rooms. Day care for babies. Six other centers. Continuity and organization so that we could work with the same person at the same time on the same day for a year. Small groups. Groups of three or four. So they could give each other help and so they wouldn't feel they're all alone. That would be important. It would take money, and more teachers. I could organize a dozen groups. I could get together college kids I know to give a hand. We could do an oral history of ————. The stories of this city, of the GE plant, the old shoe businesses, the union stories, stories of the days when there were pushcarts, markets, clothes for sale all over town, the brickyards, and the immigrants, the stories . . . We could do it. We could open up those doors."

In five years they have worked with 1,400 people. There are over 15,000 people in the city who are said to be in serious need of educational assistance. Because of cutbacks in the schools, the numbers are increasing.

"Out in the suburbs," I say, "the kids are joking that they don't need math. They add things on their pocket calculators."

"Not here they don't. They don't use calculators in this town. They add up on their fingers."

Before I leave she tells me that she has two children who are handicapped. I ask how serious their problems are. The oldest has Down's syndrome. The youngest one was premature. He is two years old and still is in intensive care in

Boston. She seems embarrassed to be asked about her problems. "I'm managing. I'm getting paid. My husband's back at work."

It is the week before Christmas. The center is decorated with a tinsel tree. Students are waiting for their teacher on the other side of the partition.

7

The Pedagogic Time Bomb:
The Children of Nonreaders

I look at my seventeen-year-old son and my twelve-year-old daughter and I want to help them with their homework, but I can't. My son was supposed to repeat the ninth grade for the third time this year . . . He finally said he wanted to drop out . . . I see my handicap being passed on to my son . . . I tell you, it scares me.

There is reason to believe that all of this is going to get worse. Every bit of evidence we have at hand suggests that we will see an increase in the numbers of illiterate adults within another fifteen years. There are several factors which support this likelihood. In order to understand them, we might stop to take a look at certain of the changes which have taken place in recent years.

Illiteracy is not a new phenomenon in the United States. By any standard there were many more illiterate Americans 100 years ago—and perhaps as recently as 1960. In the past two decades, the number of those who cannot read at all has either diminished slightly or remained unchanged. It is functional illiteracy which has increased; this is the case because this term is, in itself, a "function" of the needs imposed upon a person by the economic and the social order. The economy and the society have changed in every age. It is the rate of change, and the degree to which it may outpace the literacy level of the nation, that determine what part of that nation is unable to survive and to prevail within the context of its times. The speedup in the rate of change, especially within the past two decades, is well known. Schools, while more inclusive, have not ceased to serve as instruments of class selection. Those who have been left behind, assigned to lower tracks throughout their education, and assigned in high school to "vocational" or "general" curricula, can no longer meet employment opportunities so easily as in a time when physical strength and docile acquiescence in repetitive operations were the characteristics that could qualify a person for a job.

Today, as the code words for survival in the hi-tech industries become "retraining" and "decision making" and "decoding," the problem becomes greater while it also grows much harder to conceal. Corporations will be able to "retrain" only those who can participate in training programs. Those who cannot read the training manuals—persons who, in another age, could nonetheless scratch out an income by the bending of the back and patient labor of the hands —may find no work at all. Even if the economic situation is improved, and opportunities for jobs expand, they will not be jobs that can be filled by people who can read at less than ninth grade level. "By the 1990s," according to Dorothy Shields, education director of the AFL-CIO, "anyone who doesn't have at least a twelfth grade reading, writing, and calculating level will be absolutely lost."

It is for this reason, I believe, that the assessment of the scholars at the Texas APL is absolutely right. Both the numbers and the visibility of functional and marginal illiterates are now significantly greater than a decade back and will be still greater in another ten or fifteen years. The present trend toward a reversal of inclusive policies, toward stiffened tracking patterns and resegregation of the poor, are likely to increase the dropout rates. Exclusion from the economic market will be more extreme, but expectations raised since 1965 may render the excluded far less willing to accept their subjugated roles. (Most, I am afraid, will nonetheless continue for a time to blame themselves and will appear to be less angry than defeated.)

There is no need for an apocalyptic overstatement of a situation which is tragic as it stands. The numbers are high. They will grow somewhat worse. They will grow a lot more visible. The cost to the society will deepen. Because the parents won't be able to defend their children against failures in the schools, nor give them preparation which might help them to defend *themselves,* the numbers served by present literacy programs will be more and more outbalanced by the numbers of illiterates emerging from the schools. It is the final point—the situation of the parents and its impact on the child—which will be the subject of this chapter.

Every autumn, as the public schools reopen, subway trains and buses moving through the cities of America carry signs that ask the parents of young children: "Did you read to your child today?"

Between one fifth and one third of all parents, over half of nonwhite mothers, cannot give an answer to this question. Some cannot answer for the

obvious reason that they cannot read the sign. Even for those among the semiliterate who can make out the question, there is little chance that they can act
upon the mandate which the answer poses.

The National Commission on Excellence in Education asked the same
question and committed the same error in the words of its report released in
April 1983. After telling the nation that our children are in trouble, that literacy
has been declining and that school performance is collapsing, the panel ended
its report with an old-fashioned exhortation to the parents:

"But your right to a proper education for your children carries a double
responsibility. As surely as you are your child's first and most influential teacher,
your child's ideas about education and its significance begin with you. You must
be a *living* example of what you expect your child to honor and to emulate.
Moreover, you bear a responsibility to participate actively in your child's education . . . Monitor your child's study; encourage good study habits; encourage
your child to take more demanding rather than less demanding courses . . . Be
an active participant in the work of the schools. Above all, exhibit a commitment to continued learning in your own life . . . Children will look to their
parents and teachers as models of such virtues."

Over a third of the American electorate could not read and understand the
document in which these words appeared. Virtually none of those whose children it affected most could possibly respond. They could not be models of
literate endeavor. They could not monitor their children's progress since they
had no means to study what it was those children were supposed to understand
or what progression of abilities they were expected to pursue. They could not be
examples of success as it has been defined by public education. The one example
they could give their children was the vivid evidence of failure in the schools
they had attended twenty years before.

The theme, however—"parents must help, and in the case of failure, parents are to blame"—soon grew into a chorus of unconscious but persistent irony.
Beneath the irony, a certain truth remains: Illiteracy does not "breed" illiteracy.
But it does set up the preconditions for perpetuation of the lack of reading skills
within successive generations. Illiterate parents have no way to give their children preschool preparation which enables them to profit fully from a good
school or—in the more common case—which will protect those children, by the
learning that takes place at home, against the dangers of the worst of schools.
Where schools are relatively effective, the children of illiterate adults may forfeit
much of what is being offered. Where schools are bad, the children of illiterate
adults cannot draw upon the backup education which is present in the homes of
people who can read and write.

Many people do not like to draw attention to this point. There is an
inclination (one I share) which leads us to avoid the attribution of a causative
effect to those who are already victims of an unjust social order. To concede that

certain parents, no matter what the reason, do not have the skills to help their kids is viewed as a political betrayal. It is regarded as a form of "deficit thinking" which may seem to blame the victim, not the system that has done the victimizing.

I share this hesitation; but I also feel compelled to face reality. I cannot say that children of one generation "die at an early age" and then rhetorically insist that, when those children have arrived at parenthood, they are as well prepared as anybody else to help their children overcome the obstacles they could not overcome themselves. There has to be a rational distinction between respect for dignity evinced by injured people in adversity and an obstinate denial of the diminution in effectiveness such people undergo. If, as many of us would like to claim, people who were devastated in their youth are "really doing fine without our own elitist literacy skills," then it is hard to argue that they now deserve priority attention. If, as we would like to say, illiterate people are "powerful in their own ways—simply 'different' from the ways that IBM executives are powerful," then there is no reason to propose a struggle for empowerment. Apart from loyalty, there is a point of simple honesty at stake. Doctrinaire denial of a generational injustice does no justice either to the truth or to the victims. Difficult as this will be, we have to face the facts if we intend to change them.

"It could be," writes Thomas Sticht, "that if we had put the billions of dollars [that] we've spent on pre-school children" into literacy programs for their parents, we might have gotten at "the real source" of illiteracy.

This emphasis is useful, although—like many of his peers—Sticht makes a false dichotomy between two equally important points and totally omits a third: the role of the public school itself. Both the literacy of parents and the preschool programs in which literate parents can participate in helping to prepare their child for the years of formal education are major factors in assisting children to survive the damage that may otherwise be done to them in public school. None of these three points should be shortchanged. It is the literacy of parents which has, up to recent times, been almost totally neglected.

Our severest problems, according to Maya Pines, "could be largely solved if we started early enough. Yet we recklessly ignore an exciting and persuasive body of knowledge . . . Millions of children are being irreparably damaged by our failure to stimulate them intellectually during their crucial years—from birth to six." Millions, she writes, "are being held back from their true potential."

Again, we need to be extremely careful in our use of words. Terms like "irreparable" are ill-advised. Any suggestion of absolute and irreversible damage in the years preceding entrance to the public school conveys at least three dangerous impressions:

First, it tends to let the schools entirely off the hook, absolving those which fail to serve the children of poor people on the grounds of "cognitive inabilities" implanted in those pupils prior to the time they enter school. Elementary schools, as we know well, fail millions of their pupils; and they do grave damage even to those children who have had the best of early learning reinforcement from devoted, literate, and conscientious parents. Nothing, therefore, ought to be regarded as "irreparable." This comes too close to something like a pedagogic version of original sin. In consequence, if not intent, it comes to be almost identical.

There is a second danger in this use of words. If we speak about "irreparable" damage, and if we term it "intellectual" instead of "pedagogic," we are subscribing to a point of view which, to all but the most cautious mind, may seem to hint at a genetic liability. The ease with which a casual observer may be led to see even substantial early setbacks as "inherent" (and, for this reason, not susceptible to later methods of reversal) should not be regarded lightly. Too many assumptions, incorrect and often racist, may derive from this mistake. In a reactionary decade there are many who will not be hesitant to use such statements to confirm their former views.

An additional problem with exaggerated language of this kind is the repeated evidence that even the worst of early learning setbacks *are* reversible and in fact have been reversed time and again by brilliant teachers and inspired programs at all subsequent levels of a person's education. The use of hyperbolic language is refuted by too many good examples.

"It is never too late," in the words of Theodore Sizer. Nothing we say, in speaking of the issues raised by writers such as Maya Pines, should lead us into this mistake. At the same time, we need to face the fact that the exclusion of the parent from all opportunity to do what is accepted by most wealthy people as essential for a child's early learning opportunities does make almost everything a great deal harder and far more expensive later on.

Thomas Sticht reports one literacy program, carried out in 1970, "in which parents were offered special education in child rearing and political activism. The program resulted in the parents improving their own life circumstances. It also produced a 15-point improvement in their children's IQ scores compared to a [control] group, and a 38-point improvement over the IQs of their older siblings who grew up before their parents received the special education." Evidence like this may help to put to rest the racist theories about IQ differential propagated in the early 1970s; but it also represents persuasive backup for the arguments regarding the importance of politicized and ethically impassioned literacy action that can serve the child and the parent both.

Those who read these words may think of parents who, in ways that seem to them both reprehensible and selfish, do not *care* to help their children learn. They cannot seem to keep in mind what they have heard but either rapidly dismissed or never quite believed: Millions of parents of the poorest children in our nation are excluded from an option which they cannot implement, no matter how devoted they may be, how much they love, how desperately they care.

It is no use to lecture and harangue illiterate adults as to "the beauty" of the written word, the "priceless value" of a book, "the spiritual rewards . . ." Harangue and exhortation can accomplish nothing. Lectures to the parents on their "obligations" can accomplish nothing. Condescending statements ("parents just don't seem to care") accomplish worse than nothing. Yet we hear such views too often and, predictably, from those who know the most but who betray the obligation which their knowledge should imply.

Because of the dangers of misunderstanding of this issue, I would like to quote the words of Charles B. Schultz, a friend who has advised me in the writing of this book and who has expressed his feelings in these terms:

"I tend to reject language that is even suggestive of intellectual deficiencies. I'm sensitive to that because I'm sure most teachers are convinced of one or another form of the deficit view [i.e., the "genetic" or the parent who "can't do the proper job"] and the mere suggestion is all that's necessary to reinforce them. On the other hand, I have no problem with the proposition that oppression has its costs; that parents who live in impoverishment have little resources, time, and maybe inclination to do some of the things that will prepare their child for the existing academic content of the school. Making that distinction is important."

I totally agree. The question remains: What can parents do to change this? What can they do to change the schools and *also* to prepare their kids for what the schools will offer as they now exist? The answer to one question is a long-term struggle. The answer to the second is a more approachable solution. Neither should be ignored—above all, not while we sit back and wait for the society to be transformed. If we agree to "wait" (and this is not what Schultz intends), we will be talking a great deal but doing very little.

There is a certain kind of courage, I believe, in fighting for a new world and still helping people to survive without ordeal within the one that they are stuck with. "We do what we can, not what we want," to use the words of Paulo Freire. This is why I am proposing here one lever of immediate and realistic change that might be placed within the power of illiterate adults themselves. This will happen only if a literacy struggle can be given the support and the priority that it demands.*

The idea of "a cycle of illiteracy" is difficult for many people to accept. Yet many examples of this cycle are available. One of the most frightening examples

---

* The passion with which poor parents fought for Head Start and now fight for the return of funding to sustain and to increase such programs cannot be ignored by those who are their allies. Parents I know have risked arrest in order to protect their Head Start centers. We cannot ignore the reason why.

is afforded by statistics that were given to me by the Cleveland Public Schools during a year in which I planned a literacy program for that city.

On the basis of tests given in May 1976, 75 percent of kindergarten children in the Cleveland schools appeared to be at or above the national norm. There was no significant divergence between races. In third grade, the number of nonwhite children scoring under national norms exceeded by five percentage points the number for white classmates. By fifth grade, the difference had grown to 10.8 percentage points. By ninth grade the difference suddenly exploded. Only 38 percent of white kids tested were below the norm: 60.5 percent of nonwhite kids were now below. By eleventh grade, only 28 percent of white students tested were below the norm: 59.4 percent of black kids were below. Whites appear to end up almost exactly where they started, with almost three quarters at or above the national norm. Blacks, during the same years, drop from a success rate of three quarters to a failure rate of six in ten.

Differences in dropout rates add to these bleak statistics. Twenty-five percent of whites drop out between the third grade and eleventh grade. Forty-two percent of black kids disappear in the same years. The drop in reading scores for blacks, and the divergence of their scores from those of whites, would clearly be a great deal larger if we could have tested every student—not excluding those who were no longer in attendance. We can't, of course. We cannot even guess what has become of all those adolescents. We can, however, guess with a degree of confidence that many of those former students have, during the years since these statistics were compiled, become the parents of another generation of poor children: kids who soon will enter the same schools without the reinforcement of those many forms of parent backup, not the least of them a minimal competence in reading, which the experts call "essential."

The figures I have cited demonstrate a stark divergence in the reading skills of white and nonwhite children. This divergence tells us nothing about racial differences. It tells us a great deal about class origins and economic status. There are poor white children in the schools of Cleveland. But there is a drastic difference between "poor" and "poorest." Those of the white working class, as well as those white people who depend on welfare, do not represent the hard core of the hopeless and defeated. They still have options, or they can at least remember options they may someday repossess. I have visited at length in almost every neighborhood of Cleveland. Many white people in this city are nonreaders; most of them, however, are "nonreaders by mistake." They are the persons in their social groups who somehow lost their way in public school and ended up for a variety of reasons as illiterate or semiliterate adults. It is, with some exceptions, the nonwhite adults of Cleveland who are the classic victims of oppression. There are plenty of other sections of the U.S.A. in which white people fall into this category too. In Cleveland, however, "black" is closely correlated with "the economic bottom." This is the reason why a contrast in the literacy figures for the white and nonwhite children in this city tells us something of importance about economic difference between those, identified by Carman Hunter, who somehow "fell through the cracks" and those who never had a floor to stand on in the first place.

In light of these statistics, we can guess what we might learn if basic skill exams that have been recommended by a number of the recent national commissions as a precondition for receipt of a diploma were to be administered in Cleveland, not only to students still in school but to those as well who have already disappeared. With 60 percent of all black students in eleventh grade having scored below grade level, and with 42 percent of all black students who were tested in the third grade having disappeared from classrooms altogether, we can expect that more than half of all young black adults in Cleveland would be found by minimal competence tests to be beneath all reasonable estimates of what it takes to function and prevail within American society. Whether they get a meaningless diploma or some other piece of paper ("a certificate of attendance") or are given neither, these are students who have little chance to enter the rat race of the present economic system or to make an impact on the voting process in a way that might transform that system. They will not be reading the reports released by blue-ribbon commissions. They will not read summaries of such reports in the newspaper. They will not know how many others share their situation. They will have no chance to find out why.

Why does fourth grade seem to represent the cutoff point? Why is it that fifth grade tests reveal the first sharp differential in the scores: a differential, in the case of Cleveland, which is over twice that of two years before?

One explanation (this is one that many people offer first) accepts the early reading scores as absolutely valid, points to the sharp decline in later years, and concludes that children of the poorest people could not be destroyed immediately by schools that stratify by social class but that, after four or five years in the system, they have finally succumbed to institutional oppression. Some of the same people point to cultural distinctions ("Black English" versus "Standard English," for example) which create a gulf of miscommunication between teachers and their nonwhite pupils. They argue that this is a gulf which is less damaging in early years but that it becomes an overwhelming force as kids get older. Others point to the peer pressures which increase as kids get older and to the growing force of adversary feelings which progressively set kids against their teachers as they look instead to people their own age or slightly older for the reinforcement of their feelings of resentment at an education system they perceive as hostile and unjust. Other observers would be tempted to reject the whole discussion on the basis that all testing has some bias, that the bias clearly works against the poorest children, and that all the test scores—late or early— should be viewed with much suspicion or ignored entirely.

Still others take the early scores as evidence that elementary schools are much improved and therefore no longer justify priority attention. Our focus, they say, should henceforth be directed to the secondary years. This final argument has had the greatest impact upon recent public policy. Hence the popularity and broad publicity afforded to a number of books which place exclusive emphasis upon the high schools.

Some of the preceding arguments—but not the first or last—make sense to me. Both the first and last points rest upon the faith that the initial scores are valid. I do not believe that this is so. My own belief is that the early scores mean very little, that the problems which appear in later years are present already in the first few years but do not show up on tests because these tests have more to do with the specifics of sounds, shapes, and letters than with comprehension and the confidence to venture into unfamiliar areas of academic learning. Up to the end of third grade, and for much of the fourth, the content of the books that children read is insubstantial. Starting in fourth grade, but more clearly in the fifth, content in itself grows more important. Up to that point, a child learns to read. After that point, the child reads to learn: to study geography or history or science or "The World News in Review." Without engaging in a survey of the research that exists on reading comprehension, I can draw upon my own experience as both a fourth and fifth grade teacher to confirm the basic point: Children who appeared to be in good shape on the basis of the things that could be tested in the first few years of school often proved to be entirely lost when asked to read in order to respond to subject matter. Again and again, these students were the children of nonreaders.

Any explanation based upon a single teacher's personal experience will not stand the test of all of those empirical devices (i.e., a "control group" and the like) which recommend opinions to the credence of experienced researchers. The issue, in any case, remains the subject of continuous dispute, now tilted one way, now the other, by the latest and most publicized reports. What can be stated with some certainty is that the child who received *all* of those forms of early and continued backup that the early-reading experts call "essential" is unlikely to have suffered as a consequence, while the child who has not had *any* of this backup seems a far more likely candidate for later failure.

Talking with illiterate adults, I often ask them how they could have been promoted for so many years without attracting more attention. The answer repeatedly is this: "I didn't understand it from the start. I learned to fake it from the fourth grade on."

Students who cannot read by this point do not stand much chance of making up the time that they have lost. School, for the society, becomes a holding action. For the students it becomes a period of morbid hibernation, lying low and waiting out the years. All the exhortations about discipline and rigor and the need for "tough" exams will make no difference for these students.

At worst they may improve the average scores by giving a last push to those who cannot read and are already on the verge of leaving school. This will provide illusory gains; and this, in the long run, may be the most that certain right-wing critics on our blue-ribbon commissions really want.

What happens to these children in the years that follow their experience in public school? How does society regard them? How do we justify their seeming failure—and our own? What is the national response?

Consider the child who is locked into the cycle that we have described: At some point, perhaps around the age of nine, he has been identified as "a problem reader" and has been assigned to one of the low reading groups within his fourth grade class. (We used to give these reading groups the names of different kinds of birds. The lowest groups were called "The Blackbirds" in one school in which I taught. Nowadays they may be labeled "Cardinals" or "Robins," but too many of these little birds in urban schools, as we know well, no matter what we call them, will be black or brown.) He is a "blackbird" then. He knows that this says something about who he is and what he might become; but he cannot yet imagine what is likely to transpire next and how he will fulfill the lowest expectations of the world that has assigned him his initial definition. If he cannot see into the future, many of our educators can. The "blackbird" of the fourth grade, the "slow learner" of the fifth, is likely to be the remedial student of the seventh grade and the repeat ninth grader of the junior high. Three or four years behind his class, if he remains in school at all, he goes on to high school to be placed in general or vocational courses. If he is allowed to take the SATs he is likely to do poorly and the average scores for everyone go down. The colleges complain. The school boards are alarmed. And now, twelve years too late, their voices grow stentorian and severe. "Minimal competency testing" comes to be the final answer to society's injustice. Punitive and retroactive, our decision is to flunk the student, not the school. We siphon off the child who was showing signs of certain failure seven years before, the child whom the schools promoted mindlessly throughout the first six grades—the very same child, in too many cases, whose parents or grandparents could not read to him when he was three or four.

Another generation of illiterate adults, a little larger this time than the one before, is ready to be consigned to unemployment, welfare, street crime, then the courts and prison cells which represent the final destination of the lower "track" for those whose parents could not read and whom the schools have failed to serve. The pedagogic slag heap grows a little higher. The newest generation of illiterate adults is added to the grim statistics which our politicians— solid, self-reliant, bootstrap advocates, literate all, and children of good readers —deprecate, deplore, and once again are ready to ignore.

Those of the marginal, the barely literate who have been granted clemency by the more tolerant school systems, may receive diplomas and go on to public colleges that offer preferential channels for the poor. Those who survive (eight out of ten will not) soon find themselves the objects of concern that grows at length into unspoken accusation: Courses have been watered down in order to allow them to remain in college. Their classmates and the parents of those classmates are alarmed to see the quality of academia lowered. Excellence is threatened by adulteration of curriculum. Anger rises, and the signs of a reactionary pullback from egalitarian ideals are in the air. The weary elders of the 1980s take revenge at last upon the hapless victims of the 1960s. They do not blame the victims. They know very well by now that they don't need to. The victims have been trained to blame themselves: "We had our chance. We can't complain. We didn't make the grade."

It is in this climate that a get-tough policy emerges in the public consciousness and finds its first bemused or cruel articulation in the voices of the press and certain public leaders. "Is this the price that we must pay for democratic and inclusive education? These poverty kids are bigger problems than we bargained for. Someone should help, of course. It's only fair. But it *isn't* fair to sacrifice the education of our own kids. Isn't the point to bring the others up— but not to pull our own kids down?"

Hard self-interest adds a new note to the question: "I do believe in equal opportunity. But every group and every race has got to do its part. You can't expect it to be handed to you. Our folks did it. They began with nothing but the shoes they wore, the old clothes on their backs . . . We did it. Why can't they?"

The bottom line of fear is given voice at last: "What if Sarah doesn't get admitted to Mount Holyoke? What if she has to go to Syracuse or N.Y.U.?"

The final thought: "There's always private school."

Those who do not choose, or can't afford, to opt out of the public schools begin to press for even more definitively separated tracking schemes. "Gifted classes" and intensive programs for the college bound are offered as a consolation by the school boards. Issues like desegregation go on the back burner. Excellence becomes a code word for retreat from equity.

Smith College, known for decades as a symbol of egalitarian ideals wedded to the highest pedagogic standards, announces plans in 1983 to transfer student-aid criteria from economic need to academic merit based on SATs. A black Episcopal minister in Boston speaks these words: "It is fifteen years and one month since the death of Martin Luther King. I wonder if Smith College has just put the final nail into his coffin."

A few days later, I repeat these words during a faculty colloquium at Brown. The dean of the college flinches at my language and appears offended. Later, she takes me aside and tells me in a quiet voice: "I am afraid he might be right. It seems that we are moving in a dangerous direction." She questions, however, whether the statistics for adult illiterates could be as high as I have said.

Ethical leaders step away from painful recognitions. The voices of the best are muted now and difficult to hear. The voices of the cruel are loud and clear. The worst, as always, are informed of passionate intensity.

It is at this moment, and with much publicity, that the National Commission tells the public that "our Nation is at risk." In the subsequent six months, no less than seven separate panels and commissions publish similar, occasionally varied but essentially compatible reports: The schools are failing. Secondary programs are too easy. High school graduation standards must be stiffened. College entrance qualifications must be more severe. The federal government must give direction and accept responsibility.

The President, however, makes it clear that there will be no increment in federal funds. He recommends instead: local initiative, legalized school prayer, and tuition credits for those parents who elect to send their kids to private school.

A conservative columnist, George Will, provides a more vindictive answer. The virtue of the National Commission's study, he reports, is its exclusive focus upon "excellence" and its refusal to divert attention from strict pedagogic goals to issues such as "social justice" or "equality." Both items are "peripheral," he writes, to education.

A final answer is provided by the courts. On May 5, 1983, a federal judge in Florida approves a decision of the Florida State Board of Education to deny high school diplomas to those twelfth grade pupils who do not achieve a passing grade on standardized exams intended to test competence in math and reading.

Of 3,800 Florida high school seniors who have failed the state exam, 57 percent are black—although blacks represented only one fifth of the student population. The rate of failure among blacks is seven times the rate for whites.

Those who are familiar with the national statistics cannot question that the test results in Florida are probably correct. Moreover, the failure rate would surely be much higher if the standards used in Florida had not been minimal. If the literacy tests have been in error, they have probably erred in the direction of a marginal competence which will not measure up to real survival needs. What if the tests applied next year, or the year after, should be more severe? We can expect that more than 15 percent of white and more than 50 percent of non-white students will be failing these exams. Are the schools prepared to withhold their diplomas from these students? Who then will provide for these young people? Will they soon be added to the scrap heap of adult nonreaders? Who then will be able to assist *their* children?

One consequence of the Florida ruling soon becomes uncomfortably clear. Many students still in junior high, faced with almost certain failure in the new exams, indicate that they are thinking now of dropping out of school. They will disappear from school-enrollment lists before they even get to the twelfth grade. They will never take the SATs. National scores for those who do will consequently improve. The public will applaud the seeming gains in excellence achieved by more efficient methods of exclusion. The nation's children, as the critics have demanded, will "be asked for more" and some no doubt will now be given more. Henceforth, "the best" might be given "the best." But what provision is the nation making for the rest?

No one proposes that those who have been cheated in their childhood, and subsequently failed by public schools, ought not to be punished but awarded fellowships for an intensive program of nonschool remediation. No one suggests that massive and well-funded literacy projects be established as a national imperative to interrupt that cycle of dependence which will otherwise persist. No one suggests that students like these, too often doomed to see their disappointments played out once again within the lives of their own children, might be granted the humane endowment of a kind of GI Bill to underwrite the programs that would meet their needs. The talk is all of "standards"—not solutions. "The time is over when we're going to accept a diploma at face value," according to one state commissioner of education. This is all well and good. It benefits nobody to be given the chance to clutch within her hand a meaningless diploma. But we cannot dump these people, like a toxic waste, into a barren kingdom of American oblivion. Where do we intend to hide them? Sixty million men and women cannot be concealed forever.

When high schools and state education boards insist upon a stiffening of terminal demands, in total disregard of the immobilizing failures of preceding years of school—and of the years before the child even entered school—they seem to claim they hold within their hands a golden bugle. To whom is the bugle being blown? What ultimately divisive message does it bear?

The faces of those twelfth grade students who have failed the Florida exams stare out at us, bewildered and pathetic, from the television screen.

The TV commentator asks for their reaction: "What seems to be the problem?"

The answers they give are awkward, ungrammatical, disturbing. They seem to tell us that the State of Florida is right. Twelve years of schooling, two of testing, two of admonitions, two years of extra opportunities to meet the minimal demands of these exams: still they seem unable to decipher sentences, compute at eighth grade level, or respond to TV questions with articulate replies.

This is the message that the Florida high school students on the TV screen convey to millions of Americans. They *seem* to be incompetent. In terms of what it takes to lead a decent life in the United States, the truth is that they *are*.

They might perhaps be given a new lease on life, a second chance of breaking down the barriers of further education, by an ardent and aggressive plan of all-out adult literacy action—if an earnest and high-powered plan like this existed. If they ask, however, they will learn that it does not. There are no such plans in operation. No funding for such plans is contemplated. Instead, there are a new set of requirements, new standards, more exams.

Wouldn't it be wiser, less expensive, and a great deal more humane not to have destroyed the spirits of our children in the first place?

What do those parents who read very poorly, or else not at all, experience as they look on at the declining prospects of their children?

The parents who cannot read to their own children in the years before they enter school are also those, as we have seen, who find it hardest to assess the teachers or to scrutinize the textbooks which their children are assigned in public school. The fear that holds them at a distance from the act of reading also holds them at a distance from the school itself.

Even if they overcome these fears, however, there is little they can do to rectify the failings of the public schools if they cannot even read the homework lessons which their children carry home or recognize archaic methods and materials. How could they do this? Even if they could, what educator would be likely to respond to an "illiterate" complaint?

Many parents who are not good readers can intuitively sense a hopeless situation in their child's school. Those, however, who do not possess the competence to read and write, to analyze, to research and to draw the right conclusions from that research, cannot turn their intuitions into criticisms that the schools will hear. They can raise their voices, but too often what they choose to criticize will be the least important part of a substantial problem which they have no way to target for attention.

Administrators, therefore, even when they recognize important problems which they feel unable to address, find it easy to defend the school against the accurate but imprecisely stated protests of the neighborhood or the community they serve. Devoted parents, starved of information that might otherwise inform their sensitivity with vision and concreteness, find themselves disarmed before the jargon that the school employs to guard the gates and reinforce the walls.

The children of illiterate parents, therefore, are defrauded in at least three ways: first, by loss of early learning opportunities before they even enter public school; second, by their parents' inability to analyze the problems of the schools themselves; third, by the fact that even when their parents see the warning signs of future failure, they cannot propose corrective measures in a language that will win political attention and response.

Democratic and imaginative public schools in an egalitarian society ought to know the way to overcome all "disabilities" or "disadvantages" that children bring with them, through no fault of their parents or their own, out of the first five years of life. We have very few such schools in the United States today. Most schools fail to some degree. Schools which serve the children of the cities and the rural districts with the lowest tax base tend to have the least success. Those whose children suffer most can do the least to pinpoint the important reasons and bring energy to bear upon the cause of grievance. They can speak loud; they cannot speak well. Soon enough, they cease to speak at all.

8

Breaking the Cycle:
The Mandate
for a National Response

In other words, there is a very real possibility that many, even most, of the children of the poor will become the fathers and mothers of the poor. If that were to take place, then America would, for the first time in its history, have a hereditary underclass.

–Michael Harrington

President Reagan asked that federal funds for education be reduced by 25 percent in 1981.

"These cuts are painful," Secretary Bell conceded. "They affect mainly low-income and inner-city children." Bell explained that federal funds are spent primarily on "target populations" of the poorest children. "So there's no way," he said, to make "significant dollar savings" without reducing funds earmarked for those in greatest need.

A similar apologetic was employed to justify the parsimony that restricts the funds available to educate the parents of those children. Thus, both in the home and in the early years of school, the cycle of illiteracy goes on.

The White House drew on several arguments to justify its actions—and inaction. Most of these arguments referred to state and local, volunteer and private-sector obligations. The government maintained that federal funding is an inappropriate "intrusion" on the state and local sectors, that corporate benevolence (or corporate self-interest) is a "better" source of money, that programs based on volunteer commitment represent the "best" approach to literacy action at the local level. All of these arguments are flawed. Some are misguided. Others are cruel. Many are dishonest.

•Local school boards are in no position to pick up the burden left by federal abdication. All are afflicted with a rise in overcrowded classrooms, teacher layoffs, and the other crises that accompany financial cutbacks. The public schools of Boston were obliged to fire nearly one fourth of their teachers in the past five years. Can we believe that schools which are compelled to fire veteran classroom teachers will supply the energy and funds to launch a major literacy campaign?

•Even if local school boards did not face the budget crises that have plagued them in the past few years, they would remain unable to provide the children of their districts with approximately equal schooling since their funding base, in local property taxes, is unequal. In the poorest schools of Massachusetts $1,500 yearly is invested in each child. The richest districts spent over $6,000. Even where per-pupil allocations do not vary, wealthier schools can draw upon such assets as the gifts of parents and the favors granted by the corporations in which many of those parents work. The *Wall Street Journal* recently described a classic situation, in Atlanta, where the funds available for computer software in the classrooms were three times greater in a rich suburban neighborhood than in an inner-city school. Funds employed to buy equipment in the suburb were donated by the parents or the private sector. Schools which had the most computers were in neighborhoods where students, in large numbers, had the use of home computers too.

"Schools that want to introduce computers are free to do so," said a government spokesperson. "The disadvantage is [that] there are going to be major discrepancies" between the ones that have the funds "and those who don't." As schools grow more expensive, the discrepancies grow greater. Local initiative will always be most helpful in those neighborhoods that need the least but have the means to do the most.

•Private corporations, in most cities, now report that they are being hit from all sides with requests for aid. We have seen that less than 1 percent of in-house training programs run by corporations are addressed to basic literacy needs. When corporations are in fiscal trouble, when bankruptcy is common and plant closings are increasing, we cannot expect the private sector to replace the government in funding literacy work. At best, it can sustain a holding operation.

•Private foundations, too, are being inundated by requests for help to which they cannot possibly respond. Several have been forced to cut back on their total contributions; what they do contribute must be split in smaller portions to address a wider range of needs.

•Volunteer groups cannot supervise their volunteers without a core of hired organizers. The loss of funds to hire even four or five efficient organizers means the loss of several hundred volunteers who otherwise might have been ready to contribute energy and time. Literacy groups like LVA indicate that they are cutting back or "barely holding even."

•Libraries, the obvious allies in helping to promote a literacy drive, are finding it hard—sometimes impossible—to do so. The Boston Public Library was forced in recent years to close on weekends and to shut down many of its branches in the face of budget cuts. Without external funding, even the most loyal members of the library profession cannot be expected to provide the leverage for a major literacy plan.

•Bookstores and newspapers, both self-interested parties in a literacy plan, find it difficult to give much help when many are now failing to sustain their sales or circulation and so many others have gone out of business. The singular initiative of the B. Dalton chain is a dramatic and important gesture. It remains that: both a gesture and exception. Publishers of books, an obvious third partner, have been timid and uncertain allies. Many have spoken boldly on this subject; with the exception of McGraw-Hill, they have yet to come forth with substantial funds.

•Universities are doing less than ever in the past two decades to assist with problems that appear to lie outside their own immediate domain. Despite some matching plans which have enabled local schools to profit from advice and personnel from nearby colleges and universities, most of the major academic centers have returned to obligations they define as "strictly academic."

•Married women, liberated by a growing consciousness of independence and a less restricted opportunity for good employment, are no longer able to devote the time that is required by a grass-roots program that depends on active volunteers. Middle class women, once the mainstay of all volunteer endeavors, are no longer an unlimited resource.

There are deeper problems with the government's approach.

The National Commission opened its report: "Our Nation is at risk." It did not speak about a small town in Ohio or a small school district in New Hampshire or Vermont. Although its single-minded emphasis on military needs and on commercial competition was myopic, its recognition of the national dimensions of the issue was correct. Americans work in one job market and cross school-district borders constantly in search of possible employment. In that search they bring their skills—or lack of skills—from one town, state, or region to another. The purchaser in Oregon is cheated by the flawed production of the worker in New Hampshire. The residents of both states are denied a chance to find productive labor in all fifty states. People who write poison warnings or mechanical instructions are addressing citizens in every state at once.

The danger of psychopaths who freely cross state borders to poison our medicines or to assassinate our leaders is well known. The danger of other psychopaths who, now and then, unhappily become our leaders has been recognized as well. The peaceful man or woman is held hostage to the poorly educated soldier who has never learned to read and comprehend with a sufficient skill to understand directions and may never have acquired the intelligent irreverence to refuse to acquiesce in face of criminal instructions. Airline passengers, as we have seen, are hostage to the competence of personnel whom they—too frequently these days—will never live to know.

We are one nation. We live as one. We undergo the danger of mortality as one. Only those whose heads follow their hearts into a nineteenth century nostalgia for the insular existence of well-separated regions of reality can still adhere to dangerous illusions of a nation that exists, or can continue to exist, by governance of town committees or of county jurisdictions in those areas of finance and decision that have power to protect or else destroy us all.

When hurricanes or earthquakes strike one region of the nation, when floodwaters cut a swath of devastation through one county or one state, federal funds and sometimes federal troops are sent to answer the requests for aid from state officials who do not conceal their inability to handle crises on this scale.

A federal complex—the Centers for Disease Control—exists in Georgia. It serves the needs of citizens beyond the precincts of Atlanta. When indications of a perilous contagion are discovered in New York, in Oregon or California, the answer comes from Washington and is conveyed with a rapidity that fits the urgency to experts in Atlanta.

The federal government assumes (though it does not consistently accept) the obligation for surveillance and correction of environmental hazards. Chemical wastes that spill into the water that consumers drink in Iowa and North Dakota, pesticides that poison fruit and vegetables in California—produce which, if not identified, condemned, and taken from the market, will be eaten by the residents of Illinois and Indiana—both are subject to obligatory intervention by the federal government. What of the illiterate who *uses* a forbidden pesticide in total ignorance of its potential dangers? Why do we assign less value to the cognitive environment than to the health of water, soil, and stone? Why do we perceive more danger in the presence of a toxic substance than in the innocent but uninformed illiterate who uses it?

Illiteracy does not restrict itself to city limits or the borders of school districts. Illiterates do not read signs that indicate a state or county border. Oppression does not stop at arbitrary lines.

It is a myth that education is a state and local matter in this nation. Tests are national in use and publication. Test scores are computed on a national curve. Children are slotted at national norms, above those norms, or else beneath them. Textbooks are national. They are produced by massive national corporations, sold by aggressive national campaigns, and depend for the enormous profits they accrue on nationwide acceptance. Teachers belong to national unions. They express their grievances at national conventions. They are trained in nationally homogenized curricula by uniform—and national—criteria. Children are educated to regard themselves as U.S. citizens, not citizens of Louisville or Dallas or Miami. They are obliged to swear allegiance every morning to "one nation indivisible"—not to one state or city or school district. They are indoctrinated by their schools to be Americans—not Texans, not Bostonians.

The national character of U.S. education is both evident and unmistakable to anyone who travels frequently from state to state to visit and observe in public schools. Only a year, more frequently one portion of a year, is given to local history, geography, or law. From fourth grade on, almost all social science and most other subject matter is identical from one state to the next. Details may differ. Architecture varies. Colloquial expressions may define a regional or state identification. The excellence of offerings is, of course, uneven—and calamitously so—from one state, town, or district to the next. But uniformity of content and, increasingly, of process has been guaranteed. A child can move from state to state, city to city, North to South, or East to West, without concern that he or she may be surprised by unfamiliar subject matter.

Only one serious difference does exist from city to suburb, and at times (within one city) from one district to the next: The children of those who are already literate, enfranchised, and empowered learn the exercise of power. The children of those who are not literate, who have been disenfranchised and remain excluded from the exercise of power, learn to accommodate themselves to impotence and to capitulation. Those who are privileged achieve the competence with which to shape the future. Those who are not acquire an attitude of civilized accommodation which will allow them to fit into slots that are provided for them in that future—or else to remain excluded from the future altogether. This alone is different from one district, or one classroom, or one child to the next. With this exception, it is one consistent and unbroken schooling system. National goals define it. National inequity degrades it. National myopia restricts it. But it is, for all of this, one education system indivisible, with liberty for some, illiteracy for others, the same oath of allegiance for us all.

The pledge of allegiance spoken each day by 40 million children in the U.S.

public schools implies a sacred and historic contract of reciprocal responsibilities. Children cannot be expected to take seriously an oath of fealty and faith
while those who run the government that has received that fealty deny their
obligation to sustain that faith by concrete deeds which guarantee the child's
rights. So long as two of the most elemental rights—the right to health, the
right to education—have been countermanded by the abdication of one of the
parties to that contract, it is not easy to believe that words alone, an oath, an
incantation, will be recited by a citizen as anything more binding than an empty
ritual, inert and insincere. A one-way contract is not viewed as binding by the
courts: still less so by the heart.

One of the most precious rights assured to U.S. citizens is freedom of the
press. American PEN has launched a national campaign to guarantee uncen-
sored access to the written word and to reverse a right-wing trend that threatens
to suppress such access by selective censorship of books that voice unpopular
positions. Although the organization has employed the slogan "Right to Read,"
the focus is directed solely on the act of publication and the presence of the
published work in libraries or schools. Another form of interdiction is the prior
censorship imposed upon those citizens who have no opportunity to learn what
writers have to say by virtue of their inability to read.

De jure censorship is an unquestioned evil in itself. It lends itself at least to
litigation. De facto censorship, by the exclusion of one third of our potential
readers, is a matter far beyond the power of the courts. Denial of the right to
speak is one form of injustice. Denial of the right to hear is quite another.
Writers may write, but who will understand? Free in theory, I am—even in the
act of setting down these words—denied part of my freedom by the fact that
those who are the subject of this book will never know its content. Freedom of
press, seen in this light, becomes a questionable guarantee. People are free to
choose what they believe, but freedom to choose depends on prior knowledge of
the choices.

Apart from the domestic danger of a disenfranchised population, there is
an external danger also. Other nations, some of them extremely poor and long
subjected to colonial oppression, have managed to assemble their resources to
make rapid progress in the evolution of a literate society. American chauvinism
finds it painful to concede this. It is the same arrogance, perhaps, which leads us
to disparage the utility or urgency of foreign language study in our colleges and
public schools. A nation that believes it's "Number One" may not imagine it
has much to learn from those that it considers numbers seventeen or sixty.

The truth is that we have a lot to learn and in no other area more central to
our pride—indeed to every form of international competition—than the willingness to mobilize a nation to address its inner contradictions by humane and
forceful means.

We state with a bewildered longing that we hope to win "the hearts and minds" of the poor people of the earth. We will never win their hearts or minds (nor, least of all, their loyalty or genuine respect) with bigger bombs or better marketing procedures. We just might win some lasting and unpurchased admiration if we could provide a strong example to the world of pedagogic progress on a sweeping and breathtaking scale.

When we speak of Third World competition, we think of Cuban soldiers, Soviet spies. It may be that this is not where our real competition lies. When Nicaragua started planning for its literacy struggle in the summer months of 1980, it looked to the U.N. and other international organizations for direction and advice. Not surprisingly, it found a precedent and blueprint in the Cuban model. This recognition led, in time, to the arrival of two thousand Cuban literacy workers and a scholar, Dr. Raul Ferrer, who had designed the Cuban effort back in 1961. The gains for Cuba, I believe, are likely to have been a lot more lasting than whatever gains it might have won by military aid. I suspect the same may be the case in several other nations where we focus only on the presence of the Cuban soldiers but dismiss the presence of so many doctors, teachers, engineers. History suggests that loyalties achieved by military aid, and even by the presence of armed personnel in periods of crisis, is ephemeral at best. The presence of a literacy detachment, on the other hand, may exercise an impact that will last for generations.

We cannot hope to offer other nations what we cannot yet provide for our own people. We can share with others only an effective lever of emancipation that we have first tested and found viable in our own land: in rural Appalachia, in the hills of South Dakota, in Detroit, Los Angeles, Chicago, the South Bronx.

I am uneasy at the need to offer an external motive for important social action which should be attempted for no other reason than the fact that people in our nation suffer needlessly and that we have the means at hand, if not the will, to help them to achieve a dignified existence. Nonetheless, political realities persist. So long as international competition must take precedence over cooperation, it would be too bad if competition must take place on battlefields instead of in the minds of those whom we appear more readily disposed to kill than to endow with educative options.

This, then, is a national matter too. We do not leave Caribbean dilemmas to the school boards of Vermont and Arizona. We do not leave our covert operations in El Salvador or Nicaragua to the state and local mercenaries of New Mexico. We do not leave our military interests in the Philippines, in Turkey, or Korea to the middle class church volunteers of Ithaca or Houston. I do not believe that an illiterate society—one third illiterate in verbal and in numerate respects, the other two thirds literate too often in the least compassionate and most destructive ways—can hope to prosper or compete in economic terms, prevail in moral terms, or hold a promising beacon to the wretched of the earth in any terms at all, until we are prepared to launch an all-out battle with the enervating adversary that resides in our own atrophied imagination.

In its report of 1983, the National Commission on Excellence in Education spoke of the "lowered standards" in our schools as something which an enemy nation—"an unfriendly foreign power"—might have shrewdly wished upon us in the effort to diminish our capacity for self-defense in time of military confrontation. If this had been the case, the authors wrote, "we might well have viewed it as an act of war."

More sober minds seem to have realized in short order that the adversary which had done this "damage" to our national well-being was not a distant enemy after all. Whatever certain people seem to say by careless, cruel, or mindless innuendo, it isn't the poor children of an underclass that lives, invisible or not, within the borders of our nation. The enemy remains our own short-sighted sense of class advantage at the cost of national well-being and of universal humane competence in service of survival.

Illiteracy is not the only, nor the most important, evidence of national myopia. It certainly is not the most important moral problem that betrays our honor and diminishes our possibilities for self-esteem. It is one of the few on which we have the possibility to take effective action. It is also one of the very few on which almost all sectors of the population, if they could be properly informed, might see good reason to agree. The answers, I will argue in this book, cannot be dispensed from Washington. They will be provided by the neighborhoods, the grass-roots groups, and the communities in which nonreaders live. The funding to do anything, however, must in the long run derive from national resources.

A nation's wealth is of at least two kinds. The kind enumerated by the GNP is dollars. The kind that cannot be enumerated by the GNP is dignity and decency and the informed and critical intelligence of human beings. We tend to value most what we can measure. We cannot measure dignity. We cannot measure decency. We cannot measure critical capacities. What we cannot measure we can nonetheless enhance by wise priorities. We can do this only with our full determination as a people.

9

Summer 1983

The airman is viewed as an information processing system with limited cognitive capacity.

—"Literacy Instruction in the Military"

One of my oldest friends in Boston is a woman whom, for now, I will call Ellen. She is forty-two years old. A descendant of three generations of nonreaders, she is perhaps the poorest person I have ever known. She is also a poet. I will return to this. Her background is unusual and, in one sense, symbolic. She is part white, part Mexican, part black. She might represent, within her lineage, an ethnic spectrum of America. Because she is my friend, it isn't easy to regard her as a symbol; but the symbolism seems too obvious to miss. She is, for certain, an explicit product of our nation's history.

One of Ellen's great-grandparents was a slave. Another was a migrant farmer. A third came to the United States from Scandinavia. Her grandmother was a sharecropper; her mother, a domestic maid. Ellen can read and write a little, but so poorly that the pedagogic world would have to call her semiliterate. Her oral vocabulary, however, is both searching and expressive. She sits with me in her kitchen often for long evenings and she "tells me poems." I write them down. Several have been published in fine literary journals. Nobody knows that this extraordinary verse has been composed by somebody who cannot read it.

I wonder sometimes how much beauty, how many poems and stories like the ones she tells me, must be stillborn every year, each decade, in America. How much of our possible aesthetic wealth is annually diminished, lost forever?

This would not appear in figures about GNP. Some of our citizens might think it should. But that is another story. It is Ellen's son whose story is important here.

Ellen has five children. Two of them were bused to a suburban school and learned to read quite well. Two others, who attended school in Boston, read and write only at marginal levels. The fifth one scarcely reads at sixth grade level. He is the second oldest. His name is Benjamin.

Benjamin is the only member of the family I do not know well. He was sent down South to live with his grandparents when he was in second grade. He did not return to Roxbury until he was nineteen. Since that time, he has appeared increasingly withdrawn, sometimes rebellious, but more often silently resistant to his mother's love. He was beaten as a child in the Boston schools. A scar on his forefinger is a cicatrix of bitterness that he too willingly restricts, constrains, conceals.

Still a poor reader, he attempted for six months to find a job, had no success, then fell into a grim, depressive state. For over a year he sat at home, glued to the TV. Involved in constant travel during that most crucial year, I called some friends. They did their best to get him signed up in a literacy program. He seemed to be prepared to try it, but the waiting list was long. By the time he was admitted he had lost whatever spark of interest he had felt. The program, moreover, took place in a local school. He found this painful, showed up once or twice, then finally withdrew and settled once again into the same depression.

Stirred from slumber one night by a TV plug—"Go Army! Be a man!"— he went downtown and got himself enlisted. By the time that I returned to Boston, he had managed to squeak past a literacy exam was given his orders, and sent off to Oklahoma.

It turns out, after cutting back on all the humane answers to the literacy crisis, the government provides one seldom-noted but heavily funded and distinctly "national" response which too many poor young men cannot turn down.

Those who are the children of illiterate adults, those who live their early years in single-parent families where the single parent is statistically most certain to be partially or totally illiterate, those who are obliged to go to the most underfunded and destructive schools—those, in short, who are most likely to be sent into the world without the educational resources to compete and to prevail within a print society—do have one last recourse in pursuit of literacy instruction. That recourse is the U.S. Army.

Men whose literacy is very poor but good enough to win a GED and barely to get through some very simple tests can be admitted to the U.S. Army and will be provided, in the course of training, with a special brand of militarily effective competence. What is likely to be viewed as functional in military terms may be imagined without difficulty. Nor do we need to imagine, since we already know too well—both from the words of military specialists themselves and from the experience of thousands of young men like Benjamin—precisely what they learn and how they are indoctrinated to apply that learning in the service of an institution which depends on blind obedience, fosters functionally acquiescent consciousness, and cannot be expected to do otherwise in view of its mandated role in our society.

The soldier is "trained." It is explicit. This is war preparedness. It is not ethics or aesthetics. Soldiers are not burdened with the histories of Tacitus, the fears of Madison, the eloquence of Erik Erikson, of Emerson, Thoreau, or William James. Nor are they confronted with the metaphors of Melville, Robert Lowell, William Faulkner, Thomas Mann, or C. P. Snow. Neither a love of life nor the respect for beauty that a civilized and life-affirming social order can bestir is part of the curricular endowment that a military officer is hired to impart.

"The interests of the individual," writes Thomas Sticht, one of the more knowledgeable observers of the military's literacy plans, "are subordinate to the goals and missions of the organization . . ."

We may think we can imagine both the "goals" and "missions" that he has in mind; most of us, I think, will be alarmed to see how far the vivid details may exceed our most uneasy fears.

According to Thomas Duffy, in a paper titled "Literacy Instruction in the Military" (January 1984), "Armed Forces personnel must operate and maintain some of the most sophisticated, costly, and dangerous equipments in existence." Literacy, for this reason, "is perhaps more critical in the Armed Forces" than in any other sector of society.

Forty percent of all recruits who enter the armed forces every year read at eighth grade level or below. Many read at only grade school levels. The volume of technical documentation needed on the job in military service is extensive. "A single stack of all the documentation required to support the equipment" on a single nuclear submarine "would be higher than the Washington Monument." Over a million pages of reading matter "are required to support the operation and maintenance of the B-1 bomber."

In one instance, Duffy writes, technicians must refer "to 165 pages in eight documents . . . just to isolate and repair one fault in a radar system."

For these reasons, "there is a formal requirement in each service that personnel must use the technical documentation during all maintenance work. Failure to have the appropriate manual turned to the appropriate page can, and has, led [sic] to disciplinary action." Forty percent of new recruits cannot meet these minimal demands.

There was a time, writes Duffy, when education in the military was offered to meet broader purposes than those described above: "The instruction [of an earlier age] seems to have been offered for the good of the individual and society and not necessarily for the good of the service." This error, Duffy indicates, has been corrected.

By present guidelines, instructional courses in the military are provided through two different offices. One is labeled education. The other is described as training. "The training command . . . constitutes the bulk of the instruction. It is also the instruction that is judged as essential to the maintenance of military readiness . . ." In order to be sure that new recruits are able "to deploy equipments," Duffy writes, it is the "training" factor, not the "education," which receives the burden of attention. Training is taken "during normal duty hours and is considered part of 'the job.' " Courses under the education command, in contrast, are "not considered essential to the job."

What, then, falls into the category termed essential?

It is essential, Duffy writes, "that everything needed to perform the job is taught but that there is no instruction on irrelevant or unnecessary topics or skills." In electronics training, for example, mathematics is restricted in two ways: "First, only that mathematics instruction deemed essential to successful performance in the electronics area is taught." Second, students "are not taught general mathematics nor are the formulas presented in abstract terms, e.g., $A = BC$." The purpose, he explains, is to spare the student "the extra burden of generalizing . . ." This, he says, is viewed as "quite unnecessary."

Today, writes Duffy, literacy programs in the military have been rendered uniform in order to conform to the requirements described above. This is all the more important, he remarks, because "the move to the all volunteer force . . . was seen as greatly reducing the quality of personnel . . ." Indeed, he says, "the percent of Army recruits in the lowest ability category [has] increased from ten percent in 1975 to 31 percent in 1981 . . ." The Department of Defense, to use his technocratic words, is suffering today from "decreased access to desirable individuals" in what he calls "the primary assession pool."

Illiterate and undesirable are treated as synonymous.

Even as late as 1983, despite all of the emphasis on mechanistic skills, education still appears to have been getting in the way of basic military needs. The General Accounting Office reported, with disapproval, that "general literacy" was still pervasive in the U.S. Army programs and was undermining emphasis on "job-related" skills. The GAO recommended that these programs (educational, not "relevant") be "terminated."

Duffy feels convinced that military policy will henceforth be in line with this directive. The Navy, faced with the "undesirable" influx of "lower aptitude personnel" (the Navy's term), now guarantees that "content is specific to the . . . training area." The Army, quick to be attracted to the technological approach, now insists that 50 percent of its curriculum be "computer-based." Both the Army and the Air Force seem to have brought technological and fragmentized ("specific") skill-instruction to a level that will satisfy the GAO.

The Army, according to Duffy, because it operates a number of small and isolated European bases, cannot afford to offer on-site literacy training taught by an instructor. Videodiscs and microcomputers therefore take the place of teachers. The computerized system, known as STARS, "has the positive feature," in the words of Duffy, that it can be used without instructors. The video material, suggestive of a kind of space wars fantasy that sounds a great deal like the content of the comic books and television programs aimed at fourth or fifth grade children, "provides a strong motivational context." Duffy adds that these materials are "excellent . . . enticing." Instruction is presented "in the context of the student [as] a member of a space team who have numerous tasks to perform . . ." One of these tasks is the demonstration that "a time machine really works." The videodisc presents "the motivational context of the space ship and coworkers . . ."

The desiccating jargon used repeatedly by Duffy in describing all these programs ("motivational context," "primary assession pool," "lower aptitude personnel") would not warrant our attention if it did not crystallize so well the values and the ethos of these military efforts. It is all the more disturbing because these, the jargon and the ethos and the shabby values, permeate civilian pedagogic discourse too. The language represents a perfect paradigm for the renewal of a disciplined, a punitive, a tightly stratified, and (most of all) obedience-based education system, structured to assure perpetuation of a fragmentized but useful population.

"The airman," in Duffy's words, "is viewed as an information processing system with limited cognitive capacity."

We might like to speculate how Jefferson or Tocqueville, Orwell or Bonhoeffer might respond to these extraordinary words. A dark voyage threatens to entice not just the soldiers in their isolated capsules of computer-based instruction in their European missile stations but the growing children and the semiliterate adults who live right here within our own hometowns.

C. P. Snow once asked a man about his taste in books.

"Books?" the man repeated. "I prefer to use my books as tools."

Snow seems to have reflected for a while on this answer. "It was very hard not to let the mind wander—what sort of tool would a book make?" He wondered aloud: "Perhaps a hammer? A primitive digging instrument?"

These are questions which would not be asked in military circles. Books or manuals, lists of truck or missile parts, instructions for dismantling a gun—all of these are clearly viewed as useful tools. If they were not, they would be excluded from the body of instruction Duffy has described. They would then be viewed as "education" and would, for this reason, be in conflict with the guidelines of the GAO.

But Snow's speculations and his puzzlement might give us pause to ask if we can tolerate the "missions" and "objectives" that the military has in mind for those that it defines as undesirable and lower aptitude personnel.

"Perhaps a digging instrument?"

If our government continues on its way, and if we cannot denounce the people who contrive these programs for the art of killing while they starve civilian programs for the art of life, who will there remain to use these instruments once military men have finished with their "space wars" and "deployments"? What of the rest of us? What of America? What of the world? Will there still remain a world for these robotic beings to inhabit? Who, then, will remain to do the digging?

There is something savage in this nation.

After absolute capitulation on a decent answer to the failures of the state and local schools, here is a military answer which is racist by selection and dehumanizing by intent.

Benjamin is done with basic training now. He wrote his mother a letter last month. It was his final week in Oklahoma. Since she reads so poorly, she called up and asked me to come over. It was an amazing document. He misspelled simple words like "freinds," "imposibble," and "terryfed." His spelling was perfect, however, when it came to "weapons," "enemy," "deployment."

In June he was assigned to go to Europe. He was given two weeks off in order to come home to say good-bye. Ellen used a neighbor's phone. She wanted me to come for dinner. He was not unfriendly with me. He was distant. A cynicism I had never heard pervaded the entire conversation. He looked transformed: rigid and slim. He spoke of killing those he called "The Enemy" with macho jubilation.

"Could you do it?" I asked.

"A soldier does what must be done," was his reply.

Benjamin is at an army base in Germany today. He is part of a detachment which will be responsible for the deployment of cruise missiles.

Many of the sorrows of Illiterate America, and all the dangers of the neatly functional machine that any nation can produce out of the slag heap it has first created, are at stake in this—Benjamin's story. Illiteracy: created by decrepit schools staffed by exhausted and defeated teachers, passed down through generations of nonreading parents. Next: passivity, the TV tube, humiliation, and despair. At last, the all-American and patriotic answer: basic training, absolute obedience to flag and anthem, suspension of emotion in the face of death, a certain hedonistic joy—a punk-rock fascination—at the prospect of mechanical annihilation. Yet he cannot write a simple note of love in lucid words, correctly spelled, to a good-hearted mother who, in any case, can't read them.

Benjamin is functionally competent at last. One day he may have his chance to press the button that releases that long, trim, and slender instrument of death that he so much resembles. Is this the kind of literacy we want? Is this the best that Jeffersonian democracy can do?

I will argue otherwise within this book.

PART TWO

A Plan to Mobilize
Illiterate America

10

The Myth of Impotence:
What Should Be Done?

Let us go back and distinguish between the two things that we want
to do; for we want to do two things in modern society. We want one
class of persons to have a liberal education, and we want another class
of persons, a very much larger class, of necessity, in every society, to
forego the privileges of a liberal education and fit themselves to perform specific difficult manual tasks. You cannot train them for both in
the time that you have at your disposal. They must make a selection,
and you must make a selection.

—Woodrow Wilson (January 1909)

This is a proper place, I think, to make an observation which may be implicit
but which has not yet been directly stated in this book.

Illiteracy in any land as well-informed and wealthy as the U.S.A. in 1985 is
not an error. It is not an accident. There is no way that it could be an accident
or error. Illiteracy among the poorest people in our population is a logical consequence of the kinds of schools we run, the cities that starve them, the dema-
gogues who segregate them, and the wealthy people who escape them altogether
to enroll their kids in better funded, up-to-date, and more proficient institutions.
It is a consequence, too, of pedagogic class selection which for many decades has
regarded certain sectors of the population as the proper persons to perform
those unattractive labors which no man or woman would elect to do if he or she
received the preparation for more lucrative and challenging employment. Finally, it is a consequence of the illiterate condition of the parents of poor

children—parents, in turn, who have been denied all recourse for self-liberation by the absence of a conscientious government initiative on their behalf.

Politicians tell us that they want Americans to read, even the invisible Americans, even black, Hispanic, and poor white Americans. But is this protestation honest and sincere? We read in the Bible: "By their fruits ye shall know them." We might update these words to fit the present decade: "By their fiscal allocations you shall know them. By their cutbacks you shall spy them out. By their commissions, press releases, and reports, you shall ascertain that they are not your friends."

It is the refusal to accept, or inability to voice, these recognitions which creates the climate of futility and impotence that limits the potential scope of several of the largest programs in existence. Many of the Laubach programs, to take only one example, are remarkably successful with the portion of the population they can reach; they also understand quite well exactly why they reach so very few. Peter Waite, the national director of the Laubach programs, is consistently straightforward on this matter. This is the case with many other literacy leaders. There is no point in trying to identify these people. The activists know who they are. They also speak, in private conversations, of the absolute constraints that limit their effectiveness to those who represent the least oppressed, the least intimidated and, in short, the closest to that state of mind that grows out of the confidence and likelihood that, with a modest effort, they shall win their place within the mainstream of American success.

It is these leaders and these specialists themselves who speak of the programs they conduct as "creaming operations." The "cream" that they skim off the surface of Illiterate America constitutes the 2 to 4 percent of all illiterate adults who now are reached by all the programs that I have described. If political constraints and economic fears inhibit them from speaking in these terms in publications written for the general population, it is their private honesty that I accept and it is their private recognition of an artifacted impotence which I respect.

It is not selfishness, it is frustration, and a vivid sense of stifling, of choking on the inert knowledge they possess, which seems to lie close to the heart of the paralysis that many of these people undergo. Hearing their words, I often find that I am thinking of some simple metaphors of personal frustration that are common to us all. At the risk of placing myself in a too-vulnerable position (but this is perhaps a risk that all of us should be prepared to take), I might give a very obvious and nonpolitical example of the inhibition that denies us access to the unencumbered energy that now eludes us.

I am writing this book within a house that must be heated by a Franklin stove. My only fuel is wood. For several hours, on too many mornings, I find that I cannot arouse sufficient flame to bring the large, split logs into combustion. The fire glows and sputters a bit, then dies away; the room grows chill and, as my hand becomes so cold that I can barely move my pen, I grab another log or two and stuff it in on top of those that haven't yet caught fire. It is a futile enterprise. It mocks the very words that I am trying to get down on paper. Stubbornly, I keep on adding logs. Occasionally I rip a day-old New York *Times* into small shreds and, like a little drop of pedagogic innovation added to a sullen and resistant status quo, the paper gives a sudden burst of flame and rapidly dies out.

After an hour of such piecemeal emendations to initial error, I reach a point of ultimate frustration. I set aside my work, approach the stove in an explosion of impatience, take out all the docile logs, and pile them beside the stove. Then I start the process for a second time: this time, however, from the bottom up—as any of my rural neighbors would have done the moment he began. I crumple the paper. I add a pile of dry twigs and broken branches I've collected from the woods outside the house. I light the paper. The twigs burst into flame. Two minutes later, I pile on a couple of those previously reluctant logs, watch them catch the fire on their bark and soon break into cheerful conflagration. Then I pile on another six or seven logs. Ten minutes later, the fire is blazing and the room is warm. I return to my desk, cross out the last three paragraphs of hesitant and ineffective prose, and—as the fire crackles like a reassuring ally at my back—I finally get down the words I meant to write since I awoke.

There are times in life, no matter how grand or minuscule the enterprise may be, when a fire will not burn unless we are prepared to start all over, to do it as we should have done right from the first, not to add another hopeless log to a despondent stove but to concede initial error and to try it once again—beginning at the bottom, not the top. Once those good dry branches start to blaze, the water in the larger logs begins to sizzle, fizz, evaporate into the morning air, and soon they too (the biggest logs: commercially acquired) take on the furious intensity of one gigantic fire.

"Something we were withholding made us weak," wrote Robert Frost. Those words of my New Hampshire neighbor seem to mock my trivial but obstinate frustration. What I was withholding was the willingness to sacrifice a foolish vested interest in the useless efforts I'd already undertaken. Once the forfeiture of vested interest (pride, in this case) is accepted, a certain liberating anger starts to soar. The fire roars. The logs are profitably consumed. Out in the woodshed there are plenty more.

What should be done?
We need an all-out literacy war in the United States.
The war must be launched by the millions of people who will never read this book, who cannot wait to get their invitations from their benefactors, who need to start the process on their own but cannot know what they must do

unless their allies or exceptional covictims can draw, out of such words as they *can* read and understand, some hint of where the origins of freedom may reside. We need, above all else, to do away with the idea of literacy as training for domestication, contrived to fill existent or imagined lower-level job slots and consumer roles, and search instead for instruments of moral leverage strong enough to scrutinize those roles and to examine the political determinants of subjugation: examine, study, stand back, and reflect upon their purpose and, by virtue of reflection and examination, first to denounce and finally to transform.

Literacy, so conceived, is civil disobedience in pedagogic clothes: a cognitive denunciation of dynastic power, an ethical affront to an imperial injustice. Critical and analytic competence on such a scale is more than "functional." It is a literacy for human liberation. It is cultural action: an event, not an idea. It is political; it is endowed with anger; it is not neutral.

Those who speak as I have spoken in these pages can expect to be accused of advocating agitation, of aspiring to awaken discontent, to muddy the waters, to confuse the pedagogic goal with a political intention. The waters are already muddy; the discontent exists already; politics is present in the heart of this injustice.

When nearly half of all adult black citizens in the United States are coming out of public schools without the competence to understand the antidote instructions on a chemical container, instructions on a medicine bottle, or the books and journalistic pieces which might render them both potent and judicious in a voting booth, who can pretend that literacy is not political?

When over one third of the adult population is unable to read editorial opinions, when millions cannot understand the warning on a pack of cigarettes or comprehend the documents they sign to rent a home, to buy a car, to purchase health insurance, who can persist in the belief that literacy is not political?

When the government itself has been elected by exclusion of one third of the electorate, when the third which is excluded is the third which also gets the most deficient nutriment, least adequate health care, poorest housing, and which has an infant death rate twice that of the middle class, and when that government—having arrived in power—has actively engaged in the reduction of all services and funds which might at least alleviate the pain if not the cause of so much needless subjugation, who can still adhere to the belief that this is not political?

The answer is that no one can believe this. The most that we can do is to *pretend* that we believe it. It is a fragile pretense, and it will not hold.

When people are powerless, when they see their children rendered powerless, when they recognize that one essential aspect of that impotence is inability to read and write, to understand, *to know*, they are obliged to ask themselves the question which the students of the State of Florida were forced to ask: "Am I inherently deficient? Am I lacking in intelligence? in energy? in will? If the answer is yes, I am inferior. If the answer is no, I am the victim of injustice." Those who settle for the former answer are the victims of pathology. Those who can emerge from this pathology to choose the second answer are political.

The politics of literacy are nothing new. Long before the politics of racial segregation in the schools came to the national attention, long before Woodrow Wilson argued for the merits of class stratification in the public schools, long before laws throughout the nation made it a crime to teach black people how to read and write, long before the U.S. Constitution measured the black citizen as three fifths of a man, one hundred years before the present government existed, a powerful leader, Sir William Berkeley, governor of Virginia, stated his views in clear, unflinching terms. "I thank God," he said, that "there are no free schools nor printing [in this land]. For learning has brought disobedience, and heresy, and sects into the world, and printing hath divulged them . . . God save us from both!"

Today we do have printing; but we can be certain that whatever heresies it may convey will not spread their dangers to the masses that Sir William Berkeley feared. Today we do have public schools; but we can assure ourselves that they will not bring disobedience into the minds of those whose confidence has been already weakened by the time they enter grade school, broken by junior high school, and defeated by the time they are sixteen. If all of this is not political in purpose and result, if it is all a matter of "defective methods," of "inadequate technique," it is remarkable with what sustained coincidence we have assigned the worst techniques, the least efficient methods, to the poorest people in our nation.

But we know well that none of this is true. It isn't coincidence. It isn't technique. It isn't the wrong method. It is, in William Berkeley's terms, precisely the *right* method. It is a method that assures perpetuation of disparities in power and of inequities in every form of day-to-day existence. The only honest answer to political injustice is a humanized political response that substitutes a passion for "a program"—that substitutes a movement, both political and plausible, for a decade of ephemeral and arid "plans." Those who, lost in their own neutralizing jargon, tell us otherwise do not merely carry out an exercise in futile aspiration. They are the perpetrators of futility. So long as we attend upon their words we will remain powerless as well.

Those who are silent cannot expect that those who profit (or who still believe they profit) from that silence, from that inability to struggle and fight back, are likely to be burning with the wish to sacrifice the power they possess. Those who are cheated cannot be expected to believe that anyone outside their ranks is likely to "deliver" freedom. Freedom is never delivered. It is never offered as a gift. Freedom is a conquest. To go on bended knee in order to request "permission" for that conquest is a pre-planned exercise in self-defeat.

This would be like asking Mississippi voting registrars in 1963 to strike away exclusionary rules so that the disenfranchised blacks who lived within their districts might attain the voting strength to put them out of office. It didn't happen in this manner, as we know too well. It never does. It never will.

In 1972 black children in the segregated Boston schools were taught by texts and teachers to pursue a set of standardized curricular activities in seeking social change. One of those activities was a time-honored ritual known as "The Letter to Our Representative in Washington." Our congressperson in that era was a woman named Louise Day Hicks, an undistinguished politician who had been elected in a gerrymandered district on her reputation as an adversary of school integration.

"Dear Mrs. Hicks: We are the students of the fourth grade in the Wendell Phillips School in Roxbury. We have had 17 substitute teachers this year. Last year, we had 24. Our books are old, our building is collapsing. Nobody is learning how to read and write and do arithmetic. We would like to go to better schools—the same schools that are serving children of white people. Please, Mrs. Hicks, will you do what you can to help us with this problem?"

Teachers who allow this kind of lesson to take place, and who pretend to children that by exercises of this kind they are engaging in "collective processes of democratic practice," do not merely leave unchanged the impotence of children who have been entrusted to their care. They *advocate* impotence. They *teach* futility. They train their pupils to accede to rituals of guaranteed debilitation. The lesson, once it has been taught, remains to curse the learner with a set of inhibitions that will guarantee a lifetime of surrender: "Ask, try, plead, fail. Puzzle a moment on the reason for your failure. Maybe the letter was not spelled correctly. Maybe it was not properly addressed. Maybe your penmanship was poor. Now it is time to move on to your next surrender."

One of the corporate groups that has an interest in the literacy issue is the advertising industry. Certain corporations will be logical participants in literacy action. In the case of advertisers, it is difficult to know what they can do which would not undermine the very essence of the struggle I propose. To point to only the most glaring contradiction: What kind of literacy would they be eager to advance? Could they have in mind the inculcation of an analytic, critical, and shrewd capacity for seeing through the doublespeak of advertising copy? We know this is not likely. We know that advertisers have a vested interest in their power to suspend our disbelief. We know this is the very opposite of an informed irreverence. Yet we have seen too many of our colleagues acting on the fond belief that groups like these are going to provide the lever to emancipate illiterate adults from their domesticated status. All of the benign pronouncements that may issue forth from those whose very reason for existence is the exploitation of persuasive language for the management of public consciousness must not be mistaken for the one thing they can never be: a call to critical and literate rebellion.

So long as we believe in these enticements, so long as we remain the plaintive applicants for fiscal sustenance from groups like these, we are condemned to an exhausting process of defeat disguised by only the most insubstantial gains. We lose our years and hours to the exercise of writing grant proposals, making carefully tailored presentations, denying the truth we live by, and, in subtle but inexorable ways, losing at length the sense of truth itself. We come at last to be the lies that we purvey. We forfeit indignation for politeness. We forfeit urgency for tremulous accommodation. We enter the network of nothingness. We become a piece of all that we despise.

There are only two approaches, in this century at least, which have made a major dent on literacy crises like our own. One is the mobilization of a national campaign sponsored by dynamic government leaders and involving mass participation by the people. In the absence of an effort that is organized and orchestrated by a nation's leaders, the sole alternative is grass-roots struggle fired from the bottom up and governed in ways that do not cause dependence, foster impotence, or reinforce existing feelings of futility. This kind of struggle still requires money. It also calls for bold and gifted leaders: articulate men and women who are able to give voice to longings seldom vocalized by others yet who remain in close enough communion with the people whom they lead to crystallize emotions that exist already. The catalytic force of energized protagonists on those whose inarticulate despair provides the light and fire that illuminate and burn away the encrustations of apology and hesitation from a purifying rage—this interaction represents the minimal precondition for a struggle of this nature.

Mobilizations of the former kind (with government support) have proven their effectiveness in recent years in Cuba and in Nicaragua. Americans find it very hard to look without extreme antipathy on any undertaking that has taken place in either of these nations. Those who wish may gain the necessary information from UNESCO.

Similar campaigns have taken place in several other nations. Paulo Freire's work among the people of northeast Brazil during the early 1960s is one instance of a government campaign which takes its energies from the illiterates themselves. The work was carried out with funds and organization from the Ministry of Education, but government sanction did not undermine the passion of the local efforts. Literacy was closely tied to the political realities of land and food and health care and the personal empowerment of people who were victims of oppression. Initial stages in the work encouraged students to reflect upon the reasons for their status, as one basic portion of the struggle to attain the use of words. The word was not divorced from the world. Literacy was not conceived as mechanistic. It was perceived not as a weapon of domestication to incorporate the poor into "available employment opportunities" or to acculturate the poor into conventional (acceptable) political ideas. Literacy was not perceived as pacification. It was not a form of pedagogic counterinsurrectionary warfare. It did involve leaders, organizers, scholars. It did result in a remarkable proliferation of resistance groups, politicized communities, and critical consciousness of an unprecedented nature in the newly literate adults.

Its greatest success, in the opinion of participants, was the power of illiterate adults to view themselves, for the first moment in their lives, not as the objects of historic process, nor as the immutable and subjugated products of the wishes or imaginations of another set of men and women, but as the subjects of their own reality, the active agents of their own self-authorized existence. By this experience they were enabled finally to overcome the myth of impotence, to recognize that it was a creation of those forces (even sympathetic forces) which derived their sense of authenticity from institutions that depended on disparities of wealth: in short, from their oppressors.

One other aspect of the struggle in Brazil provides us with a vivid contrast to the programs that exist today in the United States. Because of the grass-roots fervor that created the emotional arena for their work, literacy workers were not caught up in the alienating jargon that we know so well in the United States: a language that has been described by Freire as "narration sickness" or, in another context, "empty words." There were no "grant proposals," "need descriptions," "evaluations," "feasibility examinations," "pilot projects"—nor "outside consultants." To the extent that people had to struggle against drowning, it was not a struggle against jargon. The struggle was clear and strong and uncomplex. The adversary was injustice. The goal was liberation.

Americans who label themselves "realists" tend to dismiss the struggle in Brazil for several reasons: The atmosphere was openly political. The bias of the work was undisguised. The program aroused alarm within some right-wing sectors of the population. A military coup was carried out, and a repressive government was placed in power. Freire was arrested and, for a time, imprisoned. Those who would not choose, in any case, to take the struggle in a Third World nation as a model for our own are able to exploit the repression that resulted from the struggle in Brazil as justification for dismissal of the model altogether. But in those nations (Cuba, for example) where a very similar campaign was carried through with real success, the same "realistic" North Americans condemn the program for the character of its success. Either way, they have been immunized against a foreign model.

Where the struggle is defeated by right-wing reaction, they dismiss it as an injudicious effort that "brought on" its own demise. Where the struggle was too strong to be defeated, they view it with abhorrence as a triumph for an adversary nation. In one case, they say: "It was a decent effort, but it failed; its failure indicates that it was flawed by ideology." In the other, they say: "It seems to have succeeded; its success must have been engineered by ideology. This kind of success is no success at all. It is indoctrination . . ."

Misguided pride leaves us impervious to any version of success that does not bear the patent of our system. If it does not say MADE IN THE U.S.A., it has to be a fabrication or a well-intended failure.*

There is no need to overstate the case for what has been achieved in Cuba, nor to make unwarranted comparisons between the situations faced and victories achieved within that nation and our own. Cuba has a small and homogeneous population. Its literacy struggle rode the crest of revolution. Moreover, the Cuban struggle, carried out in 1961, did not seek to bring nonreaders much beyond a third grade reading level. It has taken twenty years of follow-up to reach a universal sixth grade level; and the time-line for achievement of a universal twelfth grade level will extend into the last years of this century. The Cuban pedagogy, in addition, was directed closely toward political consolidation of the people: a goal which was regarded as essential to defense of an embattled revolution but does not accord with my reiterated emphasis upon informed irreverence which can foster meaningful denunciations in the face of governmental actions. The Cuban achievement was spectacular. Only the most narrow jingoism can allow us to deny this. The lesson offered to us by the Cuban struggle is a lesson not of how to do it but of the fact that something of this magnitude can actually be done.

The point that matters here is that we cannot learn from the real victories of other nations, nor can we transcend the limitations of those victories, if we cannot bring ourselves to look with open eyes and honest recognition at the enterprises of our neighbors. The absence of all reference to the undertakings of the Third World nations in the literacy discourse of the U.S.A. (and, to be a little more precise, the terror of red-baiting that so many scholars feel when we suggest the possibility of looking at such programs) represents an arrogant betrayal of the interests of our own society, both of the poor who suffer and of the rich who pay one price today and will be forced to pay a more alarming price in generations hence.

Nationalism of this kind does not serve our national advantage. It is, in its effect, far more subversive to our interests than the "worst" success that we refuse to countenance in Cuba or Brazil. Neither of these nations hesitates to borrow good ideas from the United States. Why do we hesitate to learn from

---

* All U.S. educators are not equally determined to discredit the achievements of the work that has been carried out in other nations. Thomas Sticht, a political conservative whose observations on the generational injustice that perpetuates adult illiteracy in the United States have been quoted earlier in this book, served on the UNESCO jury which, in 1980, unanimously voted to award to Nicaragua the gold medal granted yearly to the nation, or the institution, which has made the most dramatic literacy gains.(See NOTES.)

them? It is understandable that right-wing leaders wish to close their eyes to matters of this sort. It is not so understandable that educators also feel reluctant to accept, or else determined to discredit, the success of others.

"If it could work we would have thought of it ourselves. If we haven't done it, it may be that it cannot be done . . ." This is one aspect of our fatalism and paralysis. But there are others; some of them are easier to pin down.

The dean of faculty at one of the large universities in the Midwest voiced two of the familiar inhibitions in a question that he posed to me during a seminar two years ago: "First of all, I'm not convinced that people who have been illiterate for their entire lives, who have experienced repeated failure in most other areas of life as well, are likely to feel the motivation it would take to enter upon an effort of this kind. Is that motivation really there? Or can it be aroused? If it can, wouldn't this awaken an entire transformation of their expectations? How could such expectations be fulfilled? The economy would still remain unable to include them; certainly it would be unable to accommodate the wishes of invigorated people who would not be willing to accept their permanent status in those lower-level job slots that exist. How would they react to a deficient health care system? Wouldn't they demand the same degree of medical excellence that is afforded to rich people? This demand cannot be met. Wouldn't this be a way of cheating people, of deceiving them, of building them up for bitter disappointment? Is it ethical, is it responsible, to do this? Wouldn't it lead to dangerous unrest? Is this a danger that we can accept?"

The first of these points, regarding motivation, is not difficult to lay to rest. My own initial year of literacy work confirms for me the presence of a limitless degree of motivation. In less than sixty days of three-hour sessions in the basement of a church in one of Boston's poorest ghetto neighborhoods, twenty-five workers—nonprofessionals like myself whose only preparation was a ten-day course provided by a militant young teacher—were able to bring 250 adolescents from a reading competence equivalent to that of second or third grade to a level of effectiveness that corresponds to sixth grade competence within a good suburban school.

The class I have described took place during my first year as a teacher, long before the founding of the school described in Chapter 6. Neither I nor any of my fellow tutors had been trained in schools of education. None of us had any background in the literature discussed within this book. Most, however, were immersed in other struggles of the same community. Some of us lived within the neighborhood as well. All of this informs my strong conviction that the motivation of the learner is by no means the real problem; but it also reinforces my belief that personal immersion on the part of tutors is a crucial factor in awakening a motivation which will seldom be apparent in a neutral setting or an outside (institutional) locale.

It is probably correct that rapid progress in this situation was encouraged by the fact that many of our students had not yet completed public school and others, some of them as young as fifteen years or less, had already been expelled or had dropped out of public school as early as the seventh grade. Because they had not been exposed to all of those humiliations that illiterate high school students often undergo as they sleep out their years in hopeless academic situations, it is likely that they had not yet developed the extreme antipathy to written words and the abhorrence (loathing even) of the learning process that the full regime of secondary schooling might instill in many persons who are twenty-two or older. I am convinced, however, that this represents at most a relative advantage. Dozens of tiny groups throughout the nation have reported similar success with people of all ages. Most of them could not work with students for three hours every day. For this and other reasons they required a much longer period than sixty days; six months to a year was probably the average time involved in making the initial breakthrough. Whether sixty days or sixty weeks, the gains were rapid and the victories were real.

The key, in every case, was to abstain from any inclination to provide the motivation as an outside force (the common professional question asks: "How can we motivate these kinds of people?") but to discern that motivation which exists already in even the most seemingly disheartened human beings. Very few people I have known would acquiesce, if they had any choice, in a subservient position. People who are not in love with death do not choose to live within a state of bondage.

Once, during my year of work in Cleveland, I was involved in a discussion with two dozen people in the crowded kitchen of a dismal flat within a housing project. I asked a woman, barely literate herself, whether there was something she could do to help those of her friends who could not read or write at all. "What could I do? I could sit down every night and teach them right here in *this* kitchen. Just give me help. Just show me what to do. And tell me what day we begin!"

Answers like these come forth from every corner of the nation. Week after week, throughout the past four years, I have received handwritten letters asking, with all possible evidence of motivation, for anything that might provide a man or woman with some concrete help in learning how to read and write. Most of these letters, written by a friend or neighbor of the person seeking help, were only semiliterate themselves. The urgency of longing was intensified and rendered more compelling by the awkward syntax and disoriented spelling:

"HELLP ME TO LEARD. THE WALLS ARE UP."

Can we pretend, in face of words like these, that we are dealing with a lack of motivation? I find this unpersuasive.

What of the fear that raising expectations might, in some sense, be "unfair"? What of the possibility that literate and critical adults will soon confront the obstacles of many other forms of long-established North American injustice and that the walls will either crush their reawakened dreams or crumble from the force of their assault? The fear that temporary disappointment may ensue is realistic. The possibility that walls might crumble as the consequence of an emancipated underclass in motion ought to be viewed not with alarm but with a sense of celebration.

Too often, those who caution us of certain dangers in the heightened expectations of a newly literate adult are using a compassionate mode to voice their own fears of the possible societal disruptions that frustrated expectations might awaken. Now and then, the real priorities and the concealed agenda do break through the pretense of compassion. One shocking revelation of the secret fears of some of those in dominant positions speaks for those of many who are more discreet. "Spending on education should be reduced . . . ," a writer for the Heritage Foundation recently proposed. Workers, he said, should not be educated "beyond what the system is likely to require . . ." Critical competence in literacy skills—or "overeducation," in his words—might lead to "greater discontentment and still lower productivity." Coming from a man and institution with direct ties to the White House, these concerns cannot be viewed as so exceptional that we may casually consign them to a right-wing fringe of odious opinion. The fears of William Berkeley are resilient.

If lobbies can form, if neighborhoods can coalesce, if people can organize, cease to request, and learn how to demand, if newly literate adults should find that work appropriate to their abilities and energies does not exist within the economic framework of America, if 60 million people rising from dependent status find that their acquired competence cannot receive a dignified accommodation in this nation, then they will set out with a constructive vengeance to transform that nation and to reconstruct that crumbling economy. What is the greatest danger that this may portend? It is the danger that we shall be forced to live up to the promise of democracy. If this is a danger that society cannot afford, I do not believe poor people can afford to live at peace with this society.

Might violence result?

Those of us who have been working with illiterates for many years have little reason to believe this. Much to the contrary: Those who, in the present context, have no other recourse but to violence (those, for example, in the prison population; those who are not yet in prison but who have no other means of feeding their own children, or of finding even the most futile forms of vindication, than the violence of street-crime and the dark pathology of drugs and prostitution) would at last discover an effective instrument of self-assertion in the lever of political organization and the power of a shrewd, informed, and well-timed impact on the outcome of elections. No nation that was worth perpetuation was ever disarmed by critical and analytic competence within its population; but many civilizations which are now extinct might well have been saved by such a population.

Apart from the tip of the iceberg which we can perceive in crime statistics, violence is with us now in every aspect of the life of an illiterate. Medically unnecessary death is violence by abdication. Nutritional starvation is a form of violence as well. Exclusion of one third of the electorate does violence to all that we pretend by our adherence to democracy. Martin Luther King, whose energies and tactics are a proper model for the struggle I propose, was sometimes accused of propagating insurrection by the lifting up of people's hopes and demolition of restricting walls. History honors him as a man of peace. It is the violence of the society he had the courage to confront which finally was used to silence him. Gandhi was denigrated by the British viceroy for stirring up the seeds of discontent. He fought against the prior violence of hunger, sickness, subjugation. The British killed his peaceful followers with bullets made in English factories. He died of a weapon, fired by one of those British subjects who had learned too well the violent methods of their rulers. American union organizers in the early 1900s were regarded as subversive persons preaching violence and unrest. They fought against the prior violence of child labor and starvation wages. They were attacked and often killed by hired thugs employed by factories they sought to organize.

Violence is not initiated by the victims of an unjust order. They are responding almost always to a prior violence. I do not believe that violence could possibly result from literate upheaval. But it *will* be an upheaval. It will be a massive mobilization. If we conceive it as anything else, it cannot be successful.

I have participated long enough in various symposia and panels to anticipate how certain people may respond to much of what is written here.

The experts nod across the seminar table. They hear my words. They do not disagree. They are polite. "This is important. Something should be done. We ought to form a new commission . . ." I offer a plan; too timid, too reserved. I speak about the nations in which problems of this kind have been addressed courageously.

"Interesting . . ." The words come back: a counterpoint of sensible rebuttal to implausible suggestion. They listen a while; at length they shrug it off. "Somebody ought to organize a thorough study of this problem."

We do not need another study. We do not need a new commission. We know exactly what needs to be done. We do not have the right to find retreat in earnest indecision. We have the obligation to take action.

Unearthing Seeds of Fire:
A Plan to Mobilize
Illiterate America

In any case, and from any point of view, the moral obligation is plain:
there must be a crusade against this poverty in our midst.

—Michael Harrington

It is now self-evident that we cannot afford to wait for government—not for the
present government at least—to take the lead. It is equally apparent that a
governmental definition of our goals (even assuming that the government should
ever choose to deal with literacy at all) is doomed to be a mechanistic definition.
The government might like to see a functional society. It will not be eager to
initiate those steps which would enable that society to function in unmanage-
able or unexpected ways.

It is believable that, in the years ahead, a new administration may discover
that it has no choice but to respond to an existing groundswell by providing
funds to launch a national campaign. The War on Poverty, enacted into legisla-
tion under pressure from the White House in the days of Lyndon Johnson,
represented a response to passionate actions undertaken in the previous ten
years by students, activists, poor people, and some highly charismatic leaders
such as Martin Luther King. Head Start, Job Corps, Upward Bound, the Neighborhood Youth Corps, Vista Volunteers, and other programs came into existence as an answer—one that was, by then, politically essential—to the civil
disobedience, the mass arrests, the freedom schools, and major mobilizations
which began in places like Montgomery, St. Augustine, and Selma. In the same
way, it is believable that an administration someday in the 1980s may decide

that it can see political advantage in support of an on-going literacy struggle. The definitions and the aspirations must, however, have been carefully established in advance of any government .participation. Some of those goals have been discussed in the preceding chapter. In this chapter I will try to make the details more specific.

Who will teach? How many? Where? And where will they be found? How will they be organized, assigned, and supervised? What might it cost? By what methods, first and foremost, will illiterate and semiliterate Americans be found, recruited, and involved?

Before proceeding with some of the answers, I should place those answers in the framework of my actual intentions. I do not intend to turn this into a prescriptive handbook. There are others who have more experience than I and who can more suitably spell out the details of a plan that seems to serve the needs of a diverse variety of situations, neighborhoods, and human beings. All that follows, then, might be construed as a scenario, a landscape of American potentials, not as a fixed inventory of sequential stages in a predetermined plan.

Some vision of the possible is nonetheless required. I will do this in progressive stages. First, I will describe a number of approaches which appear to lie within the realm of realistic action in the years immediately before us. Then I will suggest a means by which these early efforts may be lifted to the status of a national imperative, a mandate that can be translated into the specifics of a national campaign. Finally, I will draw a model of the kind of program that I have in mind. I will derive this model from a struggle that is under way today.

The first stage will receive the most attention. This is because it is the stage at which we now exist: the part we can discuss today and do tomorrow morning. It does not require research. It does not require further outlay of our money for consultants. It does not require waiting for the next six rounds of subcommittee hearings to be held in 1986 or 1994. This is why it may offend some people. I do not believe that Benjamin will be offended.

•*How do we reach them?*

A woman in Cleveland offered an impatient and exhilarating answer to this question:

"How do you reach them? You cannot do it by sitting downtown and mailing out brochures. You need to find the kind of person who can walk the neighborhood—someone with a heart and soul. A foot-walker. Someone like that would know very quickly who was illiterate and who was not. That person has got to be able to overcome the illiterate's terror of the outside world, as well as the feeling that there's nothing out there they could even *want.* Sojourner Truth said: 'I cannot read, but I can read people.' So, too, can many of the poorest people in their own communities. We had better send out people who are not afraid that somebody might have the wit to read a message in their eyes. This is a tremendous challenge: to be unafraid to speak to the poor of reading problems in their midst because we are not frightened to be read *ourselves* and to be discovered lacking in conviction.

"There are lots of people who are going to respond because they want a decent chance to earn a living and to have a comfortable life: if not for their own selves, then for their children. But we can raise other possibilities as well. Black people, for example, need not imitate the worst of white competitive consumers. They can forge some other values of their own. I say to competitive blacks sometimes: 'You're letting your white brother live inside your head rent-free!' Competitive verbosity is not the same as real communication. Knowledge has to be a deeper thing than setting out to see how many people you can beat . . .

"I would like to see some emphasis on oral history. This might lead, in time, to duplication of some inexpensive books made from the stories people tell. It gives us a chance to smash some of the stereotypes—about the 'typical' family, for example. All of our families aren't the same. A lot of our one-parent families are much closer and more happy than the ones you meet out in the suburbs. This is a fact that has not been reflected on TV."

I will return to the idea of oral history in the next chapter. For now, I think it is important to contrast the recommendation for "foot-walkers"—"the kind of person who can walk the neighborhood"—with the common assertion of so many groups that "door-to-door" solicitation does not work and, in particular, has not been successful with the persons they describe as "ghetto prospects." The question we need to ask is who is *doing* the "foot-walking" and what kind of message can be read within that person's eyes. Suppose, for example, that a door-to-door campaign were carried out not by outsiders but by literate (or, for that matter, semiliterate or even totally illiterate) insiders. Suppose that college students who have family roots in the communities in question were to provide the vanguard for this door-to-door campaign. These are people who might well succeed in getting past the door, in going beyond the standard pitch that traveling salesmen have purveyed forever—and beyond the instantaneous distrust that most outsiders both elicit and deserve. They might find themselves asked in to sit down in the living room or kitchen, share a cup of coffee, join in conversation, summon up their memories of mutual friends, and in time direct that conversation to the goals of the campaign and to the needed input of direction and ideals that may be offered by the people it intends to serve. It is very, very hard for anyone who represents a totally unfamiliar world—whose style, clothing, eyes, and mannerisms all reflect that difference—to win the trust of people who will have no reason to be sure if trust in this case, unlike many others, is deserved.

"I cannot read, but I can read people."

Even the most unselfish people carry certain meanings in their eyes. One of those meanings surely is the sense of power, of mobility, of open option that has allowed us even to decide to make this visit. It is, I would guess, precisely for this reason that so many literacy advocates run into resistance from "the ghetto prospects" (and from the poor white "rural prospects" too) which cannot be explained entirely by the presence of those masking strategies we have described above. This, in turn, explains the misconception, which the press noncritically repeats, that the major obstacle we face is the reluctance of illiterate adults to face up to their needs.

"Any meaningful attack on illiteracy," a recent story on the front page of the *Wall Street Journal* charged, "depends on the willingness of the afflicted to seek help . . . Persuading people to face up to their handicap and present themselves for remedial instruction is a major problem." Words such as "handicap" and, even worse, "afflicted" offer us some vivid hints of what is going wrong. As long as illiteracy is so perceived, as long as oppression is defined as an "affliction," as long as an injustice is reduced to something so inherent to the individual as a "handicap," as long as the illiterate himself is regarded as "a deficit commodity" in our society, we can believe that the message which is read by those whom we are hoping to recruit will not be one that wins an unambiguous response. This is the case (and I believe this point is most important) even when nothing that we do is "wrong" or "condescending" or "unkind." It is simply the fact of who we are; and this is not our fault—nor our "affliction" either. It is, on the other hand, a clear imperative to turn to methods which will be successful. The admonition of Sojourner Truth should serve as a commanding challenge to us all.

We should also look with caution on the word "attack," used in the reportage I have just quoted ("any meaningful attack . . ."). "Word-attack skills" is another term that has a similar effect. It seems so natural to use this phrase that we too easily forget its implications. Do we consider "words" to be our enemies or friends? Do we intend to kill them, take them prisoner, or ask them in to share in our existence? Literacy experts often use such terms. Another is a common reference to illiterate Americans as "the target population." Words like these are borrowed, I believe, from business terminology, from marketing and advertising firms. Innocent and unaware as those who use such terms may be, they do compel us to ask certain questions: Who is launching this attack? Who (or what) are we attacking? If there is a battle to be launched, from which direction are the generals and the tacticians viewing the terrain?

The War on Poverty, at its least enlightened, was satirized often as "a war against the poor." We need to be sure that we do not confuse the process of victimization with the victim. This is one reason why I find that "wanted" poster, used by organizers in the Florida campaign, so lacking in taste, so cruel, so ill-advised. I spoke, in that context, of the connotations of the posse, of the hunt. Terms like "target population" summon up a similar mood of "rounding up the suspects" for arrest. Many outsiders (policemen and court officers, for instance) do arrive at the doors of poor adults with court injunctions, warrants for arrest of juveniles, demands for payment, and the like. We should be certain that our metaphors do not so closely simulate reality of the most undesired kind.

If it is injustice that we set out to defeat, we should take measures to be certain that the war—including the initial skirmish—has been launched from the right side. Recruitment, therefore, poses more than questions of approach. We have to ask: not only how to do it, but who does it. This is why organizing in the neighborhoods themselves, helping those neighborhoods to generate their own agendas and their own "foot-walkers" from the very start, seems elemental to our hopes of real success.

Once the question of *who* has been resolved, we can explore more of the questions about *how*.

Radio and TV plugs have worked for certain groups. To the extent that print advertisements are used at all, we should keep in mind that we are reaching only those who need our help the least but that such announcements can be useful for another purpose: not so much to reach illiterates directly, but to mobilize communities to launch their own recruitment efforts. This does not mean simply to enlist a lot of people to go out and knock on neighbors' doors. The first stage is to reach existing grass-roots groups in order to encourage them to place this issue on their own agendas, then to adjust the terms of those agendas in accord with their own needs and through the course of neighborhood meetings which involve those (the illiterates) whom they can reach in helping to devise the way a local effort might take place.

There is a tremendous difference between knocking on a door to tell somebody of a program that has been devised already and which they are given the choice, at most, to join or else ignore—and, on the other hand, to ask them to assist in the creation of that plan. I do not mean that organizers ought to abdicate the knowledge they possess and take an utterly passive role with people whose passivity already represents one portion of the problem we confront; nor do I mean that people from outside the neighborhoods in question ought to adopt a neutral posture and deny or even mute the insights they can bring to bear. But there is a difference between provocation and control. Some of the best ideas that I have heard have come out of discussions held within the neighborhoods themselves. People, moreover, are far more likely to participate in something which they or their neighbors have been first invited to assist in planning—and something in which ideas that they have offered have been more than "heard" but given application.

I know of groups which, hoping to pull out a crowd, have advertised that something like "refreshments" would be served—and found, to their dismay, that nobody appeared. When, on the other hand, a potluck supper was announced and the word was subsequently passed from friend to friend, and house to house, and block to block, some of the poorest people in that neighborhood appeared, each with something good that they had managed to prepare. There is a reason why this invitation was attractive: A potluck supper cannot work if people don't appear. Anyone who chooses not to go will know that there will be exactly one less dish for everyone to share.

A potluck supper happens to be a method of recruitment that has worked out very well in certain situations, especially in urban neighborhoods where people live close to each other and already have some sense of common cause. But it is less as method than as metaphor that it is mentioned here. "People don't like you to 'do' for them," one woman told me during my year's work in Cleveland. "They have their pride. They also have the bad experience of social workers, salesmen, other people who have announced what they would do for them and then turned out to do them *out*, or do them *in* . . . When you recruit, you don't want to present a package: 'Take it or not. It's already been wrapped.' You want to ask them to put something in that package, even a little something, even one word of caution, one idea. You want to ask them to bring something to the meal."

An elderly nun in the same neighborhood remarked: "Breaking bread together is a beautiful idea. Helping to bake the bread is even better."

Once an idea has been proposed, no matter how modest and how simple it may seem, other people in the neighborhood begin to offer their elaborations. During gatherings I have in mind in Cleveland, men and women who had previously been reticent, withdrawn, at length began to speak. "Could you do it in a place that's got a kitchen? You've got to have a stove to make hot coffee. You'll need refrigerators too. Most of the day-care centers and the churches have a kitchen . . ."

"Try to think of some rewards for coming. Cookbooks maybe—something that could help us with nutrition. Health emergencies. Something like Dr. Spock . . ."

"Something else. If you could get some company downtown to offer a reward after we have read a dozen books . . . A bookshelf for the children . . . Something that could go beside their beds . . ."

There is eloquence and gentle wisdom and humane excitement here. It never fails to happen. I am convinced that those who share in conversations of this sort will be the best recruiters for a plan they have contrived.

• *Circles of Learners: "A Unit of Instruction"*

In some of my earlier writing I have argued that instruction should be one-to-one. This is the approach employed by many of the Laubach groups. I now believe that my insistence on a one-to-one relationship was based on limited information.

For certain people it is probably true that privacy, at least in the beginning months, may seem to be of help in overcoming inhibitions fostered by the stigma that attaches to the status of illiterate adults. In rural areas, moreover, there will frequently be no choice. Distance and the consequent dilemmas of logistics will often make it difficult to work with more than one man or one woman at a time. Wherever possible, however, I have come to be convinced that groups of six or seven learners and one literacy worker represent an ideal unit of instruction for this plan. The presence of a circle of a half-dozen friends or neighbors helps to generate a sense of common cause and to arouse a sense of optimistic ferment that is seldom present in a one-to-one encounter. It may also cut down on the learner's fear that he or she is different, or deficient, or unique: "There are six of us here within this room. All of us are engaged in the same challenge." Finally, from the literacy worker's point of view, there is the advantage that our power is reduced by virtue of the fact that several people in the same room at the same time constitute a total field of preferences and options, and of mutual reinforcement in those options, which (in its totality) is greater than our own. Sensitive literacy workers feel uneasy with the disproportionate esteem that may attach to them by reason of their singular stature as "the one" who has the needed skill. The longing to create a dialogue of equals is often undermined by the unquestioned power of the one who seemingly "possesses" what the others need. Once a group is formed, the learners and the teacher too are given some relief from this imbalance. Although one person in the group brings to the session something that the others do not "have" (something, indeed, they came here to "acquire"), the collective wisdom and experience of several learners in a dozen other areas of needed skill add up to a healthy counterbalance to the literacy worker's competence in one specific realm.

Humor also leavens the mood, and is much easier to come by, when the tension felt by one participant is allowed spontaneous release by another person's impulse to remark upon the nervousness that everybody feels. Both in teaching and in prior organizing stages, I have found this feeling of good-natured communality a blessed respite from the underlying tension which I may unconsciously create by my determination. In the periods in which I first began to seek suggestions as to organizing and recruitment plans, first in my own neighborhood of Boston, later on in Cleveland, meetings with individuals were less productive than the sessions held with a small group of residents within a single block or single building of a housing project. People who had uncomfortably deferred to me in first encounters suddenly became relaxed, and then impassioned and inventive, when we met a second time among a number of their friends. Humor and anger, and eloquence too, began to flourish once the solitary mode—"the interview"—had been replaced by something less austere.

There is another point which has some bearing here. Literacy, by definition, is shared knowledge. As such, it is collective by necessity. Eccentrics talk to themselves; some of us address incessant memos to ourselves; many people write in private journals. But few of us, with the exception of extreme psychotics, would persist for long in writing words which nobody else will ever have an opportunity to read. Words, with few exceptions, have historically had meaning only as a method of communication. Even in repossession of the past, reading has been valued not so much as private acquisition but as a collective process of retrieval of shared values, precedents, ideals. Young men of Jewish faith learn to read Hebrew not in order to pray alone but to join in groups of ten (no less) in order to participate in shared communion with their heritage and with their God. They read in order to enter a community of conscience that is based on knowledge of the Pentateuch and the ability to read or to recite from memory the words that they have proven they can understand. They do not need a sacerdotal figure, a religious hierarch, in order to pray together. Many non-Jewish people do not understand that rabbis are not members of a priestly caste. The rabbi is a learned man selected by the congregation to fulfill a number of important roles; but the power to sanctify, to bless, is not one of those roles. We sanctify ourselves through literate participation in collective reverence for our past.

Literacy, when viewed as a collective process, helps to reduce our feeling of dependence on a special person, an anointed individual (whether that person is the leader of a literacy circle or the rabbi of a congregation) and, in this way, heightens our autonomy and guards against our passive acquiescence in an arbitrary "truth" dictated by a person who appears to be above us. If one precious goal of literacy struggle in our nation is the inculcation of informed irreverence to defend us against verbal domination, whether corporate or demagogic, then the initial stages of our work ought, so far as possible, to pose the vision of emancipation from a word imposed upon us by a person to whom, temporarily, we find ourselves subordinate.

Learning in groups, people at length will generate group leaders; because these leaders will emerge out of their ranks, they will remain susceptible to criticism and correction. At the same time, because of their point of origin, and their proximity to pain, they may be in an ideal position to discover and encourage others. A snowball effect is the desired goal. Those who learn may soon be prompted to share what they learn with others. Learners may in time be teachers, or at least the organizers of those teachers. People like this can do a lot more than to teach their neighbors. They can also teach the "outside teachers" how to see at last some of the deeper contradictions of their nation—contradictions they may subsequently be willing to address with a more partisan resolve.

• *What categories of instructors ought to be involved? Where might they be found?*

For now, I will not undermine the reader's optimism, or my own, by legislating an astronomy of numbers. Whatever the required figure, we are speaking certainly of massive numbers, merely to address the needs of those who, at this time, are scarcely reached at all. I am going to suggest a teaching force composed of three essential parts. We might look at each of these three groups in sequence.

(1) College and high school students represent one very large potential source of literacy workers. Despite the recent furor over an apparent drop in SATs, poor composition skills, and other symptoms of "diminished excellence" in public education, millions of students between the ages of fifteen and twenty-five are fully competent to share what they already know. Dozens of conversations with young people in the past few years convince me that a reservoir of pent-up energy exists throughout the university and teenage population. In the course of visits I have made to schools and colleges from 1980 to the present, over 10,000 students have supplied me with their names, addresses, and phone numbers and have sometimes added a brief note of urgency: "When do we start?"

Student apathy receives the press attention; much of that apathy, we are obliged to recognize, is very real. A larger part, I am convinced, derives from the predictive power of the press itself, sometimes from parents and from faculty as well. Energy without a moral focus does at length turn inward to the sneering hedonism or the narcissistic selfishness which journalists both document and foster. This was very much the mood in 1958 and 1960. It required only the keen sense of focus, in a concrete, readily comprehended, ethically important context, to transform the uncommitted children of the age of Eisenhower into the devoted activists of SNCC and CORE, followers first of Dr. King and then of Dr. Spock.

Those who assign immutable reality to fixed compartments, demarcated by the arbitrary borders of a decade, can too easily forget that less than thirty months of soaring ethical momentum in the early 1960s marked the passage from congealed and dreary stasis to a social revolution that transformed the legal status of black people. It is the focus that does not exist today. I am proposing one such focus in this book.

Comparisons to the 1960s can, of course, be risky and misleading. Invisible victims do not win our loyalty so rapidly as those whose sufferings are vivid and enacted nightly in degrading rituals of crude evisceration on TV. The unmistakable oppression and injustice represented by the redneck sheriffs and the clubs and cattle prods employed by Southern whites in efforts to perpetuate race-segregation are not present in this case. Economic factors represent another problem. Students today cannot so easily neglect financial worries as their prede-cessors twenty years before. Both of these matters are relative, however. Neither eradicates (nor should be permitted to eradicate) one of the great and natural prerogatives of youth: namely, to act in decent ways on decent principles and dreams. The dreams are there. The decency cannot have died entirely. The focus still remains to be made real.

Additional impetus might be afforded by the universities and schools if they were to grant a student academic credit for a year of literacy work. The best of colleges (not necessarily the most "elite") might dare to do this. Certain universities and public schools might even choose to make this kind of work a firm requirement for graduation, especially at college levels for those undergrad-uates enrolled in areas like English literature, philosophy and history, and other subjects where the range of study ought to comprehend some sense of civic decency as well as private satisfaction. In a recent study, former U.S. Commis-sioner of Education Ernest Boyer recommended that a stipulated period of public service ought to be a part of the curriculum for secondary students. If this recommendation is accepted at the high school level, it is difficult to know why it should not be viewed with favor at the college level too.

There is one obvious risk in these suggestions. Service, where rewarded by credentials, credits, and the like, loses a certain portion of its idealistic thrust. More important, it may undermine to some degree the atmosphere of urgency, excitement—of a "grand endeavor"—that is basic to the whole idea of youth participation. The same reservation applies, although with greater force, to liter-acy work that is "required." If reward diminishes the sense of decent struggle to a minimal degree, requisite participation undermines that attitude still more. Whether with university or high school students, my own inclination is to view required service as an unwise policy but to view rewarded service as a workable approach if it is governed by some sensible conditions.

Even from a purely pedagogic point of view, suggestions of this kind appear to be received with warm approval by sophisticated school administrators. "Two-way tutoring" has been acknowledged for some years as one of the most promising approaches in the effort to advance the math and literacy skills of young adults. Secondary students, for example, who can read and write at mod-est high school levels, but whose competence is not yet equal to requirements for university admission, often rebel at being pressured into "programs of remediation." Already physically and psychologically mature, they find this sort of program juvenilizing. The very same students, on the other hand, often gain enormous confidence and soon discover an unprecedented surge of motivation once they are offered an occasion to share what they know with someone else. In the process they have seldom failed to gain in competence themselves. They gain in skills. They also learn something apart from better skills: They learn about some better *uses* for their skills. This, in a competitive and frequently unmerciful society like ours, may be a form of competence that we should prize above all others.

In the area of social science too, there is ethical attraction on the side of this idea. There seems both sanity and poetry at stake when we release our students from required courses like "The Problems of Democracy" in order to allow them to go out into the world beyond the school and have a chance to *solve* one of those problems. The sense of unreality that gives to much of secondary education the appearance of a simulation game might, to some degree, be punctured by such means.

Teachers, too, might be awarded credit toward seniority and tenure for participation with their students in a "literacy team." Again, a year of literacy work by would-be teachers might be established as a precondition for certification by state boards of education. This seems politically unlikely in the present climate of the nation. It is a seed that may be worth the planting nonetheless. Teachers, after a practicum like this, might better understand why many parents do not answer letters and announcements sent home with their children. They might also have *reduced* the number of nonreading parents by significant degrees and might, in this manner, have improved the future classroom situation for all children.

The problems inherent in any system of required service will remain. There is the additional problem that too many classroom teachers, long accustomed to regarding "pupils" as equivalent to "children," tend to approach adults with some of the same attitudes that juvenilize the total learning process and, for illiterate men and women who have suffered through the years of public school already, may well replicate the very atmosphere that first prevented them from learning. It is probably the case that certain teachers (especially student teachers) would be able to adapt superbly—and that others should not be involved in this at all.

(2) Students, in any event, appear to represent one large potential source of vigorous participation. Elderly people, especially retired persons, represent another. If students have not yet incurred the obligations of a mortgage, of a family, and the like, millions of people who are in their sixties and much older are already done with bringing up their children and have long since finished paying for their homes. The largest number of letters I receive from those who offer their resources, and especially their time, come to me from retired men and women. The second largest number come from students. It is, then, both the youngest and the oldest of adults who seem to me most likely to be willing and available to join within the struggle I propose.

Convenience, however, is hardly the main point. Basic compassion, not just for the old but for the younger generation too, lies at the heart of this idea. The segregation of old people from the mainstream of activity in the United States has been discussed by many authors as a tragic sacrifice of wisdom and experience in a society which needs to learn all that it can from those whose vigor and longevity enable them to see beyond the amputated present tense to which the young have been consigned by our contempt for history. Our disrespectful treatment of our parents and grandparents is not just a symptom of a certain heartlessness within our social order; it is a metaphor of our neglect for what one thoughtful scholar has described as "conjugated truth." It resonates with our despisal of the continuities of time.

The Eskimo, according to a story told to children in a standard lesson planned for the fourth grade curriculum, places his aged parents on a frozen island or an open boat and leaves them to confront and then succumb to winter's elements alone, unmourned and undefended. Americans congratulate themselves that we are not so harsh with those we love. We send our elders to an old folks' home or, in the modernized form, "a senior citizens' retirement community," too frequently a high-rise institution on the outskirts of our memory and recognition, which sometimes has the aspect of a cheerful condominium but is, in its effect, a color-coded concrete anteroom to death.

Enforced retirement comes a lot too early in this nation. We lose not just the energy, the work potential, but the courage that experience affords and the compassion that the recognition of mortality so often fosters, even in those who have, in early years, been just as restless and competitive as we.

At the opposite extreme we tend to view our adolescent students, once incarcerated in their public schools, as if they were preparatory humans—"people in training," in the words of one headmaster—trapping them in an interlock of school-mandated numbers (six years, then another six, then four) from which there seems to be no plausible escape. In such a way we have excluded them, for almost one fourth of their biological existence, from any sense of useful and enjoyable participation in the world outside of school.

Even worse, we have denied them opportunity to learn from those who have been born as much as half a century before them and who, if these needless walls of demarcation could be broken down, might well join with them in common cause to do what those who stand between them, busy with their getting and their gaining, have neither the time nor, often, sensitivity to undertake. Incarceration at both ends of the continuum of our existence isolates those who have the greatest need to learn of history from those who have the most to teach because it is a history which they have helped to shape and one within which they have led their lives. Who remains to wage the battles and to sound the trumpets? The field is left to those who, caught up in the rat race of ambition and sometimes of fear, do not believe they can afford to dabble in such matters as injustice. If it were not for these unfortunate divisions, future and past might be enabled to combine their gifts in order to endow the present with informed compassion. A coalition of the young and old might, from even the most tentative beginnings, grow into a formidable force.

In an elegy for Sigmund Freud, dated September 1939, W. H. Auden wrote these words: "All that he did was to remember/like the old and [to] be honest like children." The joining of forces of the young and old represents a literal means of reconnecting tenses. It offers the potential for a generational alliance, one in which both honesty and memory combine to forge a struggle in which biblical traditions and the most utilitarian requirements of present times are richly intertwined. The gift of energy imparted by the young is stabilized and given reassurance by the quiet optimism of survivors.

Those who are closest to the finality of death might, in this way, help us renew our affirmation of the worth of life. If we could think of literacy in the United States not so much as a technical tool, an instrument, "a piece of skill" designed to win "a parcel of reward," but rather as the elemental link between the world as it has been before our times and life as it may someday be when we are gone, then we might also think of literacy instruction, shared by the young and even very old, as something which may help to sensitize our souls, to open our hearts, to teach us that faithfully recorded words may help forgetful nations both "to be honest" and also, in the words of Auden: "to remember."

(3) At last, there is the central role of the community itself.

"We shouldn't forget," wrote Yves Dejean, "that the illiterates are scattered all over . . . Since the situation is not one of existing 'illiterate communities' but rather of the presence of illiterate adults among, by and large, literate communities, there is a practical consequence in terms of recruiting volunteers. Why should outsiders be recruited except very rarely? Let the literacy workers be members of the community, not outsiders. The majority of members of even the poorest of American communities are literate people!"

It is not quite accurate to say that we have no "illiterate communities" in this nation. Hunter and Harman have asserted what some of us know also from day-to-day experience: There are considerable stretches of our urban neighborhoods in which the numbers of illiterate and semiliterate adults are high enough to justify the generalized label of "illiterate communities." I also disagree with the assertion that outsiders have no role (or only "very rarely") in the struggle I propose.

Despite these reservations, the main emphasis is right. It also serves as a reminder that I am not recommending a domestic Peace Corps but a literate upheaval. The Peace Corps, even in its early years, existed to attenuate the likelihood of social transformation, not to accelerate its pace nor build the preconditions for its victory. Vista volunteers in the United States discovered soon, if they did not know it when they first enrolled, that anything resembling political participation even in the most accepted and responsible endeavor (a consumers' boycott or a rent strike, for example) often was the first step to dismissal.

Even this, however—an external veto—is not usually the most restrictive factor. Government constraints, in the majority of cases, are less powerful than those exerted by our own acculturated inhibitions, acting often in anticipation of a top-down reprimand. Many volunteers, moreover, are attached to certain aspects of a privileged existence which may be endangered by the liberation of a powerless class of persons who, once they have gained the needed skills, will surely seek an equal share in what is now enjoyed by those who can afford to volunteer. Decent people may believe that they are willing to share power; many are undoubtedly prepared to do so. We will see examples of such people later in these pages. Others, however, may not wish to share that power with so many millions, silent and inconspicuous for now, who may be expected to engage in ardent competition for the jobs, the college admissions, medical school and law school places, and the other options we enjoy. Even where the willingness exists, can it escape the subtle inhibitions of a neutralizing state of mind?

None of this countermands the points stated above. All that I have said about the shared participation of the young and old remains unqualified. I still believe that these will represent two basic elements of a successful national campaign. The same two elements exist, however, *inside* the communities themselves; and this is the first place we should look to find them, to enlist them, to assist them in assuming governance and, where it is possible, entire control over the work of all who are involved: not excluding those who have recruited them to start with.

If 44 percent of black adults are totally or partially illiterate, 56 percent remain to form the vanguard of a neighborhood campaign. If 56 percent of all Hispanic adults are illiterate in English, 44 percent are not. Millions of white and literate people also live in neighborhoods in which as many as one quarter or one third of all their neighbors are nonreaders. These, then, are the population groups in which our search for literacy workers should begin.

"Neighborhood people who already read and write," one organizer said, "ought to be paired with those who don't: a kind of buddy system. Among black people, this is an idea with some historic roots. When Southern blacks first came up to the North, it was conventional for other blacks to take them in. Many mothers and grandmothers did this. They would provide a home and teach them first to read and write. This has been done in hundreds of thousands of homes throughout the Northern states. It offers a substantial precedent for what we're thinking of right now."

If we are wise in this respect, we will pay attention to the words of those who are, or were, illiterate themselves: "I had a fellow in here a while ago. He was trying to make me out a check. It was all signed in my name, made out in my name and everything. All he got to do is write in the figures. He was kind of gruff and all. I knew, from the way he was acting, what was going through his mind."

An interviewer asked: How did you know?

"How did I know? 'Cause I been through it all so many times myself. When that guy is squirming like he wanted to fall right through the cement— you *know* that feeling! So I offered to do it . . . So he handed it right over quick. And when I wrote it out, I says, 'Don't feel alone. I used to be just like that. Not too long ago, either.' I told him, 'You don't have to be like that.' "

A person who knows this, who has been "like that" himself, who has taken the risks, and fought, and won, can say this as no outside literacy worker can. If this is the case, why shouldn't that person *be* the literacy worker? Or, if not the worker, then the organizer who recruits and offers counsel to the ones who do the work?

There are some places where this is done: too few, and far too seldom given recognition. In a two-room literacy center in a mixed white-and-Hispanic neighborhood of San Francisco, I was asked to join a Sunday evening session, low-key and relaxed, a celebration (so it seemed to me) more than an organized "discussion." Several illiterate people spoke to me, and to each other, of the problems they had faced in school and of the reasons they had come at last into this center. Finally I turned to a young man who happened to be sitting next to me. His name was Fernando. He was one of the directors of the program. "I can tell you why I'm here," he said. "I came in four years ago because I needed help to read and write. I still don't write as well as I'd like. But I know well enough to teach. So I'm teaching, but I'm learning still at the same time. One day they said they had a job for a part-time director. That's my job. I'm getting paid. It's not much money, but it pays the rent. Besides, I don't have children to support. I want to write. I like to teach. I'm going to write poetry someday."

As I was leaving he handed me one of the poems that he had tried. I liked it and, rereading it now, I like it still; I have it here, along with several other poems that he has sent me since, posted across my wall. But it is the poetry of his existence which I find most moving.

Why is it that programs of this kind, the ones where people like Fernando can commit themselves at once to learn, to organize, to teach, are always found in tiny overheated rooms within the shabbiest surroundings, while those who are the experts, the proprietors of words, conduct their esoteric sessions of professional discussion next to the open bars and underneath the dripping foliage of Hyatt Regency hotels? Maybe we ought to take this as some sort of clue as to the difference between activism and intention, the difference too between a true emotional upheaval and "a modest inclination" to address "a certain documented need." The greater the distance from the place of pain, the less the reason to remember its intensity: and, also, the less our opportunity to learn from those who do remember and who, in the strength of memory, have chosen to return what they have learned to those who are not free to choose at all.

Even when we speak, therefore, of outside teachers, we might keep in mind that thousands of poor people like Fernando are enrolled in colleges and universities today. When we speak of college students, we are likely to imagine only those who come from affluent families and are students at prestigious schools like Antioch or Wesleyan or Reed. Students like Fernando (he is now at San Francisco State) represent a bridge between two of the three groups that I have described as elemental to this plan. They know the inside (it is inside of *them)* and oftentimes, as in Fernando's case, they have chosen to remain inside the neighborhood for reasons of their own. At the same time, they study on the outside; they have the opportunity to learn, therefore, how many options still remain not only a bit beyond their reach but also past the margins of imagination. This leads to a final question that we ought to ask in reference to the three-part teaching force I have proposed.

In view of my attraction to the whole idea of bootstrap mobilization, of former illiterates "recycled" in a sense into the activists and teachers of their own communities, sensitive readers may ask once again why there is any need for even the most energized outsiders.

There are several reasons why I still believe that outside help and even, at times, conspicuous participation by outsiders are essential. First, there is the undeniable fact that people who are very poor and also illiterate are burdened with a broad array of problems, economic worries, health emergencies, many of them unexpected, unanticipated, unpredictable by definition. Most of these matters take priority over a reading problem. Even for those who do already read and write, and who therefore offer to help others, there may be innumerable pressures which necessitate extended interruptions. College and high school students, on the other hand, who have committed themselves to a specific teaching obligation—two hours nightly, three nights weekly, forty weeks in sequence for one academic year—can be expected to perform their tasks with regularity and to adhere to a routine which is established in advance. The same is true of persons who, although retired, are still strong and healthy and who have not only days but months and even years to spare.

There are at least two other roles that outside allies logically might fill. One is to provide a fiscal link to people and to groups that can enable shoestring efforts to get off the ground and then survive for long enough to build political momentum. Nobody hustles money quite so well as someone who participates in such a program. Retired persons, working in a grass-roots center several nights a week, are often shaken by the sudden contrast to the affluent surroundings of their weekend's relaxation. Many of those people, in my own experience, have turned a wince of guilt into an ounce of gold and come back frequently with contacts to substantial charitable sources that their newfound allies and co-workers could not dream of. All the contradictions notwithstanding, I have yet to find a grass-roots literacy group which felt that it had lost its soul or its political integrity by the deposit of a check which somebody they never need to know has written at the urging of someone who works beside them.

The most important role of the outsider, after all the rest is said, is purely pedagogic. It is to introduce an element of option, an aperture to unimagined possibilities which people, locked into the narrow information access represented by neighbor's conversation or by radio and TV, cannot desire since they do not know that they exist. Most of us have heard the bellicose demand of certain dogmatists: "Keep away the liberal outsiders. People will choose the things they need! Let the illiterate men and women tell us what they really want to read . . ." This is a self-defeating argument. It is fine to announce that people should be free to choose what they desire; but freedom like this has little meaning if desire has been circumscribed by ironclad parameters of print. Nobody walks into an airport and requests a flight to Rio de Janeiro if she does not know that it exists. People can only choose things they have heard of.

The role of the outside teacher or of the paid professional staff worker is that of a person who already knows the map, has traveled freely, and who knows the range and nature of a thousand unimagined destinations. It remains, nonetheless, the primacy of the community itself that matters most. All of the airline maps on earth cannot be of use to those who are afraid to buy the ticket or who lack the vital insolence to hold the passport in their hands and to demand the necessary visa. This is the reason why the neighborhood itself remains the heart of the entire plan. We may call it a community of struggle, a community of learning, a community of shared endeavor; when it is warm and close and strong, as in the program I described in San Francisco, it is at length no less than a community of conscience. Political in texture, energized by anger and informed by love, groups like these begin to build their own emancipation by the application of a single rule: "Those who know, teach. Those who don't, learn." In practice, the line between the teacher and the learner will repeatedly be obscured. The learner will come to understand the word. The teacher may come to comprehend a broader vision of the world. The learner of one year will, at times, become the teacher of the next. A mutuality of learning, then, becomes the quiet if unstated goal.

• *Where might programs of this sort take place?*

"Let me tell you where to hold these classes if you want it to work out. We have empty apartments in every building of this project. If you could get a few of those apartments for this program, the people who live here would come out and fix them up. We'd do the work to clean them out and paint them, raise some money to buy furniture and lamps . . ."

Similar suggestions have been offered in a number of different conversations I have held in neighborhoods all over the United States. Most of the large programs in existence at the present time tend to favor institutional settings. Public schools, sometimes public libraries or buildings like the YMCA are the most familiar choices. Because the facilities afforded by these institutions are at times attractive, well-equipped, and modern, it is difficult to argue that they ought not to be used. Difficult or not, I nonetheless believe that we should seek less formal settings.

Schools, for almost all illiterate adults, remain the scene of former failure. (Most illiterate Americans have spent at least eight years in public school.) Libraries are a better choice; but here there is the problem that the setting remains formal. Those who enter public libraries are instantly obliged to see themselves within a context of successful readers. The library is, and cannot help but be, "a palace of the book." For those who are already reading at a modest level, this might prove to be an optimistic factor. For those who suffer from the greatest reading problems, on the other hand, it is anything but optimistic. A citadel of knowledge is approached and entered only by a drawbridge that can span a dizzying void. People already burdened with anxieties and fears should not have to cross this drawbridge too.

Transportation represents another problem. We have seen how many factors can discourage an illiterate adult from wandering far, on unknown streets whose names she cannot read, using public transportation which is often unreliable and always time-consuming. Those who are already overwhelmed with daily problems in their homes, with children's needs and uncooked meals and unwashed clothes and unpaid bills, are easily deterred from launching out each evening or each afternoon, knowing that they may spend two hours traveling for every hour that they spend in actual instruction. What, in any case, are young adults to do with infant children? For those who work or who have other daytime obligations and who therefore need to come to class at night, how much trouble will they find in making sure their child is secure while they are gone? How many needless obstacles like these should be imposed if we intend to work with someone several nights, or every night, a week?

My own belief is that the ideal place to teach illiterate adults to read and write is in the neighborhoods in which they are condemned to live, within which they can see the walls that have contained them, and in which they can find easy access to the friends and neighbors who are best equipped to give them help.

If not in schools and libraries and other public institutions, what kinds of housing might be found in which to organize and carry out our plans? Vacant units in the housing projects represent one obvious location. Outside the projects, but still in urban areas, hundreds of neighborhood "literacy houses" might be adapted from existing structures. Teams composed of literacy workers from outside the neighborhood, working at the side of those I call "the inside teachers" and with their potential students too, might devise the means to gain possession of those many buildings left behind by landlords who desert the city but whose houses may be rapidly repaired by common effort of a neighborhood committee and an outside literacy team. Out of the physical work it takes to get a building into shape, as well as the political inventiveness required in order to expropriate these structures for the common good, a healthy sense of camaraderie, of sweat and toil, even of enjoyable conspiracy, might naturally evolve. Nothing, in my own experience, can help to equalize a group of persons quite so rapidly as several weeks of hammering and painting, measuring and balancing, and hanging doors and fitting windows to their frames, beneath an August sun. Problems of measurement and calculation which arise during these days, difficulties too in the reading of instructions, might provide some natural clues as to the needs of those who will be coming to these centers for instruction.

Process and purpose, in this instance, coincide to build a real, not simulated, sense of common cause. Proprietary feelings, and the satisfaction of creating one's own citadel in company with friends, instead of venturing out alone to enter someone else's building in a world one scarcely knows, add metaphor to practicality in this proposal.

Convenience, of course, remains the chief advantage. Child care, for instance, could be far more easily arranged. "Neighborhood mothers"—women who are paid by welfare agencies to care for children in their homes while the parents of those children are at work—would be a natural adjunct to this plan. Grandparents, too, might fill a crucial role, for some in child care, for others in the process of instruction. Providing for children, in any case, would be a far more simple matter in a program which took place in the same block, or even the same building, as the home in which the child lives.

Other types of buildings might serve just as well: churches, if they are close to home; community centers; day-care centers, if they have the extra rooms to spare. In practice, it is realistic to concede that very few groups, if given the chance to use a small branch library or local school, would find it very easy to say no. Even in these cases, organizers would do well to contemplate a spin-off system of much smaller satellites, established in liaison with the larger center but filling the more intimate role of "neighborhood houses," as I have described. People with easy access to these houses would no longer be obliged to go out in the snow of winter or the heat of summer, suffering the cost of public transportation and the psychological deterrent of "strange places" in order to reach a close and friendly room of passionate and mutual reaffirmation.

In rural areas, another body of suggestions would be called for. I have spoken here primarily about the inner-city neighborhoods that I know best. The Highlander Folk School, identified for many years with Myles Horton, offers one of the most interesting models for a rural area. Here, in a single center, art and music, oral testimony and folk history, are skillfully combined with literacy work, as well as with its practical correlative in voter education, to create a total climate of empowerment and of collective self-respect which has been admired, but too seldom given the attention it deserves, for something over fifty years. It is from Horton's work that I have drawn the title of this chapter.

Whether we speak of villages in Appalachia or of crowded urban slums in Boston or New York, I have attempted to establish the idea of literacy as a community endeavor, as something close to solid ground, surrounded by the fabric of emergency and human pain that are so easily forgotten in a bureaucratic plan, something too that is infused with a reminder that, in speaking about written words, we are speaking by necessity about shared knowledge and that the way to gain that knowledge is by common, not competitive, endeavor.

• The Second Stage

The previous pages, read in isolation, might too easily suggest that universal adult literacy in the United States will be achieved by nothing more ambitious than a number of barn-raisings: "good folks meeting at the village square" to solve their problems in the manner of a country celebration ninety years before. This is exactly what the federal government would like us to believe. This is precisely what has been attempted in the past. This is precisely why we have not reached more than a fraction of the people who are now in deepest need.

Virtually every private program which exists today regards its work as an alternative to federal programs run with federal funds. I regard the build-up I have just described not as an alternative but as a prelude and a provocation to a national campaign. What I have proposed above will surely reach a lot more people than are being served today. It may double or quadruple present gains. Even at the very best, it cannot reach more than ten million people.

Up to now I have described a grass-roots movement. From this point I will be speaking of a federal plan.

Any mobilization, if successful, mobilizes people for a further purpose. The "further purpose" in this instance is a multi-billion-dollar national imperative that places universal literacy in the United States on just exactly the same level as nutrition, health care, unemployment compensation, and defense.

In an essay published over seventy years ago, William James proposed a federal program for regeneration of our nation as a "moral equivalent" to war. Much of what he recommended was effectuated in the 1930s by the federal programs known today by their initials: "CCC" and "WPA." Each of these models offers us both precedent and admonition.

The CCC addressed itself primarily to conservation. The same word might be used in speaking of the purposes we have in mind today. This time, though, the work should be adjusted to the goal of *human* conservation: not to build impressive dams to hold back and to harness swiftly flowing streams, but to open conduits that will let those waters flow into the heartland of an arid consciousness. Human ecology has been repeatedly short-changed within this nation. Even the most eager activists of 1965 soon headed for the hills of Santa Barbara and the communes of Vermont. When I met them ten years later, I would ask them whether they were still involved in social change. "I'm out of that," one man replied. "I'm into rivers now." Like many other people, I appreciate clean rivers and unspoiled forest lands; but all things are not equally important. It would seem cruel to watch clean rivers flowing sweetly through a heartless and divided nation.

There is another reason why the CCC is not a perfect model. The military ran the programs of the CCC. It stubbornly insisted that the educational uplifting of participants must not be allowed to interfere with "realistic" goals. When President Roosevelt authorized employment of 10,000 jobless teachers in the CCC, military leader Colonel Duncan Major bristled at the dangers he foresaw: "We are going to be hounded to death by all sorts of educators." Instead of teaching men to do their work, he feared that he would be impeded by "the wishes of the long-haired men and short-haired women" who would push for education. General Fox Connor, commander of the First Corps Army, issued instructions to "abolish forthwith" what he termed "cultural courses." Disciplines like history, philosophy, and foreign languages were deemed to fall into this category. Administrators went still further and attempted even to prevent "discussion" of political and social issues. One corps commander banned all books on sociology on grounds that sociologists "were somewhat radical." Unrestrained discussion, he believed, would foster discontent. The military attitudes we see today are rooted in a grim tradition.

WPA programs offer us a better model. Even here, there was consistent fear of anything that threatened to shake up the status quo. A WPA administrator in New York, General Hugh Johnson, carried out a witch-hunt which anticipated well the later work of Joe McCarthy. Despite these obstacles, the programs managed to achieve important gains in literacy work. "Literacy classes, during a five-year period [ending] in 1941," according to the Russell Sage Foundation, "were estimated to have helped more than 1.5 million adults to read and write." Expenditures on education programs between 1935 and 1941 totalled $228 million: a yearly average of approximately $30 million. Adjusted for inflation, this would be $225 million yearly in the present decade—more than twice the sum provided by the federal government to Adult Basic Education.

The major thrust of WPA projects was not, of course, toward education but employment. Much of this employment was directed to construction. Over 100,000 buildings—chiefly libraries and schools and other public structures—were constructed or restored. In all, from 1936 to 1941, the WPA expended $11.4 billion. In constant dollars, this is nearly $90 billion in the present year.

The allocation of these funds was possible for several reasons. The ranks of the unemployed were vast. The nation perceived itself to be in danger. Substantial possibilities of popular upheaval, mobilized by a vigorous left, were very real. Finally, there was a leader, F.D.R., who lent much of his personal charisma and political imagination to effectuate these plans. All of these elements do not exist today. No president in eighteen years has chosen to invest his energies or our tax-moneys in a moral venture on this scale. The left is hardly vigorous today; and, for the moment, there seems little chance of mobilizing a conservative society.

Unemployment, on the other hand—especially among the ranks of urban youth—is very high. The nation's leaders, corporations, and some academics have begun to see themselves in urgent danger from the consequences of a work force and electorate which are one-third illiterate. The building of a national upheaval is the purpose of this book.

In a lecture recently presented to a conference sponsored by the leaders of the life insurance industry, Democratic Senator Paul Simon spoke these words: "Unemployment is a permanent phenomenon. The demand for unskilled labor is going down; the pool of unskilled labor is growing . . . We must turn the liability of unemployment into an asset . . . We did it once before in the 1930s under the WPA . . . We ought to do [today] what we did then . . ."

Senator Simon then made this proposal: "What if—in addition to planting 200 million trees," as well as doing other things that benefit society—we were to take "the unemployed with skills" and to apply those skills to those "who cannot read and write?"

Here, then, is a man in Washington who has the wisdom to assert what no one else in his position has had courage to suggest. This time, instead of building more brick libraries to hold the books that people cannot read, we might at last unlock those books by hiring the unemployed to teach the nation how to read them.

The WPA is a precedent. It need not be regarded as a model. Our needs are different and our emphasis this time must not be placed upon the mechanistic infrastructure but the human soul of our society. The WPA had some spectacular results. Anyone who rides along the East Side Drive in New York City is enjoying something that was built by those who, were it not for WPA, would have seen their families starve during the 1930s. What of a plan to make it possible for millions of illiterate New Yorkers to decipher signs that might enable them to find an entrance to that highway on their way to paid employment and to have some opportunity of reading exit signs before they end up in the harbor?

Here, then, are some efforts at a very elemental arithmetic calculation. I have spoken of "circles of learners," five or six at most, in place of one-to-one instruction. A minimum of five million literacy workers would be needed to participate in ratios of one to six, in order to teach 30 million people—or one half of all illiterate Americans.* Some, as I believe, will work for no remuneration. These are persons, for example, who belong to two of the three categories (students, older people) that have been described above. Others would require part-time pay. Others still—the unemployed within the poorest sections of our nation—would need full-time remuneration. Minimal allocations might require average stipends of $2,000 to five million people, with a range beginning at or close to zero and approaching, at the upper level, something like $10,000. I will not pursue these long projections any further. It is enough to state that any government which hopes to cut the numbers of nonreaders by one half within a serious campaign would have to speak of yearly allocations of at least $10 billion.

Does this strain our credibility?

Inevitably, it does.

Let us place this figure next to several other numbers for a moment: $20 billion lost each year for the support of unemployable, imprisoned, morally disheartened, or emotionally ill people who do not have the opportunity to rescue their own children from a similar dependence in the years ahead; $11.4 billion spent in 1930s dollars for construction of the libraries illiterates can't use, the building of the highways that they cannot drive; additional billions spent for conservation of the rivers they cannot enjoy because those kinds of rivers do not flow through concrete alleyways and high-rise projects in Los Angeles and Boston; $26 billion now projected to deploy the MX missile; billions more for B-1 bombers and for weaponry in outer space to terrify the stars . . .

I have spoken earlier of certain dangers in "rewarded service." The context to which those cautionary words apply will have been superseded by the point at which a mobilization has achieved its goal. When and if that point arrives, we may hope to limit government participation to the role of the exchequer. It is a wistful hope perhaps. No money ever left the federal coffers without carrying a baggage of conditions, guidelines, and restrictions. The question, then, is not if there will be constraints (there will) but, rather, how restrictive such constraints may be. The answer depends, to some degree, on the effectiveness of those who have been active in the intervening years. If the ethos and objectives have been burningly defined, if leaders emerge, if activists are trained, these are people who will take a central role in every local program financed out of federal funds. Those who work today on shoestring budgets within grass-roots operations would be best prepared to take control, to supervise, to train; they would also be the vital counterforce to top-down efforts to disarm and to domesticate their goals.

Experience reminds us that this is not easy. The man who pays the piper does his best to call the tune. The piper, of course, can pick his own tunes too. If we have already had some years in which to learn some music of our own, we

---

* This number is a cautious estimate of those who will be less than functional by 1990.

might also have the will to keep on singing. A certain amount of discord might result. When has social transformation ever taken place in two-part harmony?

"The last thing an Establishment would do to consolidate its position," wrote John Carroll and Jeanne Chall, "would be to promote literacy unless it were in order to dictate what should and should not be read." This is correct; and, in a highly structured situation like the U.S. Army, there is little chance of countering such goals. Would this be the case in a civilian program too? The government would surely try to dictate. Would we be compelled, like timid clerics, to "take down" that government's dictation? I do not believe that this is so. As long as a free press prevails, even a biased press, how could a newly literate sector of the population be constrained to read only established texts and learn by only one mandated method? What is to prevent so many millions from creating their own primers and from speaking their own words?

Pressures toward the mechanistic and the acquiescent would persist. Conflicts would unquestionably arise. Compromise, at many levels, would be called for and, at times, it might appear to be degrading. I do not know any way to get around this. Unless we wish to view Illiterate America as an eternally embattled body of nonviolent guerrillas living in imagined mountain strongholds of internal exile, we will have to face up to the tough realities of a negotiated ardor. This is the price that we must pay if we expect to win the funds that it will take to serve not just a hundred or a thousand neighborhoods of verbally excluded men and women but to evolve at last into a total nation of electoral participants whose grasp of precedents and whose retrieval of the past is equal to their longing to transform the future.

• *The Third Stage*
I have spoken here of only 30 million people: those who are the most oppressed, the less-than-functional and those who cannot read at all. These are the people virtually excluded from existing programs. A final stage (but one which may not be entirely "final" in some ultimate respects) must address itself to all of those we have described above and 30 million more. It is impossible to know what this would cost and how long it might take before all of our fellow citizens have passed that always-moving line of "competence equivalent to present needs." What is designated as an "adequate" proficiency today would need redefinition in a period ten years from now when technological advance will have transformed the nature of the workplace and, far more important, when the democratic process of our nation (not even to speak of the survival needs of an ever-more-tightly-wired and imperiled world) will call for a degree of analytic vigilance which none of us can plausibly assess.

We should accept that many years would be required to achieve this goal. In some sense, it is a goal which will forever be before us; and the work that we anticipate, therefore, is one that properly should never end. But this leads into some other areas which are beyond the focus of this book. I am speaking of the present and that portion of the future which is still within our power of imagination.

With proper funding and enormous nerve, it seems realistic to believe that we could drastically reduce adult illiteracy in the United States within the next ten years. I would like to add to this that we could totally eradicate the hard core of the crisis by the year 2000. To say this much, however, is to take too many risks. Too many imponderables (political conditions, international disruptions, for example) would affect whatever timeline we might offer. Two things, however, seem beyond dispute:

It need not take forever.

If it takes us more than fifteen years, it is not clear what sort of nation—or what level of democracy—will still exist to profit from the consequences of our work or even to cast a backward look upon the accuracy of these predictions.

•*To envision the dream:*

I find it uncomfortable to look so far into the future.

One group I know has placed this slogan over their front door: "Battles big enough to matter, small enough to win." It seems to me a healthy slogan; and it summons up a cheerful and invigorating mood. Both for the learner (in approaching any part of a large challenge) and for the teacher and the organizer (in attempting to persist in piecemeal efforts without fear of the unknown and, for the moment, unattainable), it seems to me a wise approach. It is dangerous, as I have said above, to fix our eyes too long on something that we cannot plan tonight, discuss tomorrow, and begin on the next morning. Those, for example, who await the presence of a charismatic and empowering leader such as Martin Luther King too easily forget that Dr. King himself began the work that grew into a national insurrection in a single place, a single city, with a single issue forced upon his own (and on the city's) consciousness by one small act of courage on the part of one heroic but entirely unknown woman. No one in Montgomery that year was waiting for "a national mobilization." By a fortunate coincidence of local guts and national conditions, they managed to begin one.

Dallas Wilson, executive director of a grass-roots program in South Carolina, summarized his sense of struggle in these words: "The needs of the people we serve are so intense that, when we reflect those needs, we shine with a light so hot and brilliant that nothing can stand in the way that we have taken. As we look back upon ourselves, we also keep an eye upon the future. We like to shine. Our challenge is to be a beacon, continuously reflecting the concentrated and powerful rays originating in the pain of a suffering people."

These words help to bring us back to solid earth.

To those who join us, whether as insiders or outsiders, we should speak in words like these: "You are going to teach; but, as you teach, you will also learn.

You are going to learn much more than you can possibly teach, and in the end you will feel as grateful to your students as those students will feel to you for the dignity that you create together."

To those who are our fellow citizens, we ought to speak in words like these: "The goal of this struggle is greater than to teach poor people how to write and how to read. The dream is to enable those two portions of the population who have little means to know (and less to trust) each other at the present time to find a way to repossess their shared humanity. We will need all of our people in the wheel of one great task. We need to do it with the energy of an entire nation —and by a heroic rhythm."

If all of this sounds a little grand, I do not believe that it is therefore grandiose. If it sounds a bit romantic, then perhaps it is romance like this that any wise society should treasure and should count upon in difficult times when it is searching for an hour of redemption.

Words like redemption sound romantic too: but there is a great deal in American democracy that needs to be redeemed.

Case Study: April, 1984

He began twelve years ago. Fresh out of college, and aware that a white person who had just completed studies in New Haven might not be entirely welcome in a black community, he had started out by working for a black-run group directed by a man who wore a skullcap, black dashiki, and a black fist hanging from a chain around his throat. Like many young people of his generation, he dressed in blue jeans, wore the oldest clothes that he could find, and tied his uncut hair with headbands that he had recycled from the J. Press neckties he had worn two years before.

"If you would agree to wear your neckties properly, around your neck instead of up around your head, you might be some help in raising funds."

Heeding this counsel from his newfound black allies, he did succeed in raising funds: $50,000 from the federal government, $20,000 from a local bank.

By 1974, the group had shifted its priorities from education into neighborhood development. One of the leaders of the group, however, wanted to continue with the emphasis on education. Encouraged by each other, they decided to break off and organize a program of their own. A decade later, both of them still live in the community. Perpetual migrants, they have had to find new housing for their center several times. Today they are in an old, abandoned public school. A year ago they worked in a church basement. By around this time next year, they hope to be established in a building they have renovated on their own—and with a dozen of their students.

The two cofounders have split up their jobs into "director" and "head teacher." The director is thirty-five years old. He is unmarried and receives a salary of $7,000. The man with whom he joined to start the program is head teacher. He has a family. He is paid about $12,000.

They now have eighty students. Half of them attend a morning session. The others come here in the evening after work. Applicants are not accepted if they can already read a daily paper. This is a program for the absolute nonreader. Students receive two hours of instruction nightly, three nights weekly, for the best part of a year. At the end of a year (about 250 hours of attendance) they will read enough to understand the front page of a tabloid paper. By the end of a third year—in some cases, by the second—they will be reading at a solid sixth grade level.

In the first week of September, when the year's cycle begins, emphasis is placed on dialogue, on conversation. "Dialogue" is a fashionable word in literacy work in the United States today; the dialogue that takes place here is a departure from the fashion. Discussion centers on the demythologizing of the written language, on the reasons why these men and women did not learn to read in public school, and—above all—on the large number of skills they have already learned: caring for children, hustling for jobs, dealing with health problems, coping with anxiety, overcoming pain.

"All of this is learning. Many people never learn to manage these dilemmas. Never forget how much you've done, how much of life you understand, how many things you have already learned. There is nothing different about reading. It will be tough work, and you are going to work hard. If you don't, your classmates will not want you in this program and, at length, you will not want to stay. But you've won some other battles in your life before today. You will win this battle too."

The program is built upon phonetic methods. But the value of sight recognition is accepted. The head teacher sums it up for me like this: "Too many people learn to read exclusively by decoding [i.e., by the breaking down of every word by sounds]. If they cannot quickly gain sight recognition of familiar words, they will learn to read but it will be a case of endless 'sounding out' with every word they meet. So we look for certain areas of quick success. Within three weeks, they've got to see that they can handle some familiar words by instant recognition. Phonics and sight recognition are not incompatible approaches. It is too bad that many of the groups we know insist upon one or the other method with a cultish fascination. There is no need to make religion out of pedagogy."

The director adds: "We are eclectic, but this does not mean that we are random in our style or approach. Everything we do this year is carefully thought out.

"In the first-year cycle, virtually every word that is employed emerges from direct experience: that of the students in this group or else of others who have been here in the year before. Only in the second cycle do they move beyond this to the exploration of additional vocabulary needed to participate in areas of understanding that exceed their present needs.

"We do not avoid long words. One of the words that is employed in the initial week is 'independence.' This word is perfect. It reflects the dual emphasis that I have just described. Independence is a generative longing for these people. It is also a word which lends itself to good phonetic use. The letter *e* appears here in three of its most familiar sounds: the long *e* and the short *e* and the silent *e* of the concluding syllable. We do not attempt to foist this word upon them. It is a word which has grown out of conversation. It is also a word which offers practice in two of the consonants that are most common in the language and most frequently confused. By the second week, all but a few will have attained sight recognition of this word. To the degree that this is true, they ought to feel—and they will *be* in fact—a bit more independent . . ."

By the fourth week of the cycle, students have begun to turn to one another for correction. A woman leans across the table to a man who is discouraged by his efforts to distinguish between *i* in "bite" and *i* in "bit." "Don't worry," she says. "It's not a test." She moves her chair a little closer and repeats the sounds.

Writing and reading are not separated in instruction. "There are a thousand essays on this subject," the head teacher says. "Write first, then read. Read first, then write. Think first, then read . . . We believe that thinking, reading, writing should not be divided in instruction. How can you say that thinking is for one night and that reading's for the next? People think while they are reading. They can't write of anything that matters if they are not asked to think. Ask a writer if he separates these things . . ."

The staff consists of seven, of whom two are college volunteers. Of the others, two are full-time and the other three put in between fifteen and twenty hours weekly. One of the part-time workers is a former student in this program. She had made it to the tenth grade in the public schools but never learned to read. At the age of twenty-five, she entered Adult Basic Education. "They started too high. Most of them do. I was at zero. This is the first place where they start at zero too."

That was six years ago. She still has trouble with the spelling of some words. The difficulties that remain to plague her also function as encouragement to those whom she comes here to teach. "I could do it. So can you. They know that I'm still learning . . ."

I visit on a night in early spring. I ask a question I have asked with many groups before: Why do the students come? Why do they stay?

Three answers are given. No one speaks of money, jobs, promotions.

A woman who works as a domestic maid supplies this answer: "How can I tell my baby I can't read? How can I tell her that I cannot help her when she brings home lessons from the public school? So I figure this is something I can

offer to my baby. I can't give her money. I can't buy her pretty clothes. I am
making just enough to pay the rent and buy the food she eats. So I figure this is
one thing I can give her." Choking up, she hesitates. "There's something else. I
tell you this. My baby isn't going to go down on *no* one's kitchen floor! She isn't
going to be working for no lady . . ."

A fifty-year-old man gives this response: "I go to church. The deacon walks
around. He points to someone in my pew. That person's supposed to read. I've
been shaking in my boots for twenty years that he would call on me. Some day
soon, when I am called, I am going to stand up. I am going to hold that Bible in
my hands—*and I am going to read!*"

A married man who works as a custodian in his building gives another
reason: "Sunday mornings, people in my building go downstairs and get the
Sunday paper. They come upstairs and sit around the breakfast table. They flip
through the pages. They relax. They pour some coffee. Then they find a story
they would like to read. Someday I would like to do that too. Sunday mornings
. . . Drink my coffee . . . Read my paper . . . Just like other people in
America can do . . ."

It is April 25. In eight more weeks, at least half of the people in this group
will dare to stand up when the deacon calls. They will buy the Sunday paper
after church. They will not understand it all. They will understand enough to
know that, in another year, they will be able to enjoy it. Maybe, if they stick it
out into the third year of the cycle, they will understand the editorials about
illiterate Americans.

I question the director about national projections. Could this be replicated
nationwide? What would it take?

"It would take a lot of money. You could not just throw the money at the
people. It would take some models of success. You would have to look at places
where it works. You would also have to give the money over long-term spans.
Don't give me $300,000 and announce that I will have to use it in one year. Tell
me that the money's there, that I can put it in the bank, that I can use it as I
need. Maybe I'll be using only $50,000 in a year. As it is, we never know where
we will be within another year. I spend over half my time in trying to raise
funds. Last September, they cut off our federal grant. We opened with a thousand dollars in the bank. It was an act of faith to open up and know that we
might not have any money two weeks later. It would be an act of faith if
somebody in Washington could understand this too . . ."

Will this ever happen?

"I'm not sitting here crossing my fingers," he replies.

The program I have just described is still surviving. It does not survive
within one city only. I have combined here details from three programs that I
know and whose directors, students, and ex-students I admire greatly. I will not
name these groups. All of them have seen enough of curious reporters. All of

them have told their stories countless times beneath the bright lights of TV. As it is, they have enough to do in order to be certain that their staff is ready and their doors can open when the people who have already been waiting for a year, or for a lifetime, start to line up on the sidewalks next September.

12

Oral History:
The People Speak Their Word

Do you think the porter and the cook have no anecdotes, no experiences, no wonders for you? . . . The walls of [their] minds are scrawled all over with facts, with thoughts. They shall one day bring a lantern and read the inscriptions.

–Ralph Waldo Emerson

Most of the major literacy groups make use of books prepared commercially. Certain organizations print materials of their own. All of the writing, however, has been done by specialists, reviewed by editors, homogenized by publishers for national consumption. Only one national program (that of LVA) has made consistent use of stories told by the illiterates themselves. Some of these materials are very good. They are exceptions to the norm. Too frequently, whatever sense of oral history may have existed at the start has perished on the road to publication.

Oral history, if it is the history of people who have been oppressed for generations and if it has not been polished and refined beyond all recognition, will often find its energy in language that bespeaks a wealth of long-concealed and pent-up indignation. While much will be joyous, and some may be mundane, a good part of the history that illiterate people tell us, if they are not first conditioned to tell us only what they think we will allow ourselves to hear, will be at once a chronicle of longings and a history of secret grief.

Several small but energetic literacy groups have already begun to build a literature of oral history within the neighborhoods in which they work, and have begun to use this literature in ingenious ways to give one generation access to the voices of the one that came before. Here is one way in which this has been done:

The literacy worker, once having established intimacy with the learner, poses questions to elicit answers in the form of personal narration. Those stories that appear to draw upon the deepest roots of passionate conviction are then transcribed from taped narration into brief and only nominally edited scripts. The worker draws out of the narrative a body of words which meet a set of parallel criteria. The first criterion is the intensity with which the word is spoken. The second criterion, a bit more calculating, is the phonetic makeup of the word. We need to look for words that will include the units out of which a maximum of other words can be constructed. The literacy worker needs to look ahead: Will this be useful? Will this enable us to build a dozen other constructs based on some of the same sounds?

I have taught many students by these two criteria. In Boston, some of the first words that were offered up by students were surprising. "Cadillac," "Yastrzemski," and "conviction" are three of the unexpected words that I recall. Sexual terms were also common. Some words were sad and some were words of soaring jubilation. Many adolescents whom I knew could spell a word like "Cadillac" when they could neither read nor write a word like "mathematics."

Carl Yastrzemski was not of much help to me, or to my students, in developing a body of familiar phonic units. Other words—"Cadillac," for instance—were composed of syllables and sounds from which a number of other words could soon be built. I learned very quickly that it was not necessary, and it was not helpful, to select only the simplest words. Words like these are the familiar choice of most of the "high-interest/low-vocabulary" primers now in common use:

"Jack gets a job."
"John gets a car."
"Susan gets a baby."

Reliance upon short and boring words like these permits an early introduction of full sentences; the loss, however, is not worth the gain. Better to begin with one electric provocation—"Thunderbird" or "Skylark," for example—than to insist on little words like "drive" and "car" that cannot fail to put to sleep learner and teacher both.

Words that grow out of a personal narration are not always angry, but they almost always carry possibilities of danger. Paulo Freire speaks of words like these as "generative" words. I call them "dangerous" words, because they are responsive to the dangers that poor people undergo but also because they do portend some danger for the social system as a whole.

A practical man once posed to me the obvious concern: "Isn't there some danger in the use of 'dangerous' words? Wouldn't they be dangerous? What kinds of dangers would we need to face?"

Selfish or not, the question should be posed. Will people who do not have access to appropriate facilities for medical protection grow disruptive once they read enough to recognize the difference between the medical attention they receive and that to which the affluent are accustomed? Will they be dangerous once they can read enough to understand the lease that they must sign in order to inhabit an apartment they cannot abide for payment of a rent which they cannot afford? Will they be dangerous once they possess a license to drive a mediocre car out of the neighborhood in which they are obliged to live, into a neighborhood in which they still are not permitted to obtain a home or send their kids to school?

Words like "lease" and "license" are employed already in some literacy plans, but always in the strictly denotative sense that robs them of their ethical potential and strips them of their connotative force. A lease may be a useful piece of paper that protects a man against eviction; it may also bring to mind some other thoughts: a lease on life, a lease upon a dignified, empowering existence. A woman may desire a driver's license: She may also long to have the license to stake out her own autonomy, to win herself a decent place beneath the sun. Words that have been stripped of connotation by so many of the reading methods used today deny the poetry of human longings and reduce our language to a lexicon of mechanistic needs. A constant movement from the denotation to its connotative possibilities enables us to move beyond the stated and initial goal and to respond in this way to a deeper aspiration which the wish "to get a license" often masks. The power to transcend the frozen stasis of a total syndrome of depression—not just to acquire a Plymouth and to drive to the next town—is often at the heart of these requests. Unless we wish to lock our students, and ourselves, into a prosaic consciousness that always states but never can suggest, that timidly asks but never can implore, we should hear both the specific and implicit meanings of the words that they bring forth.

Doctor, license, lease. Words like these, if undiminished by our mediation, do convey a certain danger to established patterns of injustice; but if these, in fact, are words that people need in order to express their views, teachers have no right to draw away in search of language that appears more "seemly." More to the point: These are precisely the allusive words that people need to use if they are to find avenues of exit from the crowded prisons of their souls, to give voice to their longings, to give both lease and license to their rage.

A man who lives in Lexington, an affluent suburb to the west of Boston, was honest enough to give voice to this danger: "The incidence of crime within some urban areas may not make the movement of illiterate—or recently illiterate—adults into the suburbs all that attractive to some people. If they can decipher street signs and can earn sufficient funds to buy a car and read enough to get a license and to follow highways past the limits of a rapid transit line, some of them may soon decide to follow signs that lead into the neighborhoods in which we have our homes."

He spoke of the alarm with which some of his neighbors had reacted to the possible extension of the urban subway system, past the nearest suburbs, into the next circle of exclusive neighborhoods in which they live, divorced by fifteen good commuter miles from the inner-city tensions that they read about in their newspapers. If a subway system threatened to extend mobility beyond the limits of its presently secure parameters, what would they say of the more ominous mobility afforded by aggressive literacy programs that engendered economic aspirations which might lead, in turn, to unaccustomed neighborly proximity?

"The same old liberals who have had second thoughts on metropolitan school busing once it threatened to involve their children," he observed, "may not be delighted with some of the more ingenious details of your plan. People who can drive into our neighborhood might choose to *live* there. They might like to see their kids go to our public schools. Some of those kids might like to date our daughters and our sons. I am not saying this is *my* concern, but I can tell you what I hear around me. Liberals might volunteer to drive into the city once a week to teach somebody how to read. I'm not sure that they would like to see their students buying homes in Lexington . . ."

Governor Berkeley's warnings and his gratitude to God return to haunt us once again. "Dangerous words" do represent a danger to divided and unequal social systems. Virtually any word, even a street sign, once regarded from this point of view, contains a certain danger. Words that matter most to subjugated people surely contain *more* danger than the kinds of words the advertising industry, the realtors, or the mortgage officers of major banks would probably prefer to use in literacy work. This is one reason why the programs staffed and organized exclusively by outside volunteers have come into existence with a built-in guarantee of limited success. This is also one reason why even those groups that have attempted to elicit oral history as one ingredient of their tutorial attempts so frequently elicit the most dry, mundane, innocuous of tales, a history of insignificance, at best of technical utility, seldom of anger, rarely of irreverence, almost never of political intensity.

Few Americans would willingly imprison one another in a cell of silence or a city of despair; but certain forms of cruel self-interest are at stake in this discussion. Most of us would like to see a nation that can read. What that nation reads, and how it makes use of its skills, convey some dangers to convention that all citizens will not find reason to applaud. Illiteracy is guaranteed domestication. Informed irreverence carries certain risks into the heartland of self-interest.

A footnote is required to the theme of dangerous or active words. Words in themselves are seldom either active or inert. It is the context which infuses any word with powerful connotation. A better term, therefore, than "active" might be "activated." An activated word might be defined as any word placed in a context such that it takes on emotional intensity. We have seen the use of words like "independence" in the context of a program which is truly dedicated to reducing the dependence of illiterate adults. There are many other words which do the job as well, but only when the context does not undermine their passionate potential.

The word "revolutionary," for example, might appear to be the paradigm of active language in a literacy struggle that is rooted in the anguish of impoverished people. Here, in a single adjective which dominates the public dialogue of hope and fear, are all five vowels of the English language, four of the more common consonants, the difficult suffix "tion" which is used in several dozen common words, as well as the occasional vowel *y*. (In passing, it is curious to notice that a word so common, so important, and so eminently suitable for phonetic practice rarely if ever appears in the materials prepared for literacy programs financed by a government which owes its origins to revolution and which celebrates that revolution with a dazzling display of pyrotechnic jingoism every year. Not so curious, on the other hand, if terror at the possibility of foreign revolutions—at the possibility that other people may respect and wish to emulate our own—has been allowed to shadow and eclipse the truth of history.)

The word, however, cannot be immune to a dilution by its context. Whether in the noun or adjectival form, it ceases to convey much of its literal provocation, and indeed it comes to be a vapid and domesticating term, once it is employed to advertise "a revolutionary new detergent" or "a revolution in the women's undergarment market." The word "sleep," on the other hand, might be regarded as a rather ordinary and uninteresting verb. It becomes an activated verb within a sentence that describes the plight of people who must sleep in rooms that are unheated or in rooms that they must share with rats.

Power exists not in the word but in the meanings which that word accumulates in a specific setting. The problem today is that the words employed in literacy work tend to be neither active in themselves nor activated by the contexts that are chosen. Certain words are certainly more susceptible to lively applications than some others; it is the applications, not so much the words themselves, which should command our chief attention.

I am speaking, then, of oral history as literacy primer, history that has been mediated only in the terms described above: first recorded, next transcribed and edited with selectivity that serves phonetic purposes, finally returned to the illiterate in written language that can be employed in several concrete ways.

One of those ways, designed for literacy workers in the Cleveland area, is the use of stories told by parents and, in certain cases, by grandparents in an early learning program organized for preschool children. In order to serve at once the needs of children and of those adults who wish, but do not have the competence, to reinforce their children's readiness for public school by early storytelling, the program draws upon a mother's, father's, or grandparent's love as motivation for two different but connected forms of learning.

It is one thing to have the chance "to tell our story." It is a better thing to know that there is somebody for whom the telling of the tale will hold a special meaning. In cases where young parents do not have the need or opportunity to be participants, it is frequently the older generation, in some cases men and women in their seventies or eighties, who take up the challenge and pass on their knowledge, through the vehicle of words that they have newly learned, to four-year-old grandchildren.

"It is all very well to teach adults to read and write. What can be done to guarantee that children now in school, or those about to enter school, will not become *another* generation of adult nonreaders in another ten or twenty years?"

The question is familiar. It cannot be dodged. One part of the answer is provided here. A literacy plan that ties the learning of the parents and grandparents to the elemental needs of preschool children serves at once preventive and corrective roles. It also helps to answer the familiar question about adult motivation. We have seen the anguish that young parents undergo in recognition of their inability to help their kids to read:

"Donny looked at me . . . He's only five. He knew I couldn't read . . . Oh, it matters," the child's mother said. "You *believe* it matters!"

Since it does, and since the mother understands this very well, it would be tragic if we did not have the sense to draw a strategy out of necessity.

"My baby already wants to read. She asks me to read her stories. I can read. I read to her every night at six—and then again before she goes to bed. I worry about the kids in other homes nearby. Many of the parents haven't had the education. Some of them ask me for advice. I wish that I could help . . ."

Even excluding something so self-evident as parent motivation, there is also practicality at stake. Those with children have to make provision for those children while they are participating in a struggle for their own empowerment. We have seen the many problems this presents. We have also heard the recommendations that provision for concurrent child care is elemental to success in building an uninterrupted continuity of work. Logic suggests a final stage in this progression: Child care might be conceived not merely as concurrent with, but also as connected to, the learning of adults.

"They're going to bring the child anyway," one organizer said. "Why set up a child-care center in a separate building? There you go—cutting off the young ones from the older ones again. You'd have to have some separation. It would be chaotic otherwise. That's common sense. It would be stupid, though, to lose the opportunity that all of this presents. We're going to need to hire someone good to take care of those children: someone who can help the older ones with schoolwork, somebody else to take care of the little ones, to tell them stories, read them little books. In another room you've got that child's mother or her father pouring out their stories to somebody else! Somewhere down the line, you ought to put those two ideas together . . ."

It is a good idea: one that has been generated in the hearts of those who love their children most and know those children best. Dozens of scholars (Theodore Sizer, David Elkind, and Jeanne Chall are three with whom this plan has been discussed) have expressed their strong concurrence with the views already voiced by the illiterates themselves. It represents the germ of an idea which someday might explode into a national objective. For now, I want to focus on the simpler point from which this possibility emerged. Literacy, for whatever purpose it may be pursued, represents in every case some sort of answer to a universal need for vindication and for self-perpetuation. Oral history, established as one honored centerpiece of the entire undertaking, represents an answer to both stated and unconscious needs that virtually all men and women know.

Stories that have been transcribed and edited as I propose need not be extravagantly praised by eager literacy workers.

"Sarah has a brilliant mind. She can't do commas, but she writes like Flannery O'Connor!"

Adults do not need to be rewarded by implausible flattery. In any event, it seldom works but comes across as unintended mockery. Many semiliterate people know the Bible. Most, whether they can read or not, have heard the Bible stories from their preacher. They understand that they are not competing with the Song of Solomon or with the Hebrew prophets. Many, however, at some level, may correctly recognize that what they are doing is not unrelated to a biblical tradition and that the inheritance of "the word"—no matter how simple and how modest the initial word may be—has something in common with the beautiful tradition that created Scripture.

The unpretentious aspect of this undertaking is important to an uninhibited approach. The booklets that have been transcribed by literacy workers need not have a national or even citywide appeal. They do not need to be contrived and tortured into "works of lasting worth." Local in character, private in value, situated often only in the urgent present as it grows out of a very recent past, books like these—unlike the massive textbooks and the million-copy primers that are marketed by major publishers for twenty years of sale—do not need to reach beyond one time, one moment, or one geographical locale.

Local place-names, radio call letters, names of local churches, politicians, allies, enemies, or friends can therefore find expression here. (This is something no commercial publication, standardized for use in fifty states, can ever hope to do.) If they are useful, if they are successful, if they can achieve the goal we have in mind, they will have become expendable a few years later on. Indeed, their value may, with some unusual exceptions, be identified precisely by the speed with which they prove to be archaic. The little book that does the job in 1985 will not be needed, though it still may be admired and remembered by its author or that author's child or grandchild, in a later generation.

Oral history is used effectively by some of our best authors in the search for raw materials from which to forge important and sometimes extremely moving books. This time, oral history might stay in the community from which it has emerged. Its first and frequently its only audience may be the child of the man or woman who has drawn that story out of lived experience and passed it on to add to the experience of those who will live on to tell *their* stories to their children and grandchildren too.

If this is a simple use of oral history, leaving no riches to the social anthropologists, the publishers, or literary critics, it is this fact—the modesty of the entire enterprise—which gives it a value few of us would not find eloquent. This is one example of the virtues of a literacy war whose methods are as old as Scripture and as new as inexpensive tape recorders, whose mode is humanistic, angry, honest, and capacious, whose consequence may be the transformation of at least one tiny portion of an unjust social order which has relegated millions of young people to an isolated present tense to which the past is never prologue and for which the future has forever been imperiled.

Santayana has admonished us that those who cannot learn from history will be condemned to re-enact its errors. This is a warning most of us would like to heed; but those who do not know of Santayana cannot profit from his admonition. Oral history is one of many ways by which we may restore the continuity of time—what we have called a conjugated truth—for those who may not know that it exists, or where it leads or whence it has emerged, but nonetheless, like all of us, are doomed to lead their lives within it.

There is another virtue in the oral history approach. Books, in themselves, are obviously intimidating to a person who can't read. Those who have seen stories of their own turned into books or booklets, and employed for purposes they understand, are able to some degree to demythologize the whole idea of written words.

First, they learn: "A book is something I can make and something therefore which is not divorced, except in incremental ways, from my potential power first to shape and then to comprehend."

Some books are better, wiser, more complex than others. This is something they will surely learn and perhaps, in almost every case, already recognize. But the idea of the printed word becomes less terrifying, less bizarre, as they participate in the creation of a literature of their own intimate conception.

Second, they learn that books are vulnerable objects, that they did not come out of the forehead of a god, and for this reason are susceptible to error. They learn, in this way, that words are not protected by an aura of the unimpeachable. Books are inventions. Some of them are good inventions; others are profoundly flawed. Either way, they do not need to tyrannize the literate newcomer.

Sensible irreverence and discrimination might, in this way, be imparted to the man or woman who has previously regarded print communication as a finalized and hardened truth. Orders, no matter how well written, may be disregarded. Factual statements, no matter how emphatically asserted, may be held up to examination. Writers exaggerate. We all know this is so. Few of us tend to understate a point of view that seems to ratify our own belief or offer confirmation for a thesis that is only supposition. It is important that a newly literate person understand this. Anyone who wins the use of a new weapon ought to have a chance to recognize its dangers. For those who only recently have won the use of written words, it is even more important that they understand the possible misapplication of that competence by others.

"What they are doing is not unrelated to a biblical tradition . . ."
From early centuries, the Hebrew people have been known as "People of The Book." It was "The Book," not books—"The Word," not words—which gave a sacred character to literate tradition. After the destruction of the Second Temple, Jewish scholars carried on that literate tradition (one that was both reverential and defiantly pragmatic, critical, and analytic) through twenty centuries of pogrom, pilgrimage, and persecution.

The first great literacy campaigns of modern history were fostered by the followers of Martin Luther—and, with a more lasting force, during the English Reformation—out of the desire to allow religious persons an unmediated access to the Bible and to undermine the absoluteness of a sacerdotal domination by anointed hierarchs. Even the most notable of literacy campaigns conducted in the past three decades, those of the Chinese and the Cubans for example, drew much of their energy and exaltation from the sanctity assigned to other kinds of "holy writ." The writings of Marx and Engels, Lenin, Mao Tse-tung, were not used specifically as literacy primers but the ideologies and passions they conveyed surely infused with special energy both of these fervent undertakings.

We cannot artificially create a sacred writ. Nor should we even entertain a strategy so tortuously contrived and, in our situation, so unnatural. But many men and women surely must regard some of their own beliefs and memories as "sacred" in a very private sense; and most of us experience some longing to extend part of our being, of our living, to the children whom we love and, through those children, to the generations still unborn. History, in this respect, provides us with a precedent for an approach that is not simply a good "motivating" method but one that can inspire us to rise above the day-to-day banality of unreflective life and can provide an answer, even a rather gentle answer, to one of our most elemental and most nearly universal fears. Like Jacob, each of us must wrestle with our angels. One of those angels, surely one with which most of us grapple constantly after we enter middle age, remains the certitude of our mortality. Some of us may draw some consolation, and some dignity as well, out of that private scripture which, for many, might possess the value as an act of testament that the Pentateuch possesses for the Hebrew people and the Christian Covenant for Protestant and Catholic men and women.

Heaven, for most human beings, is little more than their perpetuation in the hearts of those who love them. Hell, if it is visualized at all, might be oblivion. For those who are devout in an unwavering and literal respect (very few people, I suspect, are quite so literal as this), there is the faith of "a reward in afterlife." For the rest of us, there is no afterlife beyond the bond that bridges those who live on earth and those who live within the memory of those they leave behind. If this, in Thornton Wilder's words, does represent "the only survival" and "the only meaning" of our own existence, then we might respect this longing by the reverence that we bring to language and the sensitivity with which we listen to the sacred words of every man and woman we are asked to teach.

I recognize that there is more than optimism in the statements made above. The spread of literacy has never been a guarantee that anything like spiritual conviction or aesthetic dignity would be encouraged, honored, or enhanced. "Education in twentieth-century England," Richard Hoggart wrote, "has not arrested the trivialization of reading matter. Reading, which in other settings has promoted the intellectual growth of a people, now threatens to arrest it."

He had in mind the shabby books and lurid tabloids, so much like the Murdoch publications of today, which threatened (and still threaten) to degrade the reading tastes of British people. There is no reason to believe that we are any more immune to trivializing inclinations of this nature in the U.S.A. This is one reason why, even in the midst of a specific and extremely urgent crisis, I have tried to look ahead to what we hope to gain from this endeavor. We have seen the mechanistic thrust of literacy discourse in the past five years. The reading of manuals, the understanding of instructions, and the filling out of forms have been the stated goals. It is difficult to know whether these uninspired aspirations —if they are the only ones that we espouse—are any less lurid, in a final sense, than the degrading tabloids that offended Hoggart. (We have those tabloids too, needless to say, and Harlequin "romances" also.)

It seems remarkable that, even in the midst of all the signs of a declining culture—of a people starved, diminished, amputated, by the loss of contact with the poetry inherent in their print-recorded past and by the desert of electric entertainment that admits the use of words in only the abbreviated form of captions and subtitles to those quick-fix pleasures that perpetuate the very thirst that they pretend to satisfy—virtually no one other than a handful of librarians and one booksellers' chain seems to be disposed to speak about the one most noble reason for which literacy flourished in the past 400 years and for which it might, if we are wise, flourish once more.

The Hebrew people did not strive to read and write in order to decipher technical instructions. Martin Luther, Calvin, and the Puritan reformers who first settled in New England did not struggle to advance the literacy levels of devoted Christians so that they could handle welfare forms, fill out applications, or contrive the most efficient means to cheat their neighbors. The primary goal was to empower people to read words in those momentous combinations which were known as covenants, as scriptures, or as testaments.

Perhaps, in the idea of oral history as it may gradually evolve, there is a quarry to be mined which might enable us someday to better guard ourselves against that "trivialization" of the word which Hoggart feared, abhorred, and carefully recorded. If we cannot realistically expect to spare ourselves the same proliferation of the mechanistic and the mediocre, we might nonetheless nourish the faith that new and stirring and transcendent works of art may gradually evolve out of the stories told, the memories regained, the past retrieved, within the process of the literacy work I have described.

It is unwise, as I remarked above, to overpraise, to flatter, to exaggerate the eloquence of the initial stories people tell us in their efforts to traverse the first small stages of their struggle to achieve the fluent use of written words. But it would also indicate a foolish arrogance if we were not ready to perceive those special moments of triumphant exposition when they do appear. I am thinking, for example, of the poet I described in Boston. How many other men and women, poor and semiliterate and unknown for now, might soon emerge out of their present silence once the floodgates are released? If and when they do, will we be ready both to recognize and honor what they give us?

It will sound extravagant to suggest that universal literacy, once honorably sought and finally attained in the United States, will suddenly and magically endow us with an efflorescence of great poetry and art. It isn't very helpful, I suppose, to hold this out as one of the immediate rewards of our initial work. The primary goals are equity and justice, respite from grief, relief from needless fear.

Still, when I talk with those whom people of another generation would have called "unlettered" men and women, I cannot escape the thought that there is an unopened vein of unimagined beauty here. A quarry is the image that comes to my mind. It requires at times an effort of will to reassure myself that there is no reason to feel awkward or embarrassed by the strong emotions that are stirred when I am sitting in the homes of people whom I never see in universities, in art museums, or other places where the cultural proprietors of our society are to be found, secure, relaxed, at ease in their domain: and suddenly I find myself reduced to tears.

Many illiterate people, at the present time, believe that they are trapped, locked in, or lost somewhere along an endless highway or, as one man said it, literally, "a one-way street." Once the traffic starts to move, who can say what beauty and what truth such people may not bring us?

In view of the preceding passages, it may be of value here to add one cautionary note.

Volunteers who are politically attracted to the notion of non-neutral education that I have reiterated often in this book are too frequently disposed to search for agonized emotions which do not exist at all or else, more often, are not being offered at the moment they are ready to perceive them. I have said that literacy instructors should not feel obliged to tie one hand behind their back and act less efficacious than they really are. But the opposite of foolish abdication is not arrogant prescription. I have argued that we ought to be aware of connotative implications in the seemingly most mechanistic needs that an illiterate may voice; this does not mean, however, that those connotations are at all times present and, like fissionable metals, simply waiting for our act of detonation.

In a setting which is keyed to oral history, especially if it also is identified with the needs of children and with a concurrent preschool literacy plan, it may be expected that a great deal of narration will be offered for its own sake only, with little conscious effort to infuse that narrative with angry implications. I am still convinced that anger, indignation surely, will pervade a lot of this material. The likelihood that this will frequently be true cannot be mistaken for the certitude that it is always so.

Exceptional restraint, therefore, is called for. Sensibilities like these cannot be "injected" into literacy workers in the course of their initial preparation. These are things that people learn as they are working at the side of others. If such preconditions as the means of governance, the physical setting, a proximity to pain, have been established firmly in advance, indignation will emerge in unmanipulated ways. I have quoted above (in Chapter 6) the words of an indignant teacher in a literacy center in a mill town near my home. She could not have learned that indignation in a "workshop" for prospective volunteers. She learned it from impoverished people who had come to her in desperation. This is why her anger, like her sense of humor, has the authenticity it does. Sectarian recipes are not a substitute for openness and receptivity to simple chronicles of love and need.

This may be a helpful antidote against one of the risks inherent in some of the words that I have written in the prior sections of this book. Perhaps it will defend us against yielding to the inclination to exploit oral history for narrow and impatient purposes which are our own but which are not (or are not yet) those of the men and women we intend to serve.

*Case Study: "Somewhere down the line, you ought to put those two ideas together
. . ."*

At 7 P.M., as the heat of early June is cooling down within the narrow alleys of the project and the voices of teenagers start to shrill across the ragged patches of untended weeds that were intended by an architect to be "small areas of park and lawn" for relaxation of the residents when he designed this urban maze ten years before, a dozen children show up at the front door of the center.

The center is, in part, a renovated three-room flat on the first level of the building. Across the hall, there is another flat—this one a little larger—and, one flight above, there are a third and fourth collection of connected rooms. Provided rent free by the city, and restored last summer from the boarded and vacated units they had been for several years, these fifteen rooms comprise one of two dozen "Family Learning Centers" in a neighborhood of 13,000 people. One third of those people are adults. About 2,000 are the parents of young children.

By 7:15, a total of over eighty children and approximately forty adults have arrived. The children are assigned to rooms on the first floor. The adults, some of whom are only seventeen years old and others over fifty-five or sixty, are heading up the stairs to find their places in the seven rooms that have been renovated on the second floor. All of the rooms, upstairs and down, are air-conditioned, cheerful—and the atmosphere is calm.

The children are divided into several groups. The youngest, who are three to five years old, are cared for by a neighborhood mother, by two high school students and a college undergraduate—all of them receiving part-time pay—and by a woman hired for this purpose by the children's section of the neighborhood branch library. Trained as a storyteller, she has also trained her three co-workers. She also knows enough about the needs of preschool children to provide activities that do not have to do with books or stories but involve a lot of listening and sharing and informal interaction. Letters and words and pictures—some of them the pictures drawn by children—are on every wall, blackboard, or room-divider. This is the largest group of children. On a crowded night there might be nearly sixty. This evening there are only forty-four.

Across the hall, a group of twenty grade school children are at work in two connected rooms. An English teacher from a local high school is moving quietly between these rooms, assisting kids in doing lessons they have brought home from their school. One of that teacher's twelfth grade students is assisting several kids with long division.

A retired executive from Polaroid seems to be preoccupied with his own reading in another room nearby. He is flipping through the pages of *The Old Man and the Sea*. Around him, sixteen others—some as young as eight or nine but most of them teenagers—are sitting on comfortable chairs and sofas. They are reading books and magazines. The man from Polaroid gets up and hands *The Old Man and the Sea* to a young woman who is staring out the window. He chats with her for a few minutes. Then he wanders over to a shelf of other books and slips out two or three which he has never read—or not for thirty years.

On the second floor, approximately twenty-five adults are now at work in two connected rooms, sitting at tables, five or six at each. The organizer of the program is a woman who lives in another building of the project. She is educated but, for reasons that nobody ever asked, is living on a tiny income with her daughter and her daughter's kids. Assisted by a twenty-year-old man who is a student of linguistics at a local university, she is guiding these adults in conversations that appear to an observer to be aimless. Every so often, a member of each group goes to a blackboard and laboriously writes out a word which has emerged from the discussion. A number of the students find this very hard. One woman gets confused by certain letters—*d* and *p*. The student of linguistics, sitting at her table, tells the group: "The alphabet has been invented by the devil." He gets up and writes out "alphabet" and "devil" on the board. He circles the *d* in devil and the *b* in alphabet. At 7:30, he distributes a phonetic workbook. For the next half-hour, they are struggling their way through words that start or end with *d* and *p* and *g*.

"The devil made projects. God made people. Good God, what do all the devils do downtown?"

It is a workbook that was written by a group of people from the council that includes the staff of all two dozen centers.

A twenty-year-old man makes this remark: "The devil deals drugs . . . There's a lot of *d*'s."

The tutor asks him to go up and try to write that on the board. He runs into trouble when he gets to "deals" and "drugs." The tutor does not speak of "consonant and vowel blends." Consonant blends, however, are the subject of the lesson they will do at the next session.

In three of the other rooms upstairs, an elderly woman with two college kids who grew up in this project and now go to school nearby is passing around small stapled booklets to the fifteen men and women who first joined this program when it still was situated in a storefront eighteen months before. Three months ago, these stories had been tape-recorded and have since been typed and edited and reproduced on the impressive copying machine which stands in a back corner of the second room. There are fifteen copies of each little book. Each of the learners is given all fifteen. Most of them check first to see if their own stories are included.

The woman from the neighborhood branch library comes into the room and takes a chair. She spends some time in demonstrating how to animate a story, how to tell it in a way that will not lose the interest of small children. They have observed her doing this before with their own children. This is a brush-up then, a quick reminder; she is done by 8 P.M. before the kids appear.

Fifteen of the youngest children come into the room. They are seated with their parents or grandparents—or, in one case, with an eighteen-year-old sister. It does not go off like clockwork. Kids get restless. Some of the adults freeze up, become uneasy, grow confused. The staff is quick to spot these situations and to intervene in ways that do not seem to add to anyone's discomfort. Before 8:30, everyone starts packing up. The children leave the room. The parents and grandparents chat with one another as they get their books together and begin to go downstairs.

Outside now, the air is cool. The voices of the neighborhood teenagers are not quite so shrill.

This is Monday. Tuesday night and then on Thursday they will meet again. On Thursday, however, people come a little earlier: soon after six o'clock. They carry with them covered dishes, salad bowls, and platters covered with tin foil. The members of the staff contribute too. The man from Polaroid brings in a couple of cartons from a local package store. Bottles of wine and sixpacks of cold beer are passed around the tables where the learners, teachers and the children sit together. There is less work tonight. Some of the stories which were first distributed on Monday will be read this time to the entire group. A few who do not dare to read aloud will ask the ones who do to read their stories too. After dinner there will be some time for people who have urgent problems to discuss them with their friends or with the members of the staff. The younger children will be brought downstairs. An open discussion of the way the program is progressing will allow some opportunity for people with complaints to have their say and for the staff to listen and respond. An announcement is made: The local tenants' council has a meeting planned for Friday. People are exhorted by a powerful-looking woman to be sure that they are there.

Before the night is over, there is time to browse through racks of magazines and manuals and to look at an assortment of job-opportunity announcements for which applications also are available. Some of those applications will be brought back by some people for assistance when they meet next Monday night.

Once a month, the dinner meeting does not take place at the center. The library has managed to obtain the funds to hold the dinner at the library itself. The library people do things right. They provide a genuine red-carpet welcome. While they are at it, they do not neglect the opportunity to show their guests around and to recruit those children and adults who write enough to sign a card allowing them to make use of the library during the year ahead.

A professor of child psychology has been invited. He presents a helpful, jargon-free, good-natured speech. A month ago, the speaker was a woman who is doing voter registration. The month before, they had an opportunity to pose some questions to a pediatrician. Next month, an organizer from a local detox center will be speaking.

A dozen teachers and the principal of the local grade school were invited to this dinner. Five of the teachers and the principal are here. They use the opportunity to get to know some of the parents who have never visited the school. Next fall, two of those teachers will be given extra pay to work here in the program Monday nights. By that time, two of the parents who are learners now and who have passed a sixth grade reading level will be working as staff members.

The program I have just described does not exist.

Modest versions of this program do—though not in air-conditioned settings with a staff of thirteen people and a photocopying machine in their own building.

What does exist?

The parents exist: some of them just barely. The children exist. Their energies and willingness and faith exist—at least they do today in 1984. The pediatrician, the child psychologist, and the local organizers all exist. The local grade school and the high schools and the nearby universities exist. Energized librarians in the branch libraries exist. The projects exist. The money exists. We know, however, it does not exist for programs such as this.

We have some fairly good ideas of where it goes instead. To take only one example, $120 billion is expended by the U.S.A. each year to keep a permanent and unloved force of U.S. military men in Western Europe: many of them, as we have seen, the rejects of the very schools which serve such neighborhoods as this. If the balance of terror in the world could possibly survive even a 10 percent reduction of this sum, we could have a program of the sort I have described in every black, white, and Hispanic neighborhood of the United States. Why is it that such programs don't exist? Why would any nation hesitate to serve its own best interests by such sensible and humane redirection of its wealth?

We may recall the words of C. P. Snow.

"They never found the will . . ."

13

Cause for Celebration (When People Speak, the Nation Sometimes Has a Chance to Hear)

But the goal must not be banalized to the obvious and indisputable need to win jobs, attain promotions, cope with mechanical instructions and the like. When we tie it to jobs, or to survival needs, we fall into the trap of mechanistic literacy. We must teach those materials for the sake of their own beauty. We must teach literacy because NOT to be literate is to be denied a portion of our own humanity and, therefore, to be denied a part of our own souls. The fairy tale, the work of fantasy and ecstasy and fun—this helps the parent and the child both to transcend mere utility. They help us to perceive the word not only as a mirror of the narrow world in which we happen to find ourselves at any particular moment in our own career, but also as a mirror of the larger world of high stakes, deep struggle and innermost human need which are the true domain of every bit of literature that genuinely counts. Only when love and need are one, and our life is lived for moral stakes—only when we value truth and beauty (the beauty of logic, the beauty of language as a logic in itself)—only then do we begin to reach the pinnacle of intellectual reward in the pleasure of the printed word, the bound and published book.

–*Currmie Price, The Urban League of Greater Cleveland.*

"Why not flood the neighborhood with books?"

"Not just the neighborhood. Why not the city and the nation too? What if, every place you turned, you found another pile of books?"

"I don't mean in libraries and stores. We don't use the library. The nearest one is nineteen blocks away. I mean: right here, right in our neighborhoods, our houses. In our lives . . ."

What if our nation were prepared to take these women at their word? What if we could summon up the willingness and wisdom to suspend our disbelief? What if it were possible somehow to flood the nation—from the smallest villages of northern Maine and southern Arizona to the mining neighborhoods of Appalachia and the streets of the South Bronx and Boston and Seattle—with three or four hundred million free and excellent and brand-new books? What if we did this, not just once, but month after month, year after year, for ten or twenty years?

This is, to say the least, a sweeping proposition. But it is a question that is forced upon me often in the course of conversation with illiterate adults.

"Make sure that there are lots of books for adults, for teenagers. Also for the kids. Novels. Histories. The lives of people who are dead. Health books for emergencies. Advice for people who have newborn babies."

"When my daughter was little, I would get alarmed. I went to the hospital every time she cried. You could help a lot of people if you gave out books to help us understand."

"Children's books cost five, six, seven dollars. I've bought a small collection. It's at home beside my daughter's bed. It's not enough. I'd like to buy some more. I look at the prices of the milk, the other groceries we got to buy if we are going to stay alive. I got the gas bill and the bill for electricity. I'm with her in the bookstore. I say: 'Shoot! I can't afford it. I can't buy that book. I wish I could. She'd read it if I brought it home.' "

Flooding the U.S.A. with books—books that are neither bought nor borrowed, but brand-new and unencumbered, free—is not an entirely new idea. A modest program known as "RIF" has, for several years, distributed free books to children. It is a good but indiscriminate and underfunded undertaking. The books distributed are far too few. They reach too frequently the people who could easily afford to buy their own. Books are chosen by potential readers, but selections must be made out of a pool of preselected titles. The books are distributed exclusively to children and, most often, in the setting of a public school. Finally, there has been no effort made to build or even find a parallel structure of instruction that might raise the likelihood that books, once scattered on the sea, will be retrieved by those who have some chance to read them. Any good idea deserves to be critiqued with reservations. RIF is a very good idea. Once carefully examined, it could stand to be corrected sensibly, freed a bit from its top-down control, and then magnificently expanded.

An emphasis on oral history remains the bedrock of the plan for which I argue in this book. The additional point, established earlier, that books at first intimidate those who have no chance to read them and who, to state it more precisely, have been led by the predictable defeats that they have suffered in the public schools to view the printed word with something close to loathing and with something more than fear—this emphasis remains unqualified as well.

The point, therefore, is not to leap, by some miraculous parabola of cognitive athletics, over the void of words and vacuum of realistic comprehensions which immobilize illiterate and semiliterate adults. All of the prior stages named above must still remain in place. The flooding of a nation—of its cities, projects, neighborhoods, and homes—with millions of attractive and enticing books is not meant to substitute olympic pedagogy for the piecemeal labors it will take to mobilize Illiterate America. For 25 million adults, ordinary trade books will at first be far beyond all possibility of comprehension. For others—organizers who may read at only marginal levels, for example—some of these books may be accessible, while most of them will represent at first an undiscovered but perhaps increasingly desirable terrain. For others still—those who can read but do not do so often and who can't afford the price of books on sale in the United States today—the presence of good literature within their homes and neighborhoods and ordinary lives will answer the same appetite that it awakens.

Whether for the first group or the second or the third, there can hardly be a disincentive in proximity; and it is not easy to believe that there would not be *positive* incentive in availability. Why not make it possible to own, right from the start, what one may someday have the option to enjoy and opportunity to understand? I should think a person would be far more likely to be eager to learn how to drive if there were a small attractive car parked out in the garage. The likelihood that one will never own an automobile cannot fail to have the opposite effect. Books are not cars, and reading is not shifting gears or turning an ignition; ownership, however, and proprietary pride may have some lively impact on our motivation.

My enthusiasm for this notion is not based on speculation. I have seen this plan in operation. A group involved with literacy work decided, some years back, to start a book collection in a neighborhood center situated in an area of high-rise projects.

Summoning their courage, they applied to several publishers in New York City. Their first attempts brought in ten dozen cartons that contained about 3,000 books. The books were not, as they had feared, the ones nobody buys. They were the residue of titles that had since gone into paperback editions. One publisher, indeed, was sensitive enough to send them first a catalog of titles that remained in stock in order that they might select the titles they would find most useful. He may have been surprised by their selections. Although they ordered several hundred copies of the kinds of titles—ethnic, women's interests, and the like—which seemed to hold the greatest current relevance for those they served, the largest number of requests was for established works of history, biography, and classic fiction. Militant leaders, when they are both militant and well-informed, do not always choose the "gritty" stuff that some of us expect.

Curious, and still uncertain of response, they put the books out on display: not in tightly crowded shelves but on a set of easels which they made from plywood planks. Most of the books were gone within two months.

The reader might already have suspected the first problem that they faced. The books, intended as a loan, were not returned. Suspicion turned to thoughts of conscious theft, then to the improbable idea of a black market, of a thriving underworld in which the currency might be a $15 book. Investigation led to a more simple explanation. People were putting their books out on display. Some of them remained, no doubt, as little more than living-room decoration. Some—too many—ended up in tatters, lost, forgotten among underclothes and paper bags and other junk that had accumulated in those crowded, poorly heated, and uncomfortable homes. The rest were being read.

Not always, it turned out, by those who borrowed them. Often, the one who brought it home had soon lost interest in his acquisition. An older brother, sister, or grandparent had picked up the book from where it had been left, soon grew intrigued enough to read the book, then gave it to a friend.

The organizers tried for a time to get the books returned. "It was as hard to get them back," one parent said, "as it would have been to get back turkeys at Thanksgiving." Trusting to their past experience, they soon agreed that it would be much easier to try the publishers again than it would have been to wander through the neighborhoods and projects in an effort to persuade their neighbors to "return a book, fill out a card, and take another." In this natural and easy way, the concept of the one-way library was born.

"The books go out. They don't come back. When we are getting down to the last six or seven hundred, we write another set of letters to our unknown friends at Random House or Doubleday or Little, Brown."

How might we apply the lesson that these organizers learned on the much greater scale of an entire nation?

Would it be very complicated or expensive to start as many as 10,000—or 100,000—one-way libraries in day-care centers, hospital clinics, laundromats, or in the vacant units on the first floor of a thousand of the largest housing projects in the nation? The books go out. If someone brings one back, she gets another. If she never brings it back, she gets five more. Wherever they are, we can believe that somebody, somewhere, must be making use of *some* of them.

To return for a moment to even the most fanciful of fears: What if, with so many millions of new books in circulation, an underground market in expensive books should gradually evolve? What if a book did actually become a "chit" for underground exchange? It isn't, unfortunately, very likely; but, in the rare event that this occurred, it is rather difficult to think of any consummation more devoutly to be wished—and celebrated! What civilized society with any vision, any sense of history at all, would not wish to beat the drums and sound the bugles on discovery of an eventuality so little to be looked for? Unlike that golden bugle used in recent years by those who promulgated warnings that one third of the electorate could neither read nor understand, this time the bugle that is being blown might also have some chance of being heard.

How might we obtain so many books? Who would supply them? Would they, as the group described above originally feared, turn out to be the books that no one really wants? There are a number of answers, some less probable than others, to these questions. One of them, however, seems quite clear.

Millions of the finest books, and more of the finest than the worst (which are the easiest to sell), are locked up in the silent stacks of buildings in all sections of the nation. The publisher's warehouse, filled with overstock of works that have been published since in paperback editions, are to Illiterate America what giant silos filled with surplus grain might represent to people who are hungry. Millions of these books are shredded yearly or allowed to rot and gather dust in purgatorial existence.

Millions of mass-market paperbacks, at the same time, are annually promoted into high-priced paperbacks and must, for this reason, be extracted from the market. A writer I know was told not long ago that one of her books had just been labeled "out of print." Knowing that the book was being used in college classes, she was startled and she asked how this could be the case. Her publisher explained that annual sales had dropped to 7,000 copies. "We can't keep a title in the pipelines if it doesn't sell at least 10,000 yearly." She asked, then, if this meant her book was dead. No, the publisher explained, it wasn't dead. It would just become a little more expensive. "Quality paperback" would be the next stage in its natural life-cycle.

"What will you do with the copies you've got left?"

They told her they would shred 6,000 copies. If she wanted, they would let her have the other thousand . . .

Millions of books, as we now know, are relegated to the shredder every year. Would it be so hard to make a simple virtue out of this bizarre necessity? The fluctuating centigrade of prices might be made to work to our advantage in at least two ways. Hardcover books cannot be sold once they have been reprinted as mass-market paperbacks. Mass-market paperbacks cannot be sold once they have been promoted in the opposite direction into paperbacks that cost $8. Literacy leaders might attempt to set up pedagogic roadblocks both ways on the highway of commercial publication. What does the publisher or author stand to lose? At very worst, some of these books might not be read.

They might end up in the trash—or used as tinder. This is not a pleasant thought, but it is a good deal less unpleasant, and a great deal less contemptible in implication, than their relegation to a shredder. Other books, millions surely, would at length be read and might, during the interim, provide a stimulus to those who cannot read them now but may in time achieve the skill to do so. There is no way this could do harm. There are a lot of ways it could do good. One of the greatest goods might be that shredders—an atrocity in an illiterate society—could at last be relegated to extinction.

It is argued that there might be one financial cost at stake in this idea. Publishers would surely lose some money in a diminution of their sale of over-stock hardcover books to discount stores. The dumping of overstock titles, how-ever, brings in very little money; it is at best a way of cutting down on ware-house storage costs. To the degree that there is any loss at all, it might well be counterbalanced by the tax advantage that could be provided. If there is any loss to anyone at all, it could not outweigh the long-term gains in an expanded future market.

A more important obstacle might come not from the publishers but from certain of the literacy groups themselves. There is an unquestioned element of benefaction in this plan. Is there an unpleasant note of "charity" as well?

My own belief is that the people are entitled to these books and that this—"entitlement"—should be mandated by the federal government just as it should mandate all the other bare necessities of food and health care and old-age protection which a decent nation owes to every citizen without conditions. Such entitlement should be included in the plan I have proposed in the preceding chapters. No human being who wants to read and own a book should ever have to go on bended knee to get it. People should be able to use libraries. They should also have a chance to own them.

What I have suggested here, like much of what pervades the other sections of this book, is offered as an interim approach to be applied during the days immediately ahead: the hours and weeks in which we work and live, the present tense in which our students now exist. I have made it clear that I do not believe in sitting still and waiting with monastic patience for divine or presidential visitations. We do what we can with what we have. We do not have a govern-ment prepared to grant entitlement to truth and history to its impoverished population. Someday we may. Until that day, we need not beg. We need not crawl on bended knees. But we should strenuously *insist*.

In practice, all of this self-laceration is irrelevant. People who care about the lives of those whom they intend to serve do not find it difficult to reconcile the kindliness or tax advantage of a corporation with their own strategic needs. I recognize that publishers will not accede to all the details of this plan. There are several complications that I have not even tried to explicate or to explore. Some version of this enterprise should nonetheless be possible and ought to be considered carefully by those in the book industry who have repeatedly announced their serious commitment to this cause. It is difficult to know how anyone, other than Sir William Berkeley and his latter-day descendants in the Heritage Foundation, could reject the opportunities and possibilities that might, with such apparent ease, be made available to every citizen within this land.

"*Shoot! I can't afford it. I can't buy that book. I wish I could.*"

Words like these should serve us as an invitation to make possible an unexpected and unprecedented feast. Gentle longings, spoken in such plain and honest words, must not be permitted to remain unanswered.

PART THREE

Beyond Utility

14

Technological Obsession

The computer has some unique capabilities. It can do graphics, make decisions and have a dialogue with the students . . . When the dimension of dialogue . . . is added, the computer takes on your style of instruction.

—advice to teachers, "Strategies for Computer-aided Instruction"

Some of those who have debated these ideas with me have argued that my absolute insistence on a human mobilization is archaic in an age of technological innovation. We have seen the dominant place that technological instruction has been given in the literacy efforts of the U.S. Army. The same phenomenon is spreading fast throughout civilian education too. It stems, no doubt, from an American infatuation with the scientific shortcut, the mechanical quick fix, the curious but abiding faith that all our problems—no matter how clear their genesis in human abdication, no matter how cruel the price that they exact in human terms—will somehow be resolved at last by the discovery of an inspired machine.

Enormous dangers lie in this noncritical infatuation. There is irony as well. We pride ourselves on individual differences, unique ideas, the spirit of the pioneers, of Tom Paine, Emerson, Thoreau. At the same time, we look for the predictability of outcome that is guaranteed by technological contrivance. Humanists and social scientists increasingly attempt to clothe their efforts in the trappings of "hard science." Not only sociology and cultural anthropology but even a field like literary criticism increasingly becomes infested with the jargon of empirical addiction.

We open a book on *Adolescence in the Hills of North Dakota* and we find more charts and graphs and loops and curves than moving verbs and connotative nouns. Evocative writing is regarded as less scholarly than strictly denotative statements, stripped of the power to arouse emotion but supported by a little robot army of hard numbers. Even the analysis of poetry and fiction is too frequently reduced to number-counts: the frequency of certain verbs, the number of times that "images relating to the sun and moon appear in Donne, Marvell and Blake . . ."

The less secure a scholar feels, the more he seems to be attracted to the need for scientific reinforcement. Numbers seem to offer absolute protection not only against critics but against our own sense of uncertain, flawed, or futile enterprise. In literacy work—an area that is regarded still as one of the least prestigious realms of academic toil—the tendency to draw for reassurance upon a technological jargon is increasingly apparent. Especially in programs run by academic ("adult education") faculties, people are overly impressed by talk of "instantaneous feedback programs," "computerized learning systems," and the like. In the old days teachers, trained to a professional constraint, only did their best to act like a machine. Now, it seems, they are prepared—eager indeed—to be *replaced* by one.

Sensible people cannot underestimate the obvious utility of certain technological devices. Those, moreover, whom we teach to read and write will need to be conversant also with technology and mathematics and computer science to survive in the job market and, far more important, to be able to assess and criticize the nature of that market. What is troubling, however, is the likelihood that newly literate men and women may be reduced, by mechanistic teachers using strictly mechanistic tools, to acquiesce before a technological apparatus that controls or replaces human beings.

Two arguments are raised repeatedly by those who are most easily seduced by technological devices:

(1) "Technology will soon make reading and writing obsolete. The Information Age depends upon communication by computer. Literacy as you define it in this book is virtually archaic."

This argument is both diversionary and, at length, immobilizing. It is correct that we are entering an age when new and unfamiliar forms of information storage and retrieval will compete effectively with printed words. The printed word remains the access route to every other form of intellectual information. How can people possibly find out what they do not yet know if they cannot read enough to understand the very books that underscore these points? Future-thinkers, starting back in 1968, have quoted the warnings of Marshall McLuhan in attempting to diminish the importance of "archaic" literacy. Illiterate adults cannot be grateful for these warnings. Even if writers like McLuhan have—or had—some useful intuitions, how is this information to be purchased and employed by those who cannot read? Will the future-thinker read McLuhan to them?

"What you don't know yourself," wrote Bertolt Brecht, "you don't know!" This is the point repeatedly ignored when those who have already had a privileged education, and are well prepared and fully competent in use of print communication, tell us of the foolishness of struggling to bring poor men and women to a level of effectiveness based chiefly on the use of written words. The idea of a "higher level" of literacy makes excellent sense for those who have the opportunity to know that it exists, but any chance of reaching such a level depends upon a prior mastery in use of written words. Until illiterate people have achieved this prior competence, who is it who will explain to them that there are other, possibly more challenging devices for communication even farther from their reach?

The answer is that people need to have the power to inform *themselves*. Those who denigrate this need ought to be asked to spend some time among real people with real problems in real places such as Roxbury and Harlem.

The worst result of futurist obsessions with computer literacy is that the humble literacy worker, and the still more humble literacy learner, can be overwhelmed by a paralysis of will created by a global sense of "all the other things we need to know." It is very hard to try to climb even one hundred yards when those who seem to be our friends keep pointing to a series of transcendent mountain peaks so far above us and so far beyond our present energies and dreams that we do not even dare to take the first ten steps. The fatalistic apathy that this creates becomes a part of the induced passivity that I have seen in thousands of illiterate adults. There are, no doubt, a limitless number of "higher levels" which a newly literate person (or one who has been literate for forty years) might well desire to attain. If we are not to despair, however, even before we find the courage to begin, I believe that we should start without apologies at the beginning.

(2) There is a second argument propounded by some advocates of new technologies: "Granted that print literacy has some residual use, granted that print information may be with us for a time, surely there are better ways than person-to-person education to eradicate illiteracy in the United States. Televised instruction, in conjunction with a clever use of home computers, can achieve the basic literacy levels we require in a shorter time, at lower cost, and with less human sweat and toil, than the methods advocated in this book. Why mobilize a literacy army to invade the colonies of Appalachia and East Harlem and the Bronx when technological devices have the power to deliver a 'first strike' that will defeat the enemy in weeks or even hours?"

The answers to this question are implicit in the previous thirteen chapters of this book. Televised instruction is, at best, a useful adjunct to the real thing. It cannot be countenanced as an alternative. The television learner is entirely passive. The television mode is intellectual disjunction. The consequence of televised instruction is a deeper balkanization of the human consciousness than anything that academic fragmentation has engendered up to now. The mechanistic dangers are no longer metaphoric but specific when we learn from a machine. The separation of a skill from a reflective understanding of its ethical or anti-human implications is enhanced (and it is often virtually assured) by televised indoctrination. The centralization of control is guaranteed. The imagination of the learner is no longer simply dominated, it is now monopolized, by the intentions of an unseen corporate producer.

If Holt, Rinehart, Houghton Mifflin, and Scott Foresman had a damaging preponderance of power over grade-school education, those who produce and market televised instruction have a nearly absolute control over the consciousness, and even modes of consciousness, of those who follow, swallow, and ingest their organized curricula. Which of us can honestly believe that corporations with the wealth and the accumulated ingenuity to offer programmed literacy instruction to 60 million isolated and dependent people are likely to inspire attitudes of critical irreverence and of analytic acumen in those who constitute already, in their present subjugated state, a captive clientele for any and all ideas, products, or attitudes of mind that U.S. corporations have to sell?

It does not require radical perspective to recognize that those who have a firm hold on the market of American ideas will not foster an ability to question the validity of ideologies they live by. Corporations don't exist to subsidize the forfeiture of their dominion. Literacy as critical consciousness for moral action will not come out of a televised production until the governance of that production has been handed over to the representatives of the illiterates themselves. We will wait a long time for that hour of expropriation. In the meantime we had better look with caution on this growing fascination.

Those who market personal computers have begun to foster an insidious idea that individual learners, sheltered in the privacy of their own homes, may now at last be able to determine, shape, and supervise their own instruction. They can determine the pace, the pressure, or the necessary repetition of a predetermined sequence of ideas. They cannot shape the content; nor can they subvert the passive stance which the computerized agenda has congealed.

People can press buttons. The buttons allow them the illusion of manipulation. It is a disarming substitute (it is much worse than this: it is, in fact, an antidote) for anything like real control over their lives. The learner manipulates the terminal that sits beside her television console; yet it is she who is manipulated by the buttons she selects. Her only option is to choose at which specific moment she will plug into the sequence of accreted information which has been approved by those who know what will be best for her, and for themselves, and who have planned the literacy curriculum with sensitive anticipation of its probable results. We think, as we sit before our small machine, that we have been empowered to design the program of our modernized emancipation; but it is we who shall be programmed by the lessons we receive. We can adjust this little instrument to any lesson that we choose; people whose interests and ideas we do not know, and never shall have any opportunity to face head-on, have already determined how we shall be programmed to accept their own interpretation of a functional effectiveness in the society to which they are, by now, accustomed and in the context of disparities to which they sensibly adhere because they are the ones who profit from them.

Except within the U.S. military, literacy instruction by computer and TV is not wholly operational today; but it is clearly in the works. We should be prepared to counter this unprecedented instrument of domination by all possible means.*

The sticking point, again, is the obsessive inclination, on the part of psychologically imperiled humanists, to reinforce their fragile confidence by imitation of hard science. Man, as Aristotle said, is an imitative animal. "But one of the sadder commonplaces about human nature," in the words of Walter Jackson Bate, "is the incorrigible tendency . . . to imitate the . . . peripheral rather than the essential things." Practitioners of the humanities, when they turn their attention to the procedures of the natural sciences, imitate not their openness, but their self-imposed limits of specialization. "In the strong initial period of specialization of a true science, a limitation is accepted as the price, not as itself a gain—a price paid in order to make strides toward the general end in mind. In this creative stage, the limitation is far from being desired as an end in itself, but the temptation in human nature is to imitate the limitation—to view the means as ends themselves—and to leave any further ends to luck and serendipity."

In areas of low prestige like adult education, the limitation is repeatedly accepted as the end. The price is an impoverished humanism: a foolish imitation of the least important values of the sciences. The wistful longings of some literacy experts to endow their trade with technological decoration is a costly paradigm of Aristotle's observation. If we could bring into the genesis of our work a genuinely scientific prescience, millions of illiterate adults would profit greatly; but the imitation of the superficial will not do the trick. We would do best to hold to an archaic faith in the persistent value of the written word.

---

* Computerized instruction may be used in ways that seem to draw entirely on the input of the learner and do not involve explicit imposition of external content. This, as we have seen, is not the way in which the military has employed computerized instruction; nor, despite the fanciful disclaimers that have been advanced by IBM and other firms, is it really possible to render this instruction wholly neutral. Mechanistic learning in itself conveys an ideology. For evidence of the totality of power that computer manufacturers have themselves articulated as a final goal, see NOTES.

Books will endure. Literacy will continue to depend upon the power to decipher words and to decode their connotations. All literacy, all language, in the long run, is a dialogue between one person and another. I cannot tell how many other teachers share this view; but I, for one, do not want to see a generation of young people, or of formerly illiterate adults, learning to read by talking to machines. We already have political leaders who speak with the predictability and anomie of a computer. In a world that lives beneath the terror of a nuclear explosion, a cataclysm that will be initiated by the pulling of a lever or the flicking of a switch, it seems imperative that we do all within our power to be certain that those whom we attempt to teach today are never denied the elemental recognition of that tender, vulnerable, and perishable reality—humanity, another man or woman—that exists behind the button and beyond the switch.

Mechanical means too frequently have mechanistic ends. Those who learn from a machine soon learn to live like one. Efficiency at the price of human decency, and of the simple recognition of the perilous and fragile nature of all human life, would not be a service to illiterate men and women in this nation or in any other nation whose existence we determine and whose possibilities of cultural extinction or survival we control.

There are some examples of intelligent and cautious use of televised instruction. The literacy programs of the BBC in England offer us one instance of a civilized approach which uses television as an aid to personal instruction; but this is a different matter from the automated methods of the U.S. military which employ technology not as an adjunct to but as a surrogate for personal participation.

In our struggle to establish universal humane literacy in the United States we should use technology with wisdom but also with a sensible degree of reticence and stealth. That reticence should be inspired by the absolute, unshakable resolve that we shall never undermine the quintessential definition of a literate human being: one soul, reaching out of the loneliness of the human condition, to find—through love—another. Love too is a part of literacy. We should not be frightened by this word; nor should we be frightened by the hardnosed condemnation which will certainly assault our courage to persist in ethical and old-fashioned goals.

15

The Obligation
of the Universities

What made him so great an intellectual figure was his capacity to
cross boundaries: between philosophy, fiction, and drama, between
politics and psychology, between knowledge and ethics.

—Richard Sennett, on Jean-Paul Sartre

Scholars in the universities and colleges of the United States would seem to have
an obligation to confront the dangers posed by mechanistic education. Those,
above all, who are committed to the study of humanities within the faculties of
arts and science would appear to be the natural participants in any effort that
attempted to infuse this struggle with a humanistic breadth. If the denial of the
written word to one third of our adult population cannot win their serious
concern and consequent participation, it is difficult to know where else within
the academic world a humanizing struggle of this kind can hope to find compassionate adherents.

There was a time when both allegiance and participation of this character
were manifested long before they even were requested. Many scholars, for example, in the Boston area offered to black activists in Roxbury a good deal of
extremely useful help during the 1960s, often in the most ingenious and unselfish ways.

In one instance, a prominent sociologist was able to help a neighborhood
group with which I was involved by redirecting research funds, so frequently
available to academic institutions but seldom to the organizations that are toil-
ing to make use of the research which has already been done. Seeing the fiscal

164   ILLITERATE AMERICA

problems we were facing, he submitted a proposal for a study to explore the feasibility of "a pilot program" that accorded in all details with the program we already had in operation. He got the money, used some of it for research, but managed to direct a good amount to underwrite our work. In this manner he enabled us to grow a little bit "more feasible"—and to remain so for the next five years.

Why is it that the same alliance is not in effect today?

One initial explanation is a false impression, on the part of literacy activists, that any struggle which is pedagogic in its nature ought to look for allies among those who are the certified custodians of pedagogic knowledge. This is a serious miscalculation. Despite the many advocates and allies in the schools of education who can bring professional intelligence and, at times, financial help to bear upon the efforts of an underfunded group, the insecurities of many faculties of education are well known. Experience ought to serve us as an admonition. Unfortunately, those who cannot read, or scarcely so, have little means to learn the history of past mistakes; few such people even know the chronicles of disappointment from one decade past. Lack of information, in this case, seduces the illiterate to seek liaison with the single group least able to respond.

Those on the other hand who *could* respond, who have the vision and prestige to be most valued allies—the faculties of English, sociology, and history, for instance—tend to disqualify themselves for lack of "special expertise" in something which appears to be so esoteric, so dependent on technique, as literacy instruction.

Working in voter-registration drives, in boycotts, demonstrations, and exuberant projects such as freedom schools in 1965 did not seem to call for an experience in detailed methodologies. The primary requirements were energy, enthusiasm, and a visceral response to an articulate and angry plea from those who, bitterly excluded and oppressed, could nonetheless express their needs in terms that could not be dismissed. Illiterates, as we have seen, cannot voice their grievances in written words; nor are the dimensions of oppression so explicit in the silent struggle of a largely leaderless and unseen population.

Even a potential ally needs to feel the first rush of adrenal urgency. Inaudible victims do not win compassionate co-workers with the ease of those who can articulate their needs in cogent words.

Conservative pressures ("excellence" and "standards") undermine in another way the likelihood of venturesome affiliations by potentially committed scholars. With the dangers of alumni criticisms ever present, and the threat of federal punishment by cancellation or reduction of Defense Department funds, academic leaders are less willing than in decades past to take the risk of helping people to achieve implicitly political objectives.

Many of the same professors, in addition, have been led (or let themselves be led) to pacify their conscience with the notion that most economic and societal inequities have been addressed for long enough, and with sufficient impact, to enable them to relegate "all that" to the nostalgic blur of "an old struggle" undertaken in the 1960s and ratified by subsequent court decisions that desegregated some of the most blatantly divided education systems. Many academics really do believe that all of us are now beginning once again with a clean slate. Once this incorrect impression is accepted and congealed, there is no commanding reason to disrupt the customary rituals of their existence.

All of this is tragic for at least two reasons.

(1) Academic humanists are potentially the most effective allies for illiterate people who have been denied, above and beyond all other forms of wealth and opportunity, the amplitude and richness of the humanist tradition: one which may be carried on to future ages by no other vehicle so fragile as the written word.

(2) If the best of humanists are not impelled to lend a hand, it may prove impossible to foster an exalted and ennobling ideal of literate humanity, rooted in high seriousness, which has the power to protect the newly literate adult from either the mechanistic competence defined as "functional" by corporations, government, the military, and some schools of education, or from the simplistic goals of a politicized but unreflective indignation.

It is the second point which we should reexamine now in greater depth.

The following scenario is one that takes place monthly, even weekly, from one season to the next: Scholars assemble in commissions or in study groups (a "task force" is the favored term: derivative perhaps from military jargon) but they soon break up into diverse subunits ("working parties") to examine separate sections of "the question"—whatever it may be. One unit is assigned the university; another is given secondary education; a third is granted elementary level; a fourth may look at early childhood education; a fifth perhaps will be invited to assess the adult literacy situation.

Just as the futurist too frequently surveys the future in apparent isolation from the past, the humanist assigned to university dilemmas tends to look at upper academic life in ways that scarcely touch the surface of the secondary school and totally ignore the lives of younger children. The problems of adult nonreaders, if addressed at all, may be assigned to "other members" of the same commission—or to "another task force" which may meet, perhaps, at some unstated future time . . .

If the analysis could have been conducted in a manner that did not assign such rigidly defined subsections to so many separate groups, it might have been possible to recognize the lines of causative connection that are basic to an understanding of each one—and all—of these subsections.

One of the constant problems faced by university instructors is the recent influx of large numbers of young men and women who are not equipped to read and analyze successfully and who do not write with adequate effectiveness to meet the expectations of professors. Discussion therefore concentrates on methods of remediation. Sophisticated teachers are aware that something might be said for a concerted drive to make remediation needless by a prior effort to address these problems at their source. Nonetheless, it is those symptoms most perceptible and pressing to the academic scholars which consume their time. If they extend their reach at all, they tend to look "above" (to graduate education in the university) rather than "below"—to the condition of the children of the cheated parents of our nation. Then too, there is at times an element of snobbishness at stake: Troubled children in the public schools do not magnetize the interest of those men and women who have spent their lives in study of Keats, Coleridge, and Yeats. Universities are their domain; high schools, elementary schools, and problems of impoverished children are the turf, and the priority, of someone else.

A separate group of specialists may speak of high school problems. Since this group, much like the group described above, is looking at one body of dilemmas out of context—and divorced from prior causative injustice—there is a familiar inclination toward a punitive approach. Higher demands and higher expectations, they appear to say, will summon forth by retroactive process the degree of excellence that they require. It is the problem of "the golden bugle" once again. We know who blows that bugle, but we also know how many millions of the mothers and the fathers of our children have no way to hear.

There is some unintended cruelty in this. A humanism that would scorn humanity and relegate compassion to "another expert" (or another subdivision of another area of special expertise) is a distorted creature that perpetuates those insular compartments, barriers and walls that humanists repeatedly condemn. To speak of the humanities in terms so narrow is to undermine the meaning of our language. The rhetoric of those who wish to see the colleges and schools go "back to basics" has been attacked, as we have seen, as an unsubtle euphemism for a retrogression into basic privileged reward for few and basic heartlessness toward those who are denied the means of access. Without the active intervention we propose, this is a charge to which there will be no responsible defense.

Education schools, cut off already from the breadth and depth of liberal academies, are fragmentized within their own departments too. Those who specialize in early childhood education read the works of Skinner, Elkind, Burton White, and Piaget. The specialists in elementary education meanwhile focus their attention on the methods and materials appropriate to elementary years. Still others, sharply cut off from the rest, address the issues relevant to secondary school. Those who are involved with teaching school administrators focus on issues of standardized exams, college requirements, general and vocational education, management of budgets, teacher tenure and promotion policies, and demographic issues that affect the operations of an urban or suburban school. Those who serve on national commissions which determine policy and have the greatest impact upon national decisions tend to be selected, largely on the basis of prestige, from upper academic levels (college presidents inevitably appear on these commissions), government, corporations, and foundations. Each group has its insular concerns and each is locked within the tunnel vision of its own experience and tangible self-interest.

Educators used to speak of something known as "the whole child." But the educator's function in the world of public policy today is less one of amalgamation than skilled surgery. One category does not "bleed" into another. Locked in the cell of himself, each specialist sees only that which lies within his close proximity. Departmental localism paralyzes our capacity to apprehend a sweeping panorama.

Those who work exclusively at upper levels of the pedagogic world rarely look at the terrain of early childhood. Early childhood specialists, meanwhile, keep their vision fixed upon the child and, at best, upon the things a parent "ought to do"—but seldom on the reason why so many parents *can't.*

The only authorized spokespersons for adult illiterates in the United States today are those who have been certified as specialists in adult education. Even those within this field who seem most eloquent have seldom studied history (nor, generally, literature) in any depth. They could not possibly have done so at the same time that they underwent the training that accredited them as experts in a subdivision of the schools of education. Adult education specialists, in any case, do not exercise much power in this nation. The very credentials we assign as rationale for their official governance of this domain represent a signal to the body politic that they are not sufficiently impressive to be feared or trusted. The dignity of humanism is denied them; the power and (to some degree) the glory belong elsewhere. Who does have power? Those who have the power are the humanists and scientists, the scholars in the faculties of liberal arts and sciences that represent the heart of all great colleges and universities: those, precisely, who have abdicated all responsibility for "unlettered" men and women because they are not experts in this field.

Even from a selfish point of view, the disadvantages of this approach must now be clear. If the colleges received well-educated high school graduates they would not need to dedicate their time to massive programs of remediation; nor would they be forced to give so much of their attention to the problem of diminished student interest in the more demanding areas of science and humanities. If the high schools were receiving students who had learned to read and write, to question, analyze, and synthesize ideas in junior high school and at upper elementary levels, they would not be driven to "enumeration of prerequisites" which cannot fail to have a punitive effect. If fifth and sixth grade teachers were receiving students who had learned to read and write and do arithmetic during the first four years of school, they would be in a position to develop competence for critical skills, research and composition, and sophisticated thinking, which would prepare their students properly for junior high school. If primary level teachers were receiving children who had already enjoyed the benefit of early childhood education, they might not see reading scores collapsing by calamitous degrees after the fourth grade year. But early childhood development, in turn, depends upon a reassuring backup from committed parents who have competence equivalent to their commitment.

A thousand problems, viewed in vacuo, as if they were inherent somehow to the upper academic world alone, could be substantially reduced if serious attention were addressed to the progression of related items I have just described.

The entire debate concerning standards of admission at the college level and the many tensions and recriminations that emerge from the idea of group or racial quotas might evaporate within two decades if the arguments for excellence, on the one hand, and for justice, on the other, were not divided but amalgamated in a single plan for universal humane literacy. Equalized opportunity from birth might enable colleges to ask for—and receive—the level of excellence which now eludes them and to do so in a context that does not deny the most essential obligations of fair play.

Unless we deal with issues of fair play as an inherent aspect of the drive for excellence, the populist/elitist confrontation will continue, and the denigration of our labors as "elitist" will be painfully deserved.

Artists and scholars from Robert Frost to David Riesman have addressed the dangers of a fragmentized perception that erects unnecessary but convenient walls between essentially related areas of our existence. Riesman has written of the departmental insularity that favors rigid borders to protect small, demarcated areas of academic expertise, then turns those borders into barriers that only the most bold and visionary dare to penetrate or to transcend. Walter Jackson Bate has written of the loss of continuities that decimates our wholeness of perception and denies us the ability to hold in mind more than one possibility, one explanation, one response. Time itself is balkanized as a result: The present does not know the past. The past is neatly segregated from the future. Localism of this sort achieves a bitter climax in the insularity of our approach to universal humane literacy in our society. Even the most thoughtful humanists disdain to speak about the problems of those men and women who have been excluded from the world of literary satisfaction which those humanists control and explicate but do not feel the obligation or the power to make visible, and then accessible, to those they never need to know.

"Before I built a wall," wrote Robert Frost, "I'd ask to know what I was walling in or walling out." Before we build these walls of departmental isolation and myopic humanism, shouldn't we ask whom we are letting in—and how many million others we have casually consigned to wordless isolation on the outskirts of the kingdoms we control?

The false equation of "humane" and "humanistic" is hardly a new problem. During the height of nineteenth century optimism, as George Steiner has observed, there was a compelling inference that "cultural transmission," if and when it could be carried out effectively, "would lead necessarily to a more stable, humanely responsible condition of man." "For both Voltaire and Matthew Arnold," Steiner writes, "there is an obvious congruence between the cultivation of the individual mind through formal knowledge and a melioration in the commanding qualities of life."

We know now that this is not so.

Without an arduous, unbroken, and sustained ideal of universal humane competence, extended through all classes and all categories of a nation's population; without a constant struggle to relate one area of sensitivity, of special knowledge, whether classical literature or Roman sculpture, African ethnography or modern fiction, to every other area of instruction; without a militant insistence on the breaking down of walls between the acquisition of a special skill and its potential applications; without a sense of history as the pervasive bedrock for all special areas of academic toil; without an ethical (not doctrinaire) intensity as a conditioning ingredient in every realm of learned aspiration; without these conscious efforts on a full, sustained continuum of time, the fragmentized perception that I have described above will not diminish. The scholar will continue to reside within a sealed compartment of ungenerous endeavor. The humanities—no matter how much vigor, depth, or excellence they may regain—will never be humane.

"Sensibility," in Steiner's words, "intelligence, scruple in learning" can easily "carry forward in a neutral zone . . ." Museums, theaters, and universities can prosper next to concentration camps. Collective hysteria, savagery—or simply quiet abdication in the presence of ongoing misery outside the college walls—have coexisted with the highest pitch of excellence and culture. "Men such as Hans Frank who administered the 'final solution' in Eastern Europe were avid connoisseurs and, in some instances, performers of Bach and Mozart." We know of personnel in the bureaucracy of the gas ovens, Steiner writes, "who cultivated a knowledge of Goethe, a love of Rilke . . . One of the principal works that we have in the philosophy of language . . . was composed almost within earshot of a death camp. Heidegger's pen did not stop nor his mind go mute."

There can be "no presumption," he writes, "of a carry-over from civilization to civility . . . Our knowledge of the failure of education, of literate tradition, to bring 'sweetness and light' to men, is a clear symptom of what is lost."

What is lost cannot be repossessed by narrow efforts at archival conservation. "Not to have known about the inhuman potential of cultured man what we now know was a formidable privilege." We no longer have that privilege.

Steiner asks the question, therefore, that should frame all of our current pleadings for the restoration of old standards and should provoke our academic humanists to cross those borders they so frequently deplore but reinforce by genteel acquiescence. "Why labor to elaborate and transmit culture," Steiner asks, "if it did so little to stem the inhuman, if there were in it deep-set ambiguities which, at times, even solicited barbarism?" Granted that culture was a medium of excellence: "Was the price paid for it too high?" These are questions that we have to ask whenever academic humanists appear to relegate the matter of unfair exclusion based on class and race to "other commissions," "another department," or a separate subdivision of their own. "Can it have been accident that a large measure of ostentatious civilization—in Periclean Athens, in the Florence of the Medicis, in sixteenth century England, in the Versailles of the *grand siècle* and the Vienna of Mozart—was closely correlate with . . . a firm caste system, and the surrounding presence of a subject populace?" What good did high humanism do?

Those who wish to repossess the richness of the past but manage to ignore the cruelty, and often savagery, which coexisted with those brilliant symbols resurrected in the golden glow of words pronounced by Matthew Arnold or by Walter Pater will not see the need to reach beyond such limited objectives as the excellence and higher standards they believe to be attainable at upper academic levels. The illiterate status of 25 million fellow citizens, the exclusion from all humanistic studies of an additional 35 million marginal illiterates, and the undeserved ordeal of millions of their children will remain for scholars of this sort a "grave concern," "a genuine injustice," but will be consigned once more to separate kingdoms of effective advocacy to be taken up by "others."

The illiterate therefore has been crippled in at least three ways: first, by economic and societal exclusion; second, by the inability to see historic precedent for that exclusion and thereby to make use of what has already been said by others; finally, by the inability to render eloquence accessible, and suffering believable, by use of written words. The dark satanic mills that Blake described are with us still; but children of the poorest people in our nation cannot even hope to find employment in those mills. The only mills they enter are those starkly lighted public schools that cannot hope to meet their needs but offer, at best, custodial arrest for twelve or thirteen years, grinding them out at last to wander back into the cycle of illiterate existence which produced them.

So long as academic humanists resist the obligation to cross borders, and to participate in unfamiliar, openly political, and therefore highly dangerous assaults upon societal injustice, there will be no potent advocates for the illiterate, no written expositions to be read by a society that manages to segregate its victims and anaesthetize itself to the persistence of an anguish it has sealed away in celluloid containers. Yet the containers do not always hold; and, in this case, the end result of our neglect is the persistent contestation that afflicts the university itself, that polarizes students while it pluralizes competence, that brings a final sadness like an early twilight to even the most insular of scholars and—at the end of a long journey—gnaws at the dream of excellence, tears at the fabric of democracy, devastates many, nourishes few, impoverishes us all.

The humanists may continue to pursue the narrow interests of their own profession, but they will not serve those interests well. Remediation at the college level will remain the only particle of decency within their reach; exclusion of the unprepared will be their sole alternative. Excellence and equity will be perceived increasingly as incompatible objectives, and the populist/elitist choice will grow progressively more bitter and extreme. The humanists, to the degree that they refuse to cross these borders, will become less human.

I have sat through numerous commission meetings in which little more than inert or "objective" sadness was evinced by even the most sensitive men and women in regard to issues which appear, despite a stream of eloquent disclaimers, to belong in separate boxes, other agendas, "someone else's study" —anyone's—not ours. All of this transpires in the midst of the most brilliant commentary on the tragedy of "fragmentized imagination" and "the balkanized condition" of American humanities.

Whatever the irony, responsibility returns at last to those who do have power. Humanists must now be asked to exercise the natural authority which they command in service of a class of persons they have managed not to know. They must be asked to draw upon the recognitions which—almost alone today —they still possess. Most of all, they should be asked to act upon their knowledge of that incomplete equation between "humanism" and "humane" which history repeatedly reveals but language easily obscures.

Many of those who long to resurrect a sentimentalized conception of the education that was granted to the children of the upper class of England in the 1800s speak with a nostalgic yearning for the university, as it has been portrayed by Cardinal Newman, and of the school that was described and idealized by Matthew Arnold. It should not be easy (but it still seems possible) to forget that Rugby Chapel and the academic life of Dublin coexisted with extraordinary cruelty and exploitation—hunger, famine, child labor, human degradation which was heightened by the growth of industry and by imperial expansion. The work of Coleridge, Keats, and Shelley coexisted with the misery described by Blake. The work of Wordsworth came into existence at the same time as the growing desperation in the cotton mills. The work of Tennyson coexisted with the devastation of an urban underclass described by Dickens. Divided consciousness prohibits many scholars from a recognition of the fact that humanism can and does repeatedly appear to flourish in the presence of dehumanized behavior.

Shelley, Keats, and Wordsworth understood this contradiction very well. "Man's inhumanity to man" is not a phrase invented by Karl Marx or by a 1960s radical. It was written by a Scottish peasant, Robert Burns, who was a compassionate and stirring poet too. Yet those who are the specialists in British literature can easily romanticize their own experience of beauty, extracting the terror from Wordsworth, perceiving the "form and structure" of a work of Dickens as if it dwelt within a separate kingdom from the suffering that it portrayed.

Even the best scholars of romantic verse do not always recognize in Wordsworth's pastoral expression a prelude to much of the danger that would brood and smolder in the century ahead. Industrial growth would heighten the divisibility of our perceptions. Assembly-line production would complete the process. The separation of the worker from his work, of the dancer from her dance, would soon become both fact and metaphor. Marx in one way, Yeats in another, understood this.

The Rockefeller Commission, in its otherwise superb report of 1980, speaks of the need to repossess a history of culture; but the act of repossession of a piece of history cannot be contained within a sealed compartment. Distortion by encapsulation is no less denial than entire neglect. Humanists, deceived by cognates, can flatter humanism in disastrous ways.

If humanism is to be associated with the word "humane," it will not be because we say that it is so (or, in the most common verb form of the Rockefeller study: "should be") but because we have engaged in a life struggle to *assure* that it is so. But this, in turn, requires that those scholars who prescribe for us the means by which to repossess and to transmit the best of what has been achieved before us must also struggle to escape the cellular perceptions which have balkanized that "best" in ways that murder to conserve. Beauty and truth, if each has been encapsulated separately, do not automatically give reinforcement to the other; and neither, in an unjust world (our own, or Keats', or that of Tacitus or Cicero, or of Hans Frank) will automatically impel a human being to be more human.

Those, above all, whose special expertise includes the origin of words ought to recall that "classic," "classical," and "class" are cognates. The recent exhortations we have heard regarding a return to classical ideals, whether we describe them as Athenian or Jeffersonian, ought to be examined closely. Here—in three cognates—etymology and economics, ethics and aesthetics, excellence and ideology do coincide and offer us a hint of our own casual elisions. Do we mean "classical" or "class"? If the former has been subtly employed to mask the venal interests of the latter, even if this has been the case without our conscious or malign intent, it should lead us to rethink our use of words and then to search our hearts.

The ominously silent heart of London that Wordsworth sensed upon Westminster Bridge—the "spleen" of Baudelaire and the "ennui" of Mallarmé—

were prelude to a holocaust that would engulf the world of Kafka, Einstein, and Thomas Mann. The humanities will serve humanity only if their great protagonists can manage to escape their labels and unmake the walls that now demean them. Bitterly enough, it still seems possible that excellence may flourish in a moral void; it may be that certain kinds of brilliance, if protected and rewarded by extreme inequity, will profit in alarming ways by the exclusion of intrusive noise created by the suffering outside the academic walls. If this is the case, we have no right to claim for the humanities the humanizing patina that glows, perhaps deceptively, in almost every grant proposal and commission study.

If we do believe in what we say, then we should accept the obligations this entails. Neither rhetoric nor an affirming faith will do the job. If excellence is never democratic, access to "the excellent places" must be. Until this precondition is established by a solemn national commitment to achieve the universal literacy that many nations far less wealthy than our own have shown the will and the determination to pursue, all the talk about the need to reach "the best" will be class-serving and dishonest. Rugby Chapel cannot be rebuilt within the shadow of Illiterate America. If we learn anything at all from Matthew Arnold, this should be a good part of the lesson.

16

Beyond Utility:
Literacy Redefined

The brotherhood is not by the blood certainly,
but neither are men brothers by speech, by saying so:
Men are brothers by life lived and are hurt for it.

–Archibald MacLeish

I have argued that the scholars in the colleges of liberal arts ought to take an active role in helping to reverse the technological momentum that has overtaken literacy work.

If some of the better humanists can be persuaded to assist us in this cause, we will need to demonstrate with more precision some of the objectives we pursue and some of the specific areas to which a humanistic breadth might be applied. It will not suffice to protest at the mechanistic and utilitarian intentions of the government, the military, or the private sector. It is essential to spell out some realistic goals.

Fundamental humane literacy is an imposing phrase. The term is not my own; it was suggested by Charles Muscatine, a teacher at Berkeley and a member of the Rockefeller panel that examined the condition and the role of the humanities in the United States. It seems to me a good term, generous and open and suggestive of a willingness to cross established borders. It also implies a broad array of intellectual and ethical ideals. Some of these require definition.

•*Informed Irreverence*

It is not sufficient to awaken in newly literate people an unreflective inclination to say "No." Imprecise denunciation, while it may attract the temporary fealty of certain people, cannot persuade those who are trained by their experience to scrutinize our rhetoric and test it against careful information.

Angry people may speak loud; but if they cannot speak well and wisely, if they must draw upon an insubstantial pool of information or if they use illogically the information which they do possess, none of their victories will long prevail. One of the most common reasons for defeat among a newly organized community of previously passive people is the imprecision of their utterance, the lack of reasoned argument, the inability to arm themselves with contradictory but essential data. Literacy should mean a willingness to synthesize conflicting points of view. Competence to write should also mean the patient work of bringing together complex information and amalgamating separate facts in ways that often lead to deeper resolutions than the ones with which we started out.

Many of us hesitate to criticize the careless statements of poor people who have only recently developed literacy skills. We are afraid of being viewed as "cultural invaders." Our greatest concern is that we may be called "paternalistic." Insistence upon truth and reason is not cultural invasion. Flattery of error, on the other hand, assures perpetuation of dependent status.

•*Tolerating Indecision*

Learning to live with temporary indecision, when it is occasioned by conflicting data, is another part of literacy that is too frequently ignored. When people are ill, or poorly housed, or lacking funds for food, or overcome with terrible depression, a certain bravado in arriving at an energizing point of view is obviously essential; but, if that step is taken recklessly, it brings only ephemeral gains. Learning to live with temporary ambiguity is often discredited by people on the left as an elitist luxury—or even as a "trap" prepared by comfortable people. So long as hesitation is a prelude to decisive action, a preparedness to live for a short time with a realistic sense of contradictions is a precondition for enduring gains. This should be a part of literacy too.

•*Political Sophistication*

One consequence of a truncated sense of history is the inability to recognize (and to anticipate effectively) the probability that ethical rebellion will be met with powerful retaliation. The shock of the left, and of a number of black leaders, at the harsh right-wing retaliation of the 1980s might have been diminished—and the force of that retaliation might well have been neutralized by shrewd anticipation—if we had been able to hold in our minds at once the present struggles in which we were engaged and the obliterating steps that have been taken in the past by those who saw their selfish interests threatened by an era of reform. Emancipation and the false euphoria of Reconstruction were followed by the swift retaliation of "the dual system," reinforced, when necessary, by the terror of the Ku Klux Klan. Early struggles to end child labor and achieve a living wage through union organization found a crushing answer in the union-busting tactics and the hired armies of industrial tycoons. Efforts to resist the arms race and establish an enlightened posture toward decolonized societies in the aftermath of World War II led to the red-baiting that is now identified with Joe McCarthy but was given strong support by much of the mass media.

Recognition of the cycle of such patterns of retaliation in the past one hundred years may enable those who join in comparable struggles in the years ahead to guard themselves against an injudicious overconfidence and may push them to solidify their gains by concrete actions (the enactment of a law, for instance) which are difficult for future decades to erode and wash away. Pendulums do not swing entirely on their own. Pendulums are swung by those who have an interest in the course that they may take. Those who have been reinforced by history have wisdom to predict, and consequent power to control, the ways in which that pendulum may swing.

•Respect for History

The organized amnesia which is heightened by reliance on mass media allows political candidates to win adherents who might never be so easily won over if they could compare the promises of one year with the shrewd deceptions of four years before. Although the written press is easily susceptible to the revisionism of a cynical politician, at least a reader of the written word has access to the yellowed pages of newspapers from the year before. Candidates cannot revise their own historic record with the same impunity before a population that has power to retrieve the past.

Even beyond the limited range of any single candidate's career, voters can look into the devious acts (and, more important, into patterns of mendacity contrived to mask or to distort the nature of the actions) of a series of historic figures who have attempted in the past the same evasions that contemporary leaders may attempt today. When politicians of the 1980s speak of peace in Nicaragua and El Salvador and Guatemala, voters are seldom well enough informed to measure those words against the previous eighty years of military intervention and political manipulation which have rendered all three countries properly distrustful of American intentions. Very few voters in 1985 have vivid memories of U.S. military overthrow and/or destabilization of the governments of Panama, Brazil, Iran, Greece, Egypt, Chile, the Dominican Republic, or Vietnam.

Voters who had some awareness of Islamic history and culture might not have been so astonished, though they surely would have been disturbed, by the spectacular eruptions in Iran during the months that followed the demise of the corrupt Pahlevi monarchy. The leaders of our nation, if they had the cultural resources, might have known enough to lay the basis for an equalized relationship with those who, after their long period of exile, might have come to power with less virulent abhorrence and less justified distrust of our intentions.

Similar dilemmas are most certain to confront us, and some comparable disasters will most surely overtake us in all sections of the world during the years ahead. How little, for example, do we understand of India? How many tragedies, not only for ourselves but more important for the citizens of India itself, might be prevented by political sophistication which derives not from strategic calculation but from deep historic understanding and a cultural respect for the immense complexities of this subcontinent? Few of us have any knowledge of the history of India beyond a superficial imprint of the role of Nehru and a vague, unfocused memory of Gandhi's ethical apostasy before the viceroy. What of the history of Pakistan? How can we expect to be authentic friends, not merely military allies, to a populace which will in time see better reasons for political alliance than the meager loyalties which can be purchased by arms shipments?

The uses of history go further back than this. Those who understand the work of Machiavelli will be better armed to deal with the manipulative ways of those contemporary "princes," of whatever ideology, who now endanger international survival. Those who can apply an understanding of the decadence of the Roman Empire to the narcissism of our own society may have some opportunity to resist and possibly reverse the crumbling of ethics and collapse of rectitude which may otherwise turn out to be precursors of precipitous and irreversible decline.

The vision that allows a blinded people to regain its past need not threaten patriotic values. Long-term patriotism, at this moment of impaired perception, may in fact depend upon the capability to sacrifice the short-term goals of an archaic nationalism. Informed retrieval of historic truth is part of literacy too.

• *Violence*

Literacy cannot wholly counteract the visual and aural violence of the mass media; but it can reduce the impact of that violence by placing it in context and by introducing counteracting forces in the form of calm aesthetic satisfactions that transcend the hedonistic thrill of instantaneous and often mesmerizing exaltations. Violent elements in our society have unbridled power to identify excitement with sadistic spontaneity by the impact of the isolated TV moment on the sensibilities of passive human beings. Electronic noise that passes for pop music, very much like those exploitation films that use such music to enhance a venomous exhilaration, purveys the cruelty of punk despisal. Spray-painted swastikas, ubiquitous graffiti ("KKK"), and other inducements to despisal of the black, the foreigner, the Jew, are instant messages eliciting an almost automatic affirmation in the consciousness of a susceptible observer.

Printed exhortations can convey the same dehumanizing views; but print is limited in its manipulating power by the factor of delay. The written word (unless it is a single word, as in a televised inducement, that flashes in and out of consciousness with the rapidity of light) allows the reader time and opportunity to find at least a silent hour of reflection. All of us are vulnerable still to print pathology. The work of Goebbels and *The Protocols* of Henry Ford allow us evidence that even the delayed response to written words does not protect the reader from a cognitive contagion. Time at least is on the side of the reflective reader.

A people that cannot read at all is undefended. American Jews, more than some other groups, must recognize the danger that exists in an illiterate underclass of unemployed and underfed and powerless poor people who have easily been tempted to seek out the scapegoats most available in time and proximate in place. Hitler's success in winning mass support among not only those who felt excluded by their loss of marginal economic status but also those who were the poorest and most poorly educated strata of the German population stands as an enduring admonition. Any minority is endangered by the one slightly less favored in a situation of diminished access to the civilizing impact of the written word. Perhaps this is one reason why so many Jewish people have been sensitive and loyal allies in the task that I propose.

• Wise Anger

The wholeness of an individual's reflective powers helps to reduce the inclination to an often cruel and narrow focus that perceives emancipation for one group of persons only at the cost of others who are only slightly better off than they: a cancerous pluralism that has threatened to reduce America into the tattered shreds of ethnic rage and internecine competition. Anger is a logical response for an exploited people, but it is "wise anger" which can serve the needs of one group without injuring another. The energy of devastation is an easy catalyst for social change, but it guarantees a reciprocity of hatred which increases the reactionary swings of social policy I have described above.

• The Arrogance of Taste

If illiterate people are denied sufficient opportunity to gather needed information, those who are already literate are now bombarded with a great deal more than they can possibly digest. Even the most discriminating citizens are buried by mass mailings, periodicals, and books, wholly apart from the unceasing flood of "headline information" that pours forth from television. Sorting skills have come to be essential. All things are not equally deserving of attention. Some ideas are better than the rest. Even good ideas are frequently contained in banal packages that neutralize the virtues they possess.

A common perversion of egalitarian romanticism insists that "everyone's point of view" deserves an absolutely equal hearing and, by implication, that all viewpoints may be equally worthwhile. This is transparently untrue; but glamorized presentation of the insignificant renders the exercise of shrewd discrimination virtually impossible for some of us and painfully elusive for us all. The worst is often passionately intrusive, while the best is readily eclipsed by noisier and more persuasive methods of dissemination. In the face of an exploding information glut, even the most thoughtful citizens are easily transformed into abject, noncritical receptacles. If we are to repossess the sense of agency that is essential to a self-authenticated human being, we must resist the false democracy of an apparent "open market" of industriously weighted values and ideas. This means that literacy must comprehend the arrogance of taste: the willingness to state that some things count a lot, others much less, and some things not at all.

The same sense of discrimination that enables people to select the stuff that matters from a great deal that does not also applies to matters of aesthetic choice. If some ideas are better than others, and some points of view more worthy of attention than the rest, it is also true that certain forms of entertainment are ennobling to human beings while others tend to undermine our taste by repetition of familiar mediocrity. People who are better able to perceive mendacity in areas of public policy may, in time, experience a comparable capacity to search after that "better truth" which is artistic excellence. Citizens, once empowered to be critical consumers of both products and ideas, may not be so readily seduced to settle for the plastic artifacts which offer delectation at the cost of satisfaction. The love of beauty is a part of literacy too.

•Global Literacy

Teachers of high school students often are appalled to recognize the inability of boys and girls to situate themselves within the longitude and latitude of demographic truth. Even the most literate of U.S. citizens have only the most casual idea of geographic reference points. I have taught college students, first at Yale, later at Trinity, who could not determine the correct location of Sri Lanka, Libya, Zimbabwe, Syria, Iraq, Iran, Bulgaria, Haiti, Bolivia, Brazil, or Costa Rica. More disturbing, they had no idea how many people (or what sort of people) live in these or perhaps a hundred other countries. With the sole exceptions of the U.S., Canada, Japan, and Western Europe—and perhaps a handful of our other military allies—we learn of the location, the political disposition, and the size of population of another country only in the aftermath of natural disaster, social revolution, or political upheaval that appears to justify the presence of American armed forces. Too frequently, Americans discover the location of a Third World country only in the wake of Soviet or U.S. intervention. (Where is it? How many people live there? Why is it they don't like us?) This is, to say the least, a costly way to learn geography.

Perhaps if our imaginations and our powers of compassion were allowed to voyage more capaciously, and at an earlier age, we would discover better emissaries for our interests than armed soldiers. Geographical myopia, much like our national aversion to the acquisition of effective foreign language skills, represents another symptom of domestic arrogance: a nationalistic self-assurance which the sweeping tides of geopolitical upheaval and transformed realities throughout the world have thus far failed to stir from an imperial sedation.

It is a great deal easier to disregard the silent violence of sickness, malnutrition, and starvation in a nation whose location we can scarcely visualize and in a population whose reality we can too easily dismiss. It is also easier to take recourse to acts of literal violence in dealing with a people that cannot make visceral demands upon our conscience. For many Americans, a large part of the world makes no greater claim, in terms of moral or emotional attachment, than a vast unpeopled desert. Even where we know that it is peopled, we cannot imagine who might live there, what they might be like, or how they might resemble people that we know and love. Hence, the strange dispassion which allowed us to regard large stretches of the South Pacific, for example, as a reasonable test site for "strategically essential" nuclear explosions and which enabled us to use in Southeast Asia chemical defoliants which we would have found it unendurable to use in Canada or Western Europe. (News reporting frequently reflects this inability to allocate reality to nonwhite and non-Western human beings: "One hundred sixty people died today in the explosion of a jet on takeoff from Djakarta. Two passengers were North American, and one was British . . .") Factual information in itself cannot assure a sensitive response to the travail of other human beings; but a total lack of information surely helps anaesthetize a nation to the lives of those beyond its borders. A world reduced by technological transformation to the size of a small room cannot survive the mortal consequences of this capability for ethical eclipse. Dehumanized behavior on a scale so wide within a world so tightly wired cannot fail to cast its darkness on our own land too.

•Decoding Doublespeak

John Kenneth Galbraith has described the power of commercial advertising to create the wants that people then set out to satisfy by purchase of goods for which they have no need: goods which frequently are indistinguishable in worth from any of a dozen other versions of the same thing packaged differently and marketed with different labels. "Organized public bamboozlement" was the term that Galbraith used to designate the orchestrated efforts to control a population in this way. The same description might be used to indicate the power of political doublespeak. It is in defense of democracy against this everpresent danger that a literacy based upon informed irreverence is most desperately needed.

All of the points discussed above converge at length upon a single theme: A nation that is drowning in the presence of false language cannot differentiate between decision and mechanical response. A population subjugated in this manner is a danger to itself and to that portion of the world which it commercially and militarily controls.

It is easy enough to recognize such dangers in totalitarian societies; yet dangers like these are no less real, and they may be a good deal harder to perceive, in a society which has been led to think that its desires are free. Orwell's warning was interpreted by the American mass media as an indictment of the Soviet system; this was in part the case but, in some of the final words he spoke before his early death, Orwell attempted to remind his readers that he was troubled also by the possible evolution of "the total state" in the U.S. and Britain. He noted the disturbing term "hundred percent Americanism" which certain politicians in this nation had begun to use, and he observed that 100 percent "is as totalitarian as anyone could wish." We might do well to keep in mind this part of Orwell's message too.

Nuclear power and recurrent foreign interventions have produced a full vocabulary of manipulative terms which would deserve a place in any glossary of doublespeak. In Vietnam, people were not "killed" but "wasted." Civilian bombing was described as causing "profound psychological impression"—a less disturbing term than "human slaughter." Friendly dictatorships are still called "governments." Those which threaten U.S. interests are "regimes." (A *Newsweek* bureau chief recently described the style guidelines used by Latin American correspondents for that magazine as "a glossary straight out of Orwell.") Invasions, if initiated by the U.S., are "incursions." Jungle fighters, if they are American, are "advisers." When they kill, it is in "self-defense." When they are killed, they have been "murdered." Governments are certified for "human rights" to the degree that U.S. corporations are allowed the right to operate without domestic opposition. What once was a department of war is now one of "defense." Espionage is called "intelligence." Other nations spy on one another; Americans simply gather information.

"Perhaps," one glib observer told me, "the illiterate adult is better off in one respect than those who are exposed to written words. Fraudulent words cannot bamboozle a nonreader." It is a gloomy argument at best. Doublespeak, purveyed through television news and cinema, invades the mind of every citizen. The passive role of television viewers simply heightens its effect. Democracy depends upon a universal capability for critical response to print manipulation.

Critical literacy, as we have seen, does pose some dangers to the special interests of some sectors of the population. It threatens jingoistic interests, textbook publishers that help to propagate such interests, teachers who have been indoctrinated to employ such textbooks. It threatens to reduce the powerless pool of unskilled candidates for military service. To some degree it also threatens the unaltered status of the two political parties which so easily trade off their four-year periods of power and so comfortably continue policies initiated by their predecessors. It raises at length the fascinating threat that we might finally insist upon the evolution of two parties that can differentiate themselves from one another with at least the clarity that separates political parties in democracies like Britain, Germany, and France. The ultimate threat is one that patriotic citizens should welcome. It is the danger that we might at last create the pluralistic freedom that we advertise and might become the democratic and compassionate society which we would like to hold up as a model to those newly independent nations which will otherwise be drawn into the orbit of the literal "total state" that Orwell has envisoned.

All of this goes a great deal further than the issues of survival which were raised in the first chapters of this book. We are speaking now of something more than the initial struggle to incorporate adult nonreaders into the accepted mainstream of noncritical America. We are speaking of a different and a better kind of literacy than that which dominates discussion and congeals imagination. We should begin with a revised vocabulary to define our goals and calibrate our gains. "Functional literacy" is, as scholars at the Texas APL have properly observed, a two-dimensional term. Perhaps it is time at last to find the third dimension.

17

Borders

The number two is a very dangerous number . . . Attempts to divide anything into two ought to be regarded with much suspicion . . . This polarization is sheer loss to us all.

–C. P. Snow

There used to be a word called competence. It was a singular noun and spoke to a singular vision of humanity. Today the word has been adulterated (school officials speak of something tortured known as "competency") and pluralized ("competencies"). "Children are expected to demonstrate mastery of the following ten (twelve, fifteen) competencies." In elementary school there may be only a few dozen. By secondary school there will be several hundred. By graduate levels in the universities there will be several thousand. Adult Basic Education, in one program that I visited in Boston, lists exactly sixty-eight "required competencies" for adult literacy instruction. The concept of fundamental humane competence—continuous, interactive, and holistic—has been pluralized.

We see this at every level from the fourth grade of the elementary school to college classrooms and beyond. Even the fashion of interdisciplinary studies cannot really deal with the dilemma. The combined discipline itself becomes a new container. Psychology may have one box. Linguistics has a second. Psycholinguistics now receives a third. It may prove to be the most impenetrable of all three.

"What a piece of work is a man," said Hamlet, "how noble in reason, how infinite in faculties, in form and moving how express and admirable, in action

how like an angel, in apprehension how like a god: the beauty of the world
. . ."

But that was before the Age of Fragmentation. It was also before the age of
university subdivisions, the infestation of our colleges by the special interests of
the graduate departments. It was also before the age of requisite and numbered
competencies and pluralized reality. It is Polonius, alas, who wins the day.

Polonius, indeed, would probably feel at home in modern public schools
and universities. In praise of "the best actors in the world," he tried to demonstrate the multitude of possible areas—within the world of drama—into which
they might apply their skills: "tragedy, comedy, history, pastoral, pastoral-comi-
cal, historical-pastoral, tragical-historical, tragical-comical-historical-pastoral;
scene indivisible, or poem unlimited." Hamlet's approach was less complex.
"Come," he said, "a passionate speech." Hamlet would not do well in modern
universities. Polonius—tragical-comical himself—would have a splendid time.
He would also be a marvelous attraction for a graduate school of almost anything. Departmental localism could achieve dimensions that would offer jobs for
every splintered soul: psychological-linguistical, philosophical-mathematical,
mathematical-illogical, pathological-divisible, much of it comical, none of it pastoral, all of it tragical. Nobody, so divided, could ever be asked to come up with
something so simple, or essential, as a passionate speech.

The use of categories, when those categories serve a useful function, is not
questioned. Language itself must, by its nature, be exclusionary. Chapters of
books, sections within chapters, sentences in sections, demonstrate our absolute
reliance upon arbitrary lines, distinctions, allocations. It is, indeed, almost impossible to think of any complicated task that does not call for rational divisions,
sequences, and borders. The privacy, moreover, which is temporarily afforded to
a specialist of any kind—a carpenter, a scientist, an artist—necessarily requires
that we close off certain options and shut down some of the circuits of communication (some of us cut off our telephones while we are working) if we hope to
realize anything of value or distinction.

"Distinction" itself is a suggestive word. We cannot distinguish ourselves in
any sense if we are not granted an exemption from eternal commerce, in order
to immerse ourselves in secretive obsessions of creative worth. This, however, is
a different thing from the construction of protective walls that separate not
temporary and essential areas of singular pursuit but interlinked and overlapping
kingdoms of societal concern. The line may be drawn between a category (useful, necessary) and a cubicle (impenetrable, difficult to open, hard to see beyond). We may also see a difference between temporary demarcations that have
been mandated by convenience, and are so conceded, and a permanent division
which is given the appearance of a natural phenomenon and which exists not to
enhance creative growth but to defend against the justified concern of others:
especially of those who may be victimized by our reclusive undertakings.

It is the hardened numbers that attach to these divisions which appear most frightening: another instance of the urgency with which the pedagogic world attempts to copy science by rendering even the ambiguous empirical. Priorities have always existed, and of course they are essential. It took the present decade to transform priorities into a verb: We now "prioritize." There is a story by the novelist James Purdy; its title bears a sensible request: "Don't Call Me by My Right Name." But everything in education nowadays must be called by "a right name" (or, if there is no right name, by a wrong name) and everything must be assigned its number.

The madness here is that it does not matter *what* we organize, *what* we number, *what* we subdivide. The subject matter may be hunger among children, problems of suburban tooth care, the Seven Major Products of Bulgaria, the Fourteen Major Facts about the War of 1812. The subject matter ceases to be of issue anymore. It isn't the stuff that we wall in—it is the building of the demarcation which becomes our occupation and obsession. Good fences, whether in grade school, universities, or Central Europe, do not make good neighbors. They have exactly the reverse effect. They make distrustful neighbors, hated occupants of segregated units of discrete realities. Classroom periods divide the day. Departmental rivalries divide the universities. Ethnic competition shreds the fabric of the nation. Nationalistic isolation tears apart the fabric of humanity. Pluralized nouns prioritize us all. We are a part of all mankind, according to John Donne, but the death of no man can diminish any other if they live in separate cells surrounded by impenetrable walls. Addiction to enumerated fragmentation is not an American dilemma but an international disaster. The bell tolls for more interested parties than the silent and illiterate adults of our society.

I wish that we could press home this idea to everyone who works in adult education and to every teacher in our public schools. We fragmentize the day, prioritize the school, divide the indivisible. It is not surprising that the center will not hold. "In the prison of his days," wrote Auden, "teach the free man how to praise." But the demarcated conscience is not free and cannot praise. This is the struggle that we must confront when we are faced with bleak and rigid concepts such as "functionally efficient literacy."

If there is a single word we would do well to wipe away from the vocabulary of a literate society, it is the invidious modifier "functional." It is a bad word, chosen by technicians but unfortunately accepted without protest by the humanistic scholar and the pedagogic world alike. Machines function. People either perish or prevail. We need to find more generous delineations of our goals.

When this designation ("functional") was used in 1973 by scholars at the Texas APL, there was an important purpose in its use. The term enabled us to get beyond the old criteria of grade-completion levels and to speak instead of what it takes to manage, to survive, within a print society. Recognition of utilitarian necessity in 1973 must not blind us to the need to go beyond the limitations of this term in 1985. The competence to function at the lowest levels of mechanical performance now must be transcended by a humanistic vision of the uses to which literate men and women will address their new-found skills. A fundamental humane literacy is one which does not demarcate a skill from its potential application, a scientific from a humanistic purpose, a selfish ambition from its frequently destructive consequences. Words that are learned not to describe an ethical arena we intend to enter but rather to delineate a moral context from which we have forever taken exile—words like these deny the decency inherent in us all.

All of the above leads to a final point.

No single goal described within this book is so important as the literate capacity for whole perspectives and for informed denunciation in the face of the increasing terror of a global war. All the issues of survival that we have discussed above must be subordinated to this ultimate imperative.

One of the most vivid instances of the divided consciousness that now afflicts us is the willingness of many literacy specialists, school administrators, and the blue-ribbon commissions to isolate the smallest and most narrow definition of a "functional" adult and to exalt that definition to the cruel apotheosis of a national ideal. Only the most helplessly divided mind could foster a discussion which incorporates the needs of industry and the requirements of military competition but does not once make reference to the most alarming and essential moral question of our times.

Literacy, if it is to be responsive to the dangers of the world in which we live, cannot restrict its definition of survival to the needs of one particular community, no matter how severe the suffering which that community endures. There is also a societal and global obligation. Nothing else that we achieve is worth the labor of its undertaking if we are not able to protect our civilization against nuclear destruction. Reverence for life remains the single indispensable ingredient of any local, national, or worldwide mobilization to enhance the fundamental competence of adult human beings.

Educators often speak of something rather mean in spirit and delimited in stature known as "coping skills." What is the worth of "coping" with our wife or husband, school, police, or grocer, doctor, landlord, or attorney, if we cannot cope with man's apparent acquiescence in the face of instruments of all-encompassing destruction? Fighting for food stamps is a necessary piece of "functional" effectiveness in Indiana, Maine, or Massachusetts; but what is the profit to a man in Indiana, a woman in Maine, a child in Massachusetts, if the world is simultaneously reduced to a defoliated and carcinogenic waste?

Sanity insists that certain things do matter infinitely more than others. The false equality of needs described above can easily eclipse our recognition of the only need without which every other will be rendered meaningless. It is with this perspective that we must approach the ideology of "neutral skills." Nothing is neutral. Competence addressed without concern for its potentially destructive possibilities is hardly preferable to a benign ineptitude. Some of the brightest products of such excellent academies as Exeter and Groton, Yale and Harvard, Berkeley and Ann Arbor allowed themselves to be the willing acolytes of murderous technicians in Vietnam, Laos, and Cambodia, and—only a few years later on—to join in the concerted undermining of democracy that grew explicit during Watergate. Men as highly literate as McNamara, Bundy, Alan Dulles, Kissinger, John Dean allowed themselves to exercise an amputated competence divorced from moral hesitations and from humanistic qualms. What is the worth of learning how to read and write, to calculate and to compute, if all that we shall have the chance to read are the obituaries of our neighbors and all that we shall ever have occasion to compute are the precise statistics of our final decimation? Human survival is the final indispensable objective of all efforts to achieve a universal humane competence in 1985.

During the years in which I have been working on this book, I have visited in dozens of public and nonpublic schools, worked in adult literacy programs, and taught for part of one year at South Boston High. Some of the most revelatory conversations I have had were not, however, with the younger pupils but with students at some of the most distinguished medical schools and law schools in the nation.

A medical student in the Boston area shared with me the following exchange. She had asked her teacher in an obstetrics class a question about the competing claims of the unborn and of the pregnant mother: a question which is on the minds of many young physicians nowadays. The professor told her that he was "not qualified" to speak about that issue. He told her she might do well to bring it up in "Medical Ethics"—an elective course that she could take the next semester. Medical ethics, however, was not offered in the medical school. It was taught by a professor of religion in the divinity school. She said to me: "There's some humor here, but there is pathos too. What do we do in later years when we are facing questions of this kind? Do we run out and call the priest or rabbi? What if the priest is occupied in prayer? What if the minister is on vacation?"

The same dilemma is addressed, in far more serious terms, when we consider military issues. J. Robert Oppenheimer reacted with irritation when, in 1961, he was asked about his role in the Manhattan Project. "I carry no weight on my conscience," he replied. He added that "the use made of these [scientific] changes is the problem of the government, not of scientists." Sixteen years before, in 1945, he had described the tight compartments that surrounded his reflections as he brought the nuclear weapon into being: "For the last four years

I have had only classified thoughts." At Los Alamos itself, after the bombs were dropped, he lectured to his fellow scientists in these words: "If you are a scientist you cannot stop such a thing . . . You believe that it is good to find out how the world works . . . good to find out what the realities are . . . good to turn over to mankind at large the greatest possible power [so that it may] deal with it according to its lights and values." According to much of the evidence we have, Oppenheimer was a sensitive and introspective man. He justified his research in the early years by pointing to the likelihood that Germany might build the weapon first. By 1943 he knew that German efforts to achieve this goal had failed. By August 1945, of course, the Germans were defeated. He was isolated then from outside condemnation, isolated within from self-condemnation, and isolated by the cubicles of time from acting in 1945 in different terms from those which he believed to justify his work in 1941: a set of terms which had already been eclipsed by subsequent events. It is correct that he was later persecuted greatly and would state, with tragic honesty after the fact, "The physicists have known sin . . ." But, at the time when border-crossing mattered most, he seems to have been surgically divorced from his most sober reservations.

In effect, what he was saying might be stated in these terms: "I am a physicist. I have no special expertise in ethics." Scholars of ethics and divinity, however, when they ask about the moral implications of this work, are told that *they* do not have "special expertise in physics."

Society cannot survive this fragmentized activity. Exclusionary practices, nourished by lifelong intellectual particularities of focus, reinforced by an intimidating jargon, lead the specialists to doubt their own good sense, while they also lead them to an underestimation of the wisdom or the basic human rights of the nonspecialist. At the same time, they force the rest of us to leave too many questions that affect our own survival to the designated expert. Whether that expert is a physicist, an obstetrician, or a biochemist, we feel unauthorized to enter the debate.

Oppenheimer seems to have absolved himself for lack of special expertise in ethics. English professors and philosophy instructors have no special expertise in physics. What, then, of illiterate adults who have been persuaded that they have no expertise in *either* area of knowledge? Scientists exclude the theologians. Humanists defer to biochemists. But one third of all American adults must patiently defer to both. The "two cultures" that were cleverly described by C. P. Snow are dangerously divorced from common commerce with each other. But the silent culture of one third of our society has been divorced from the discussion altogether.

The process begins when we are very young. We teach too many subjects to young children. We give too little time to each, and we accept too many boundaries and distinctions that can have no consequence except to render every isolated unit far less interesting while they also lay the groundwork for that fragmentized imagination which will later balkanize our consciousness, divide our world, and polarize our nation.

Many business leaders, recognizing that the high schools have neglected to provide sufficient foreign language preparation, have expressed alarm that this might harm their corporate interests. We may not be able to "negotiate" in foreign lands. Since we are a business-minded nation, this is an inevitable concern. But other varieties of negotiation are no less important. Cultural isolation may be damaging to the business sector of one nation. Jingoistic insularity is damaging to every sector of all nations. The stakes of the discussion, I have argued in this book, ought to be raised a bit beyond the entrepreneurial considerations.

Humanity has more at stake in this than business interests. If we could speak less of "humanities," more of our singular humanity, we might approach the foreign language failures of our schools—and the domestic literacy failure of our nation—with less provincialism and, at last, with more success.

In speaking of the balkanized condition of our nation, it is easier to see the questions than to know the answers. "Things fall apart. The center cannot hold." We can agree on that. What we find hard (and what appears, to some, to be immodest) is to tell ourselves and one another: why. We might take the risk of shedding some of our protective humblehood in order to suggest one possible answer.

Wholly apart from the demands for specialized and highly focused erudition created by the vast proliferation of new knowledge—"an information explosion" is the current term for this phenomenon—there may be another factor working at a deeper and less conscious level. It seems to me that there were times—even in the presence of extreme societal divisions—when unity and wholeness were much easier to find because there was a center, or there seemed to be a center, that society agreed on. For the Hebrews: Jehovah. For a later age: the Christian deity. For the Renaissance: a reverential longing to recapture classical antiquity. For subsequent centuries: a fealty to king and queen. For later days: the pride in nation-states. This is oversimplified perhaps, and certainly a bit less than empirical. But we might suggest that one deep cause, perhaps the deepest cause, of fragmentized experience within the present age is not the explosion of knowledge but the explosion of a bomb which told us in one graphic instant that all previous centers, all accepted forms of intellectual cohesion, were archaic; and that, above all else, it was the absolute unquestioned loyalty to nation-states which had gone by the board. The last safe center had been vaporized as surely as the brick and bones of Hiroshima. Although the rhetoric of national and patriotic interests would persist, and would even grow at times more strident, there must have been many who perceived that this was rhetoric which did not correspond to a transformed reality. The question that faces civilized society today is one that asks where we may look to find another organizing center.

At the risk of speaking in apocalyptic terms, and of profaning the mechanical decorum that has placed its faith in functional divisions, I would venture that the missing center is not going to emerge out of curriculum reform nor out of any national or worldwide literacy struggle of the kind I have proposed. If a unifying principle—a center—is to be surmised at all, it may be that it will find its only genesis in something like an absolute refusal to take human life and, as a corollary, in a forfeiture of every loyalty that limits us to less than universal interests.

If we can at last outgrow our kings and queens, gods, devils, academic rivalries, and national competitive dementias, there may come a time for the crossing of borders. "We should be men first," in Thoreau's words, "and subjects afterward." Auden said it in less strident words: "We must love one another or die."

A literate society is only as competent to face the dangers of the future as our definition of that adjective allows. Skills divorced from earnest applications, efficacy divorced from ethics, competence divided from compassion, no longer define a literate adult in an endangered decade. They represent instead the definition of a garrulous efficiency in service of a self-destructive goal of global domination. In this respect, few people in our nation (or in any other that I know) are truly literate. When we speak of reinventing an ideal of universal and holistic competence in service of the irreducible demands of international survival, we are also speaking of the reinvention of ourselves. Literacy, in an ennobled definition, ought to function as a border pass, a transit visa between separate kingdoms of a universe that contemplates, each day, the growing likelihood of absolute extinction. A literate world would shred its passports and, in time, its transit visas too. This would not happen as the consequence of any single national campaign to break the walls of inarticulate despair that isolate illiterate adults from the surrounding population; but literacy, defined in a new key, might be one eloquent beginning.

Whether we can project this vision to the citizens of another nation like the Soviet Union matters not at all. We do what we can within the land in which we live: a land in which we now and then do exercise some power. The same Western society which gave a new and fearful meaning to a previously innocuous term, "fission," also was obliged to coin a difficult new word by which to designate our fragmentized reality. That word was schizophrenia. Perhaps, like Daedalus, we might at last be bold enough to take the risk of burning in the fire of our finest aspirations, to fly above borders, to soar above the walls of our credentialized departments, our pluralized efficiencies, and our prioritized delimitations. Like Daedalus too, we might discover that we have no choice but to begin the search at home: in Joyce's words, within the smithy of the soul—there to forge an uncreated conscience for our age.

18

Inscriptions

And Moses rose up early in the morning, and went up unto mount Sinai, as the Lord had commanded him, and took in his hand the two tablets of stone.

–Exodus 34:4

Will anything be done?

History records too well the minor clamors and the major protestations that have led in decades past to nothing more than legislative hearings, academic institutes, and documentary specials on TV. Is there reason to believe something will be different this time than in years gone by?

We might borrow here from military jargon. We might ask the question that the Pentagon holds dear: What is the "worst-case outcome" that can be expected? What is the "best-case outcome" that a cautious optimist can plausibly expect?

Worst case: Nothing will happen.

Doubleday will sell some books. I will be invited to present some lectures and some people will write better books and give some better lectures. There will be more studies and commissions. Funds will be expended to explore the situation from a number of new angles. The government will issue RFPs. "Requests For Proposals" will elicit grant requests from universities and from consulting firms. B. Dalton will continue its good efforts but will find itself increasingly alone. Libraries will persist in their commitment but will find no funding equal to the recognized dimensions of the need. Some of the grass-roots groups will fold for lack of funds. Others will keep on but lack resources to expand. LVA and Laubach will sustain their efforts at the present levels. They will do successful work with those who need their help the least. The federal government may keep its funding at the present levels, reduce it slightly, or at best may double present allocations for the Adult Basic Education programs.

From time to time, the press will run some stories indicating isolated instances of progress. Tiring of stories about "problems," reporters will look harder for examples of success. Recognizing that they cannot run again the same disturbing "special issues" on Illiterate America they ran in 1982 or 1984, journals such as *Newsweek, Time,* or *U.S. News & World Report* will extrapolate from isolated cases just enough encouragement to justify a special issue on "The Turn-Around," "The Hopeful Signs," "Excellence in the High Schools Is Restored . . ." Citizens will accept this for reality.

The President (some president: it needn't matter which) will issue the report of a new blue-ribbon commission. The nation, we will read in full-page extracts in the New York *Times*, "has turned the corner" and "is no longer at risk." Scholars who read this will be reassured. Illiterates who cannot read but hear about this on TV will be left to think that many of their fellow victims have been able to transcend those obstacles that still appear implacable to them and that many others have been served effectively by programs which do not exist in their communities.

Black leaders will refrain from hammering at the issue out of an uneasiness at speaking about intergenerational oppression. Liberals will not wish to say what blacks have chosen to exclude from their agenda. There will be, for now, no dangerous upheavals. A modest economic upswing may relieve the worries of the corporations. Ingenious corporations may devise more skillful ways to give employment to nonreaders. The press will compliment the grocery and fast-food chains for their decision to provide cash registers designed with photographs instead of numbers as a means of giving work to the uneducated poor. Other businesses will look for ways to obviate the need for human labor altogether by the use of robots and machines for lower-level functions. For a certain period of time, this may appear to be successful.

Now and again, another conference will be held. Many of us will get together in the Hyatt Regency hotels. We will hold our stomachs as the glittering glass elevators fall through unsupported space to bring us to the open bars of scholarly receptions and will hold our stomachs once again as we attend to febrile recapitulations of the things we heard or said ten years before. Some of us will earn consulting fees. The Hyatt Regency hotels will make a lot of money. Illiteracy figures, we will learn, have shown "a slight decline." The 2 to 4 percent who have been reached and served in 1985 will rise to 5 or 6 percent—

"depending on our definition of the terms." These incremental gains will not be equal to the numbers of illiterate adults emerging from the public schools.

American society will not collapse. Academic contestation will intensify but will be managed for a time by more sophisticated methods of exclusion. The courts and prisons will continue to be overcrowded. Chaos in commercial inter-actions will grow greater. Tax expenses to support the unemployed and unem-ployable will grow, but those who pay the taxes will not recognize the reasons for these costs and will persist in thinking that the real expense derives from the dependence fostered by excessive generosity to those who do not have the will to better their own lot. Some of those who cannot read or write will be given automated jobs which they will fill as automated human beings.

Class and ethnic fragmentation will increase but, at least for one more generation, there will be enough prosperity to pacify the losers and to fend off any likelihood of a societal demise. Life will go on. Democracy will continue to be imcomplete, imperfect; but there will be voices to remind us that democracy is never perfect and "can always stand improvement" of "an incremental sort."

Authors will grow weary finally of a losing struggle. We will move on to deal with other issues: health care perhaps, or the dilemmas of the legal system. Trained to futility by now, we will be ready to engage in further enterprises of a futile nature. If we persist in sticking to this issue, we will be accused of being repetitious; at last we will accuse ourselves of the same tedious behavior. We will either quit, grow bureaucratic, or grow tiresome.

There will be a lot more accidents and several "inexplicable" disasters. Soil and crops will be contaminated. Dangerous wastes will be deposited by error in the rivers and the dump sites that endanger residential neighborhoods. More airplane tragedies will make the headlines. We will be told that there is "no real way to ascertain the cause."

We will see our leaders drawn into a sequence of blood-letting wars in Africa, the Middle East, and Latin nations. Citizens—unable to surmise the reasons for antagonistic feelings among Third World nations, unable to identify with those who live south of the Rio Grande or east of Algeciras, devoid of knowledge of Islamic, African, and Oriental culture, history, demography, or economic need—will passively submit to government inducements to send first their money, then their sons, and then their self-respect to perish in a series of debilitating wars. We will lose some of those wars. Even where we seem to win, we will not recognize our victories as opportunities for equalized relationships which can assure more than a fragile peace to be pursued by subsequent upheav-als which we will have fewer moral, economic, or political resources to resolve.

America will grow into a tougher, taller, more tormented fortress. We will be more lonely.

At some point, not in our own but in our children's or grandchildren's lives, there will cease to be sufficient funds to underwrite the growing millions of illiterate adults in life conditions even of the most denatured kind. Housing subsidies, food supplements, and health care will decline to levels that no longer can alleviate the pain. Bottom-level jobs that might be filled by those who cannot read will be increasingly exported to those Third World nations where illiterate and hungry people will agree to work all day for what would otherwise be paid per hour in the U.S.A. Illiterate Americans will swell the welfare rolls and, when the welfare funds run out, will fill the streets with an explosive clamor which will not require press release or picket sign to win attention. The disenfranchised, ceasing to be docile, will acquire methods of denunciation learned from organizers or adapted from the precedents of Third World nations. Peter may be forced to settle for a lifetime of french fries, hamburgers, and humiliation. His children and their children may not be so easily subdued. Masking skills in time will yield to a determined passion to remove those masks and to compel us to look hard into the face of every Caliban we have created and ignored. Violent disorders will become endemic. They will be met with measures that no longer seek to pacify but only to contain. America will cease to be a flawed democracy. What we will become instead cannot be named.

That, I suspect, may be a modest version of the worst.

What is the best?

I do not believe $10 billion will be allocated this year or for several years: neither by a Democratic nor Republican administration. If it should be requested, I do not believe that Congress will deliver this much money until greater public pressure has evolved.

I do not believe that publishers will make available 400 million new hardcover books to be distributed through 10 or 20,000—or 100,000—one-way libraries to poor, illiterate, or semiliterate adults in our society.

I do not believe that the Department of Defense will find it sensible to change its "missions" and "objectives" in pursuit of mechanistic skills within the bottom ranks of those who serve in our armed forces.

I do believe the following to be a realistic hope:

Grass-roots groups may build enough momentum to attract the loyalties, and then the partisan support, of student organizers and some of the more enlightened corporations. Black and Hispanic leaders will recognize the limited success to be achieved by registration of potential voters. They will see the need to move beyond a growth in numbers to a growth in leverage based on well-informed decision-making powers. By this means they may empower millions of new voters to evolve into a force sufficient to dislodge political inertia.

Progressive politicians will at length perceive their own self-interest in a voting force which is not simply larger but enhanced in its potential for judicious and discerning use of its expanded strength. A growing mobilization will compel the media to pay attention. The press will cease to speak about a problem and instead will be compelled to speak about a movement. (A "movement" is a better news event than an "injustice.") Out of these news events, the bitter truths about the real injustice will at last emerge. Liberal and moderate Americans will raise their voices to protest realities which will, by this point, be perceived as an intolerable condition of existence. The children of conservatives will bring their indignation to the dinner table. Some of their parents will be troubled; others will be scared. Many will recognize at last that they cannot escape the dangers of a nation so emphatically divided. Some will be prepared to sacrifice a short-term class advantage to the mandate for a long-term restoration of the national well-being.

Politicians will at length be forced to give an answer to the rising pressures of a broad-based struggle which includes some of their own constituents. Some may respond out of an ethical concern; others will respond out of the wish to stay in office.

Faced with the fear of more profound disorders, Washington may finally launch an all-out national campaign. Several billion dollars may at last become available. Some will go to programs that exist already. More will go to programs that emerge under the leadership of representatives of the illiterates themselves.

Organizations such as LVA and Laubach, wishing to win their share of federal funds, will form effective partnerships with the grass-roots communities. The same may be the case with Adult Basic Education. Some of these groups may soon evolve an ethos of non-neutral education, spurred by their immersion in the needs of those they seldom reach today, and may thereby grow into a single force that understands its pedagogic role as incompatible with a top-down approach or with a replication of the tone and setting of the public schools.

A powerful coalition of committed advocates will, in this way, emerge out of those modest coalitions that exist today. A network of remorseless passions will replace the network of initial hopes. Advocacy will not be seen as inconsistent with well-organized instruction.

Universities and high schools will establish literacy action as an option or prerequisite for certain students. Student groups will meanwhile have evolved politicized agendas built around the local programs in the cities closest to their schools. College activists from poor communities will bring their wealthy classmates into a political arena that will give the issue added visceral appeal. They will function as a catalytic link between the universities and the illiterates themselves. Hundreds of thousands of retired persons will become involved in some of the same programs. Retirement colonies may lose some of their clientele.

Illiterate men and women, organized by leaders—by "foot-walkers"—will remain within the forefront of the struggle and will forge the means by which to shape, if not to govern, every group that may aspire to serve them. Literacy work cannot exist without illiterates. Once the clientele perceives itself as indispensable to its potential allies, there will be a lever of wise anger to be exercised in making certain that the struggle is directed from the bottom up.

None of this can be achieved without a willingness to cross some unfamiliar borders. The inclination, which so many of us feel, to demonize those who seem to be our friends but whom we regard as condescending or uncertain allies, is a major reason for the inner decimation of a multitude of moral undertakings in this nation. I often feel that we are rougher with our friends, even potential and imperfect friends, than we would ever be with those (our outright enemies) whom we cannot approach or castigate at all. This is a common problem. People in pain strike first at those whom they can reach. Too often, the only ones that we can reach are those who have attempted to befriend us.

Openness and gentleness are never easy qualities to come by. They are all the harder to achieve when we are each afflicted by our private feelings of frustration. It is easier to speak about the virtues of "wise anger" than to be both wise and angry—and forgiving—in our work.

I have voiced distrust of certain aspects of archaic avarice. Much of that distrust is well-deserved. On the other hand, there would be suicidal blindness in an adamant refusal to accept the loyalties of those who have come forward in good faith. The promotional drive inaugurated by the libraries, B. Dalton, and some others is a good beginning. The Business Coalition for Effective Literacy, formed in 1984, includes some powerful and thoughtful members of the private sector, as well as the progressive educator Harold Howe. They could be transformed into effective allies. The Book Industry Study group, which represents some of the largest publishers in the United States, has spoken of the need for strategies that can arrest "further erosion" in the numbers of book readers and regain those who have been excluded or dropped out. We should accept these statements in good faith and should be certain to insist that they are soon translated into cash donations. Newspapers are potential allies too. Whatever their financial difficulties, they should be persuaded to provide us with that interim support which is essential in an early organizing stage. If we can approach them in a noncombative manner, many will recognize their own self-interest in expanded circulation. Others may act out of respect for human beings.

This is the best-case outcome I believe we can expect for now:

I believe the numbers of illiterate adults in the United States can be reduced by more than half within the next ten years. I believe that over 30 million newly literate adults will constitute a permanent force to keep alive a program which has given them a first taste of the meaning of deliberate and well-informed annunciation, and to insist that the continuation of this work is not adulterated or allowed to wither into routinized domestication in the years ahead. They may also bring to bear a powerful new voting force to foster trans-formations in the schools in time to help arrest the likelihood that 30 million new illiterates will otherwise emerge from public education in another genera-tion.

I believe that the book publishers of the United States may be persuaded to establish several thousand one-way libraries within the poorest neighborhoods of the United States and that they can stock these centers with 100 million copies of hard- and softcover titles yearly.

I doubt that anything can change the military programs. If, however, we are able to reduce by half the pool of those illiterate or semiliterate young men on which the military draws, it will be exactly twice as hard for military officers to find the frontline fodder for the functional requirements of war.

Narrow jingoism will persist in leading us into some hopeless wars; but a broader global vision and the voting force of people who can understand the needs of Third World nations may enable us to halt some of these efforts and to redirect our wealth into enlightened foreign programs that diminish violence and anger born of needless human pain.

The "functional" obsession is the hardest obstacle I can foresee. Techno-logical approaches hold a strong appeal for many of the governmental figures who have power to affect priorities. Enormous profits from the sale of hardware and the necessary software represent a potent force which may be heightened by promotional techniques that humanistic literacy workers will find hard to counteract. I nonetheless believe that a substantial movement toward a human-istic vision of a literate adult remains within the realm of hope, if not of easy expectation.

If we will permit ourselves to listen to the voices of the people whom we teach, if we will hear their deeply felt requests to share the testament of scrip-ture, not so much to read inscriptions written in the past but to write their own inscriptions and to read them (in the prophecy of Emerson) by their own "lan-terns," if we will hear the poetry they write and, even more, the poetry they are prepared to live, enact, and share, we may finally become convinced that these are aspirations of nobility and grace that far exceed our mechanistic expecta-tions. If this should be the case—and it can only be our stubbornness which will prevent it—then it may be that those who come to us as students will in fact become our teachers too.

I believe that many humanists and humane scientists will be responsive to the needs examined in this book. If this is an utterance of simple faith, it is a faith that grows out of the lessons learned from scientists like C. P. Snow and poets such as Auden and my own beloved and decent teacher, Archibald Mac-Leish. The evolution of this process may not be so easy as my optimistic words suggest. It will take the bold initiative of some of our most influential scholars to transform the possible into the real.

Certain elements in our society cannot be expected to be reconciled to any of these dreams. Those elements, I am convinced, remain a limited if voluble minority. With the exception of these—the cold, the narrow, and the cruel—I believe the broad-based struggle I have outlined here is possible, although I do not dare say that it is probable, within the next ten years.

It may be asked why I have argued in this book for something which I subsequently recognize to be unlikely at the present moment—and only a part of which we can expect to see enacted in the decade now ahead. The words of Auden, quoted earlier, have echoed in my mind as I have come to the conclusion of this book: "In the prison of his days/teach the free man how to praise." It seems to me we have no choice but to recite the past, find where we faltered, recognize that we may falter once again, but still persist in search of a more hopeful consummation than experience allows us to expect.

Illiteracy, when widely recognized and fully understood, may represent the one important social, class, and pedagogic issue of our times on which the liberal, the radical, and the informed conservative can stand on common ground and toil, no matter with what caution and what trepidation, in a common cause that offers benefits to all. Some of those benefits are hard and tough and painfully pragmatic. Others possess a dignified and searching character which recognize an absolute imperative to lessen the ordeal of those who are in pain and to create a less divided nation in a less tormented world.

The "best case" then must be the only case we should allow ourselves to entertain. There is another way to say this. I do not believe that we have any choice but to be loyal to our own most stirring moment of transcendence. While we toil on the flatlands of negotiated dreams, we must find the will to look back to the mountains: to remember. Martin Luther King spoke of his journey "to the mountain" in a phrase that mesmerized a generation of Americans. The first great Hebrew prophet went alone into the hills where he received the words that he inscribed upon the tablets of our conscience for 3,000 years. The challenge to transcend ourselves remains.

If we can accept this challenge, we may be rewarded by an aspect of our own potential that we cannot easily surmise. Hard as it appears, we must be willing to look back into those hills in which our heritage was born.

Where the word was given, it may someday be received.

Afterword

The Prospects for the Generation Now in Public School

What is to prevent the cyclical reiteration of this problem?

Granted that newly literate adults can do a lot to arm their children against damage they may otherwise experience within the public schools. Granted that parents, so empowered, may begin to exercise a potent force for better funding and for more effective teachers and for equitable distribution of those teachers in the public schools on which their kids depend. What is to fend off the likelihood that public schools, for all the efforts of empowered parents, will continue nonetheless to guard their citadels against the pressures of the non-professionals outside the walls and will helplessly churn out another generation of illiterate adults two decades hence?

One currently accepted answer, as we have already seen, consists of tougher policies of terminal exclusion—labeled "higher standards"—at the secondary and especially precollege levels. The other current answer is a policy of tighter discipline and more emphatic focus on the reading, writing, and arithmetic which are alleged to have been frivolously neglected since the 1960s but will now be resurrected as the cornerstone and largest portion of curriculum. The total package, known under the rubric "Back to Basics," is expected to reverse the "tide of mediocrity" that now engulfs us and will thereby guarantee that we will see no replication of the problems studied in this book.

This is not the place to deal with all the problems posed by this resurgent fashion. We need at least to clear away a number of its contradictions if we are to pinpoint certain items that may offer grounds for hope.

•There is a note, throughout most of the back-to-basics writing, of a longing to return to a remembered Eden. Much of the wording, for example, speaks not of "achieving" excellence but of "returning" to it. This is not a realistic longing. Much to the reverse, it is a subset of the dangerous nostalgia for the past, born of a basic fear to face the future, which summons up a warm and golden image of the days when conventional families drove in friendly humpbacked Fords to neighborhood stores and county fairs, and the poorest people (and especially black people) were invisible, uncounted—and did not take SATs.

If it is correct that average scores are somewhat worse today than thirty years ago, those of the social classes that did well in 1955 or 1960 are basically unchanged. If they have declined at all, such modest lowering of scores as may perhaps exist may be explained in large part by some absolutely ethical and proper reasons that a democratic social order ought to have no reason to regret.

•Most of the back-to-basics rhetoric speaks not so much of "something different" as of "something more"—more homework, more examinations, longer school days, longer school semesters. It is not clear what we may hope to gain by stipulating "more" if we are speaking only of more of the same, more hours of tedium, more school days of withdrawal and resentment, more days and years of contact with credentialized instructors more than half of whom have indicated in the latest polls that they would never choose again, if they had any choice at all, to be schoolteachers. When politicians offer us a quantitative answer to a qualitative problem, when they assume that more is better, that intensified indignity is a significant achievement, that rigorous inequity is a sagacious goal, it seems to me they show themselves to be the victims of the same consumer appetite that leads so many of their fellow citizens to see more value in accumulation of tin objects than in transformation of the tin to better metals. If I am wrong, we need to ask what kind of alchemy they have in mind. (What kind of inert metals, for that matter, do they see in the illiterate and the less literate portions of the population?)

•Testing is repeatedly extolled as one of the most useful ways to reinforce and monitor the implementation of the new demands. Testing is essential to enable us to speak about real problems. Without such tests we could not even speak with confidence of the approximate numbers of illiterate adults within our nation. On the other hand, an indiscriminate use of testing, not as a *form of education in itself* but as a terminal index of exclusion or reward, erodes and denigrates the human value of our learning. Nothing—under the sword of "measurement, prerequisite, exam"—can be pursued for its own worth but only for the cash reward it wins. The cash reward for excellence at twelfth grade level proves to be admission to a first-rate college. Excellent performance in the college years wins the reward of entrance to a graduate academy. Excellence at the highest academic level wins us the reward of an impressive income. Each stage of learning comes to be respected only as a ticket of admission to the next. The very same scholars who have authored these reports remind us often and in rather grandiose language (for example, in the rhetoric of their commencement speeches) of the virtue of learning for its own sake; yet everything in these hard-nosed studies argues the reverse.

An obstinate infatuation with the measurement of skills in isolation from a moral context or an analytic competence portends a further movement in the same direction.

•An emphasis on tougher codes of discipline pervades the recent studies. There is an ominous and familiar note of retribution in much of the language that is used in this discussion. Standards of discipline must exist and, if they are skillfully applied, they will serve their purpose better in the breach than the observance. If, on the other hand, some of our angry elders have in mind a recourse to the stick and paddle that were standard operational equipment in the urban schools of 1955 and 1960, they will not only fail to reach their goals but they will give evidence once more that they have failed to learn from history. Violence, whether by tone of voice or wielding of a stick, has never diminished student rage but has repeatedly acted as a catalyst to turn that rage into explosive actions of self-vindication.

When I was a teacher in the public schools in 1964 and 1965, students were forced to memorize a booklet of quotations on the virtues of obedience. "Obedience," one of these aphorisms told our children, "sums up our entire responsibility." That was six years prior to My Lai and nearly a decade before Watergate. It is apparent that a lot of future adult citizens learned their lessons all too well. Another quotation that the children were compelled to learn was in the form of an unhappy rhyme: "Every day, in every way, it is our duty to obey." Those children who did not accept the mandate of this little verse soon learned the consequence of disobedience. They were beaten in the basement of the school by white schoolmasters bearing rattan whips which first were dipped in vinegar or water to increase the pain they could inflict. This is the school that I described in *Death at an Early Age*.

The children I knew did not learn better how to read and write as a result of discipline like this. They are, indeed, with few remarkable exceptions, the illiterate young black adults who walk the streets of Boston now, who fill the Massachusetts prisons—or who "pull down" SATs, to the astonishment of the state board of education. They did learn one thing from "the good old-fashioned discipline" that President Reagan recently exhorted us to resurrect in public schools: They learned how to fight back. The first, most vivid instance of offi-cially legitimated use of violence in their existence was the raised stick in the hand of a white teacher. They did not forget this lesson. It made its imprint and would serve, in time, as an indelible precedent for their response.

The need for discipline is often emphasized by back-to-basics advocates as a prerequisite for excellence in public school. Do they mean that we should now return—"go back"—to equal excellence afforded by distinguished schools and teachers whose authority resides in the distinction of their scholarly achievement? If so, there is nothing to return to. Poor children never had such schools and seldom knew such teachers. Perhaps, however, what they mean is something rather different, something which can be subsumed in words like these: "Back to basic bigotry and blind obedience in the face of unjust orders from unqualified adults in an unjust society." If it is this they have in mind, they ought to understand that history will not allow them their nostalgia. They may still attempt to raise the stick; but when they bring it down, it will strike first upon the soul of the society which has denatured them and which, if we can learn no better, will in time destroy us all.

There are at least two different meanings for the word authority. Natural authority derives from the self-evident distinction and the proven excellence of a responsible adult. Credentialized authority, assigned by arbitrary numbers and degrees, attaches frequently to fools and despots. Neither child nor adult ought to respect them. There is too much respect for authority of the wrong kind in the U.S. public schools, but too little respect for moral truth enacted by societal intelligence. If there were more of the latter, there would be less need for the former; and the atmosphere within our schools might not be what we see before us now: an atmosphere of crumbling dictatorship in time of martial law.

The stick may be composed of wood or metal or exclusionary measures phrased in elegant and polished words. Exclusion of those whom we have cheated in their infancy and in the early years of school, on grounds of failures we have recognized but never yet had courage to address, seems to me a form of violence too. Those who are obsessed with longing for the good old days of 1958 need to be reminded that sadistic forms of violence to children were an honored and unquestioned method of instruction in the era they recall. Would they return to this form of nostalgia too?

•Several of the back-to-basics advocates have taken pains to list those skills (and they are specific skills consigned to strict compartments by extremely rigid lines) in ways that school boards cannot miss and testing instruments cannot ignore. The skills they list are those regarded as essential for the jobs that industry expects to make available during the decade now ahead. What of that multitude of jobs which cannot yet be named or plausibly projected since they are not known or even dreamed of? The rate of technological change is certain to outpace even the most far-reaching speculation. What of the need for critical skills and overleaping surges of imaginative nerve which would empower any human being not only to learn what we can name and readily expect but also to gain the confidence to learn—and to learn *how* to learn—what cannot yet be named?

This is an area of learning which the back-to-basics mania has overlooked. It is an oversight which was perhaps inevitable. Those who are obsessed with a nostalgic longing for the past bring with them a crippling myopia even when they try to gaze ahead. They can make out the edge of the horizon; they cannot imagine what may lie beyond. An added semester of computer skills may seem to serve the needs of 1985 or 1990. What will be needed in 1995 or in the year 2000? Since we cannot know those needs, shouldn't we take the risk of teaching people how to leap, to dare, to venture, and to overreach? Is this prospect too alarming to our blue-ribbon commissions? Are they thinking still about the troublesome overreachers of the 1960s? Should we allow the future to be held in bondage to the past because of the uneasy memories of weary academic politicians?

There is one respect in which the right-wing critics are correct. A trend emerged during the past twelve years (not, as often thought, during the 1960s, but in the years from 1972 to 1976) that tended to exalt a teaching style of essential abdication and a fascination with the whimsical, the random, and— most damaging to kids—the incomplete.

Many youthful teachers, wishing to avoid the dictatorial approach of old-time teachers who had exercised unwholesome tyranny within the isolated settings of severe and rigid schools, often made the error of believing that their only option was, in practice, to deny the knowledge of their own adulthood and to function solely as some sort of household spirit—as a "resident mystic"—in the presence of young children.

This tendency was most familiar among idealistic teachers who had over-dosed on some of the romantic writings of the early 1970s. The notion was purveyed that "none of us may really know much more than anybody else," that children should learn "spontaneously," "organically," at their own pace and whim, but that no one ought to set out with the will to *teach* them. "Teach," in effect, became a dirty word. "Learn" was the required verb for those who did not wish to be accused of speaking or behaving with the strength or knowledge they possessed. Ten years before, the teacher had too often been the only one within the classroom who had power. Suddenly now, she came to be the only one with *none*.

A fascination with crafts, with leatherwork and health foods, and an obsti-nate addiction to ambiguous expressions that were virtually devoid of denotation ("I think I feel I hear you saying that your head's not where I'm at . . .") threatened for a time to substitute a half-baked therapeutic style for all residue of syntax and of clear articulation. "Wow!" I heard one of those cheerful teach-

ers say. "We made an Iroquois canoe out of an oak log!" I will offend the
memories of many of my friends by stating once again what I replied when I
first heard this back in 1972: Nobody needs an Iroquois canoe in Boston or
Chicago. Even Iroquois do not. The Iroquois can buy aluminum canoes if they
should really need them. They don't, however. What they need are doctors,
lawyers, teachers, organizers, labor leaders . . .

In visiting an innovative public school around that time, I walked into a
third grade classroom and approached the tallest person in the room: taller by a
good three feet than anybody else. I asked what seemed to me an inoffensive
question: Was he the third grade teacher?

"No," he said, and then went off into a tailspin of apologetic and semantic
obfuscation. "Well . . . we'd rather not say 'teacher' in this school . . . We'd
rather say that I'm 'a resource person,' 'a facilitator' for the kids." Regaining
confidence, he summed it up in these familiar words: "All of us are learning and
teaching in this room at the same time."

I do not like satirizing someone who is innocent and likeable and utterly
benign. Moreover, the ideal of mutual learning is of great importance to my own
beliefs, whether with kids or with illiterate adults. But there is clearly something
crazy going on when someone who is six feet tall and twenty-nine years old, and
who has lived a while on this earth, and loved, and lost, and wept, and suffered,
and perhaps read several thousand complicated books, pretends that he is on an
absolutely equal par with little kids in yellow jumpers and red jerseys. When I
repeated his remarks to one of the black parents who had children in that
school, the parent sighed and then replied without a bit of malice but an uncon-
trollable grin: "If that's the case, if they are all as equal as he says, then I guess
he ought to split his paycheck with the kids. I can't figure what he's getting paid
for."

This was not an isolated case. Many such teachers, trapped between the
shadow of past tyranny and suddenly anarchic cults of ecstasy and whim, understandably alarmed the parents of the children who had been entrusted to their
care. It is notable that this was even more the case among black parents, who
relied entirely on the schools for the survival of their kids, than in the settings of
those liberal rich people who could leave their kids to toy around with pottery
and whim for several years, knowing that a few years hence they would be
sending them to Brearley, Shady Hill, or other prep schools to catch up on what
they'd missed.

This foolish and dogmatic fashion on the part of many youthful teachers
did substantial damage to the cause of freedom and equality which they es-
poused. Many, offended by the harsh competitive existence which their parents
had attempted to impose upon them in the years of their own prior education,
ended up by looking on the half-complete, the semisuccessful, and the inter-
rupted venture as a virtue in itself. "Beautiful failure" came, for many of these

teachers, to appear a more attractive outcome than a visible success. It seemed at times as if success and competence—the words as well as the realities—had been contaminated in their minds by their association with the vicious and persistent consummations of such unbeloved but "competent" men as Richard Nixon, H. R. Haldeman, and Howard Hunt.

Abdication moved beyond the classroom and the commune to the voting booth. Few of the young people that I have in mind would even deign to cast their votes in 1972. Even George McGovern was contaminated, in the eyes of many, by his evident persistence and success in winning nomination. Unfortunately, when people abdicate in the United States, they do not leave a beatific vacuum. What they do, instead, is leave the battlefield to those who are prepared not just to "try and fail" but who have set forth with an unencumbered will to win. In pedagogic terms, the vacuum that was left by those whom I have just described was filled in time not only by the most conservative Americans but also by those in the middle-ground who were alarmed by the excesses they had temporarily accepted and from which they now assiduously fled. The groundwork for the back-to-basics movement had been set in hard concrete. We are left to face the consequence today.

In actual fact, I doubt that the euphoric trend I have described was ever very influential or widespread. I certainly do not believe that it is this which can explain the modest drop in SATs that we have seen in recent years. Broader inclusion of the poor and the nonwhite in secondary education, and the willingness these students felt to try for university admissions at a time when scholarships were suddenly available and when affirmative enrollment policies allowed some hope that they might actually get in, seem to me the major reason (and an admirable reason) for the purported "loss of excellence" that many educators now bemoan. To state this in more simple words: "The problem" did not suddenly "grow worse"—it just grew visible. It had been there all along. "The tide of mediocrity" our government commissions now deplore is, as I have said at several points above, a not-so-subtle euphemism for the advent of egalitarian democracy within the upper reaches of the pedagogic world.

Nonetheless, the media attention paid to those who were most reckless in adherence to a style of euphoric abdication in the period from 1970 to 1976 provided an appealing straw man for those right-wing educators who had suffered through the student protests of the 1960s and now saw an opportunity to take an indirect revenge. Instead of attacking racial equity, they focused their attack on the absurdities of those who had withdrawn from any drive for social justice and who, by their withdrawal, had become in fact almost as strong a force for a renewed conservatism as the adversaries they professed to view with detestation. Instead of attacking causes and ideals identified with Martin Luther King and Malcolm X, the back-to-basics advocates were able to concoct a palpable mélange in which the ethical intentions of the 1960s were combined with drugs, wheat germ, and incoherent syntax represented by the flower children who had long since left behind such ethical ideals.

This, in my belief, has brought us to the dangerous but needless choices we are asked to make in 1985. Why should we be forced to choose between the competence of the cold and cruel on one hand and, on the other, the apparent euthanasia of the beautiful inept? Can't we conceive a better kind of excellence: one that is contained by ethics and informed by equity? Can we afford the balkanized mentality which offers false polarities and then—of two bad choices —advocates the worse?

There has to be a way to find pragmatic competence, internal strength, and ethical passion all in the same process. This is the point at which the heightened role of millions of poor parents, rising from the silence of illiterate and semiliterate conditions, may be of help in reinforcing those—the vast mainstream of teachers—who would choose for neither wheat germ nor the stick. Let us see how this idea might be made real.

Imagine a situation in which several thousand adults, many of them parents of small children, have begun to coalesce around the neighborhood centers, churches, satellites, and storefronts I suggest. Imagine an invigorating ferment of celebratory sessions that include adults who come for help in learning how to read and write, youngsters who are gaining preschool confidence, older kids who come as mentors of their younger siblings or for the assistance which is made available to them by those who are prepared to govern evening study halls. Imagine several scholars from adjacent universities, as well as ten or twenty college students and an equal number of well-educated older people, some of them perhaps retired doctors, lawyers, English scholars, scientists, or simply decent people who enjoy and want to share the pleasure that they know in reading books. Imagine, as well, a handful of committed people borrowed from the nearby corporations, hospitals, and other major institutions. (Imagine some musicians, artists, poets, too.)

Add to this scenario a rising sense of neighborhood empowerment and a capacity for strong but well-directed indignation which can aim its fire at the school as "institution" but which recognizes many teachers in those schools as logical allies and potential friends.

Imagine, finally, that many of these programs should be making use of neighborhood school buildings, in part for classes but in larger part for tutor-preparation and for organizing roles.

It is not easy to believe that teachers, once aware of all this ferment in their midst, will not be susceptible to curiosity, perhaps to fascination, or at least to a determined interest in concurrent pedagogic efforts which are taking place on every side of their school buildings, at times within those buildings, and whose consequences cannot fail in time to be perceptible in the improved performance and the heightened readiness of children entering their schools. Some of those teachers will no doubt retreat, as in the past, behind the barriers of their professional credentials. Others, I suspect, are likely to explore the possibilities of practical collaboration with a neighborhood of people whose impatience has been channeled into cogent criticisms of conditions which the best of teachers criticize as well.

Secondary teachers, weary as they are after their six or seven hours in the schools, may nonetheless be tempted to participate with their own students in the two-way tutoring which school administrators have already advocated as a useful pedagogic tool. Elementary teachers, knowing that their students are receiving help outside of school, surely will see their own self-interest in at least a casual coordination of the work they do in class and that which has been taking place during the evening hours.

All of this is optimistic; much of it may seem to verge on wistfulness and prayer. Powerful obstacles exist in the archaic notion of "professional distance" based upon a sometimes realistic fear that undefended openness may render teachers vulnerable to unfair condemnation. We know too well that it is frequently the teacher who has made herself approachable who takes the rap for those who have remained beyond the reach of an unhappy parent population. This is a case where we will have to learn from history.

I have proposed that lobbies which emerge from newly literate communities may set out with "constructive vengeance" to be certain that those schools do not produce another generation of illiterate adults. "Constructive" is a better word than "vengeance." A recognition of the best and worst within a partially deficient school may take the form of vengeance toward "the worst" or of a partisan support in the favor of "the best." Much of urban education justifies profound denunciation. The better teachers in those schools, if amicably approached, are likely to add resonance to such denunciation.

What are some specific areas to which enlightened advocates might bring to bear their energies and strength? I will mention here a few that seem to be most closely tied to problems that have been addressed within this book.

•The foolish choice between remorseless "basics" and a fatuous euphoria may be addressed, though it will not be easily transcended, if teachers and parents can participate together in achieving a realistic synthesis of needed skills and humane applications. In order for the fundamental skills to be developed without introduction of those pressure-cooker tactics advocated by some right-wing zealots, grade school teachers need to have the sense that they are doing something that the parents want and that they will be rewarded by support in their pursuit of such necessities as a redoubled funding of those elementary reading programs which were decimated by the recent cuts in Title I.

Heightened emphasis on reading/writing skills in early years of school and the fiscal allocation which can make this a reality offer teachers opportunity to better use the competence which they possess without a recourse to gestapo tactics that an understaffed and underfunded school renders almost inevitable. The same alliance can address the vastly overloaded schedules of those second-ary teachers who, as Theodore Sizer recently observed, are now responsible for teaching in a single day as many as 150 pupils and would have to be magicians to retain a memory not only of the status but at times even the names and ages of the children they meet daily.

•Most of the poorest and least literate adults whom I have known have no idea of just how undesirable and unrewarding a career in public education has become. Few college students, and still fewer of the best, are interested in teaching. Less than 5 percent of entering college freshman (1982) indicated that they planned to become teachers. (The figure was 22 percent in 1966.) Those who go into teaching are less qualified than ever. SAT scores (1982) for students entering schools of education were 80 points below the national average. Of twenty-nine academic fields surveyed, future teachers came out twenty-sixth. According to the Carnegie Foundation for the Advancement of Teaching, 55 percent of teachers interviewed in 1981 said that they would not go into educa-tion if they had the choice again.

Entering salaries for teachers are approximately $13,000; for business ma-jors, they begin at $16,000. The gap widens as the years go by. After fifteen years, the teacher may receive $25,000; the business major, by that point, may well be earning anywhere from $50,000 up. No matter what we say about prestige, professional stature, and the like, we cannot legislate prestige by rheto-ric. In a society where economic level is the one consistent index of esteem, even a series of rare incremental gains for so-called "master teachers" cannot affect the image of schoolteachers as the cognitive sediment of intellectual activity in the United States. For college graduates in 1985, teaching is the national career of last resort.

Societies cannot be guaranteed of getting what they pay for; but they can be certain they will never get what they *don't* pay for. Parent advocacy for higher pay and for progressive increments in pay for every year of provable success—not for numbers of semesters served—ought to rank high among the categories of informed (and not-so-gentle) indignation I suggest. Parents who know nothing of these matters cannot possibly address their indignation in the right direction.

•A curiously skewed disparity of income and prestige now allocates the lowest status to the primary and preschool teachers. In almost any elementary school, it is the fifth or sixth grade teacher (and, most commonly, it is a man) who gets the privilege of running workshops, supervising schedules, and—particularly important in the social context of a public school—of being accepted as a friend and confidante, a kind of "aide de camp," by the headmistress or headmaster. Middle-school teachers represent the next rung up; but virtually every eighth grade teacher I have ever known was waiting for the chance to get a job in high school. High school teachers, if they have the personal drive and intellectual imagination, frequently anticipate the day when they can get a job at junior college—or in schools of education.

The inversion of status which creates this pecking order is not only cruel to teachers but it stands in sharpest possible conflict with the difficulty and importance of the work assigned to each. This is another area where newly literate and well-informed adults might exercise their leverage in some ways that will reward and not intimidate the best of grade school teachers.

•Teaching is the one profession that I know in which successful and ambitious effort leads to a precipitous exclusion from the very place—the classroom, in this instance—in which one has proven his or her success. A gifted fourth grade teacher in the Boston schools has shared with me a classic situation. A principal who had observed and liked her work over the course of several years took her aside one afternoon in May and offered this advice: "You don't want to spend your life with fourth grade children. You can make it to the top. If you follow my advice you'll take some courses in administration. You could be a principal—like me—in seven years . . ."

To state this as, I am convinced, society perceives it: The sole reward for being any good at all at what you love to do is to be denied the chance to do it longer than the time it takes to switch to something else. If doctors are doing decent work, and feel the satisfaction of that work, they can look forward to another forty years of doing the same thing, only perhaps with growing self-esteem as years go by. If trial lawyers demonstrate exceptional success, they will win more clients and be paid increasingly large fees. Most talented professionals, enjoying what they do, can look to the future as a time of deepening maturity and broadening perspective in the same career. This is not the case with classroom teachers.

In Oakland, California, at the present time, there are ninety schools but ninety-one administrators *outside* of those schools, each of whom is earning in excess of $40,000. The highest salary for an administrator *in* the schools (a principal) is $3,000 less. The highest teacher salary is $12,000 less. Nearly one third of the budget of the Oakland schools is spent for people who do not work in a school. If we would like to find a starting point for radical enhancement of the excellence of classroom teaching in the U.S.A., one answer lies right there. Successful teachers ought to be assured that, after ten or fifteen years of dedicated work, they will be receiving for the work they were employed to do in the beginning at least as much as anyone who has escaped the sight of children for the better pay and more prestigious role of "running systems." How can parents possibly address such issues if they cannot read enough to understand the very books—the recent work of Sizer and of Ernest Boyer, for example—which can open up their minds to the inequities they have no way to understand but for which their children pay the final price?

Many poor parents ask in puzzlement how it can be that, every time their oldest child has a scintillating and effective teacher, they discover that the teacher has departed by the time their youngest child enters the same school. "Where did she go?" Too frequently, they learn that she is now curriculum assistant in "the central office," perhaps an education writer for the local paper, or (more frequently these days) "curriculum consultant" for a private firm that manufactures what are known as "teacherproof materials" for those less scintillating colleagues she has been induced to leave behind. Too seldom do the client populations have a chance to know another and more brutal reason for the loss of their best teachers. Many teachers have been bought away by rich suburban systems where per-pupil funding may be double that which is afforded to poor children and where almost every aspect of a teacher's life is more enticing.

Here, then, are some other areas where literate, empowered, and politicized adults could bring their strength to bear—if they could ever win substantial access to the facts—in making certain that they do not lose the teachers who have won their trust and served their children best.

•Teachers have been victimized by a credentializing system which requires them to sacrifice the pleasures and rewards of humanistic studies in order to receive a mechanistic preparation in "the methods and materials" of a specific craft or trade. What they get, in far too many programs, is a great deal closer to the ugly enterprise known as "Voc. Ed." than anything that honest scholars could describe as education. Those who study English as a subject to be taught to high school students learn the way to "trick" their pupils into reading authors whom they have too seldom been allowed the time and opportunity to love and to revere out of the sheer exhilaration of the work itself. Whether they ever learn to love these authors for their own intrinsic worth is problematic. Nor, in any case, do they get "credit" for such esoteric matters as a reverence for transcendent art.

In Massachusetts, as in several other states, it is virtually impossible to meet criteria for school certification and take the courses needed for fulfillment of a liberal arts degree within a single four-year span. Those who neglect to take the courses needed for certification, but who remain devoted to the goal of teaching children, are obliged to look for work at private schools like Andover and Groton. The most respected independent schools do not seek certification in their teachers. What they do require is a high degree of excellence in academic areas and an apparent gift for getting on with children. We have yet to hear a satisfactory response from the credentializing experts to the paradox that is embodied in this situation. We might hear some interesting answers from the parents of poor children if they ever had the slightest chance to understand the perfect instrument of class and economic role selection which the present system of certification represents. How can they give such answers now? We have made certain that they cannot ask the questions.

Many teachers in the poorest public schools have managed to be educated well, despite these obstacles. Others are good teachers anyway but are aware of missing areas—of gratifying opportunities denied—which might endow their work with more success and might allow them better reason to remain. Sophisticated parents might be able to advance such sensible solutions as routine sabbaticals for state-supported reimmersion—not in further mechanistic courses but in border-free enjoyment of broad liberal domains of sciences and arts. Certain colleges already run enlightened programs of this sort, but only as brief "summer institutes" for "credits" which are then translated into automatic salary increases. Fewer credits, but more satisfactions, would be a dignified and well-deserved reward not only for "the best" (who need it least) but for the total spectrum of schoolteachers.

This brings us to a controversial point which cannot be addressed with the complexity that it deserves within this book. Schools of education ought to be progressively drawn back, if not absorbed entirely, into schools of liberal arts. Scarcely more than one-semester periods of on-site preparation in the classrooms they will enter might provide all of the "methods" and "techniques" that can be used to good effect by educators who have first been educated. This, again, would call for a dramatic change in policies of state certification. Neither of these outcomes is to be expected in the years immediately ahead. It is of interest, nonetheless, to note that several recent studies have suggested, as a short-term step, that science, math, and language teachers ought to be recruited rapidly—without certification—from the schools of liberal arts. What is now suggested as a form of crisis-intervention might someday be viewed as an initial step toward transformation of the teacher-education process altogether.

I have said that it is dangerous to look too far ahead. Any major increase in the numbers of both literate and ethically effective adults in this nation would be cause for ample satisfaction in itself. The payoff for the children of those people and the dollar payoff for the nation as a whole are gains to be pursued for their own sake and with no larger expectations as the benchmarks of significant success.

A pedagogic ferment, nonetheless, can hardly fail to be contagious. If it is a ferment that produces an expanded lobby for the transformation of the schools, and above all for the betterment of work and life conditions for the teachers in those schools, then we may expect a stark reduction in the citadel mentality of many of those teachers who now see themselves endangered both by government condemnation and by adversary feelings in the neighborhoods and cities that they serve. This raises for the first time an authentic possibility that borders which now separate the school from its parental clientele may finally be crossed without alarm, and that the "crossing" may take place in both directions.

Literate adults, more confident that they are accurate in their perceptions and more certain that their recognitions cannot be disparaged for a lack of clear articulation, may find that there is less anxiety involved in visiting the school and, as a direct correlative, less pent-up venom to be visited on those whom they no longer fear but have at last some chance to understand. Teachers at the same time may feel easier in exiting the citadel of jargon and the school building itself in order to encounter parents of their students in more comfortable settings and less structured ways. The "breaking of bread" of which my friend in Cleveland spoke in reference to the neighborhood itself might come in time to be a general repast in which the child's "first teacher"—and the second and the third and fourth—may join together in a way that holds a payoff for them all.

When I was first teaching, I remember that the neighborhood in which I worked appeared to me to be a place that held a thousand perils. The greatest peril was my own imagined fear that I would not be trusted or accepted by the parents of the children that I taught. A very rigid principal enhanced this fear by her repeated warnings that we should not let ourselves be seen by parents in their homes or neighborhoods or stores. She urged that we should see them only in the classroom: on our turf.

"Let the parents come to you. Don't you go down to them." This was more than ugly metaphor: The school was situated on a steep and rocky slope.

Very few parents did come to the school. At length, encouraged by a woman who was also my co-worker, I made up my mind I would "go down" to them. With careful calculation we would pick a home in which a couple of our pupils lived; with greater calculation we would choose the hour before dinner for our visits. Most of the parents were alarmed at first to see us. Their natural assumption was that something had gone wrong at school and that we were coming to deliver a condemnatory message. "Nobody ever comes here from the school," one mother said, "unless my kid done something very bad . . ." When they realized that we had not come as messengers of imminent expulsion or arrest, they would almost always ask us to come in. Once we were seated and the atmosphere had grown relaxed, often with the welcome help of a strong drink, they would ask if we had already had supper.

"No," we said—an answer we had carefully rehearsed—"we're just heading out to eat right now."

We never did get to a restaurant those nights.

I loved those evenings. They saved me from my fear. They taught me of the generosity and kindness of some of the poorest and most poorly treated people in our nation. Many of those parents did not hesitate, during the months that followed, to come up that formidable hill and talk with me in school. I made many mistakes that year. The parents did not hesitate to tell me when they felt that I was doing something foolish and, quite frequently, when they believed that I was failing to assign their kids sufficient work. One thing I did was not a mistake. It was to cross that tiny but intimidating border. There were many rewards. One of the best was that I got some very good free dinners. There were friendships too. More than a few of them have lasted now for nearly twenty years.

I thought of those evenings when I heard that good advice about "breaking of bread." The sister said it's even better when you help to bake the bread. Most of us know nothing about baking bread. We each bring to the table what we can.

APPENDIX

Bilingual Literacy

The education of non-English-speaking people has not been addressed within this book. One reason for my choice not to discuss this matter is the tendency of many U.S. citizens to view the literacy crisis as a "special issue" forced upon us by some recent waves of immigration and extrinsic therefore to the ordinary national agenda. Too many people like to think that this must be a problem of the foreign-born, and of the children of the foreign-born, and one which therefore need not undermine our pride in the accomplishments that U.S. public education has achieved with "our own people."

There are at least two reasons why this logic will not hold.

First of all, the crucial studies carried out in Texas during 1975, resting upon data drawn from 1973, applied to people who had emerged from school at some point prior to those years. All of this antedates by several years most of the large waves of immigration from the Far East, Haiti, Mexico, El Salvador, and other lands whose citizens came to the U.S.A. in large part due to economic or political upheavals which have taken place within those areas during the past ten years. Outside of New York, even Puerto Rican immigration had not yet grown large enough to make a serious impact on the numbers of those persons who were counted as adults in 1973.

Second, despite the high illiteracy statistics for Hispanics, there is no way that these statistics could account for more than a small portion of the 60 million semiliterate and illiterate adults whom we have studied in this book. All of the Hispanic and nonwhite illiterates together do not constitute more than one fifth or sixth of all illiterate adults in the United States. Illiteracy, in short, is not, as some might like to think, a consequence of U.S. "generosity" in immigration policies. It is a homegrown problem. It would remain a serious problem even if we had no immigrants, not even the "forced immigrants" who came to the United States two centuries ago in slave ships.

Despite my choice not to address this in the body of this book, I would like to focus here on one part of the issue which is closely tied to questions raised in the preceding chapters.

The entire debate about bilingual education has been limited to questions of the rights or obligations of those children and adults who do not read or write or speak in English. A separate debate, but one which is no less intense and heated, seeks to come to terms with the reluctance or the inability of English-speaking citizens to learn a foreign language. This concern was strongly stated in the 1980 Rockefeller study. The same concern appeared again in the more strident government report of 1983. Only 2 percent of U.S. high school students take as much as three years of a foreign language. (Only 15 percent take any foreign languages at all.) Since we know how little language competence is likely to be gained in even three years of a high school Spanish class, we can be fairly sure that less than 1 percent of English-speaking high school graduates have anything approximating useful fluency and reading/writing skills in any language but their own.

With national alarm on both sides of this issue reaching fever pitch, we might look upon this as an ideal time at which to ask ourselves whether these separate "crises" may not be addressed as one unnaturally divided challenge. All Americans will need to read and write in English if they hope to share not just in economic opportunities but also in the total spectrum of political participation in a nation which relies today and will continue to rely primarily upon the English language for its governance and commerce. At the same time, millions of Americans will need to learn how to communicate with those who live within the regions of our hemisphere in which French, Portuguese, or Spanish is the spoken tongue. Mexico City alone will soon have 20 million residents—a number equal to the total population of the twenty smallest states of the United States.

Whether for reasons of politics or commerce, Americans must be conversant with their neighbors. If French remains to some degree the common language of diplomacy, and if English represents a lingua franca for the scientific world, Spanish represents the suddenly essential bridge between the First World and the Third within our hemisphere.

In light of these considerations, there is a degree of clumsiness in our divided posture on the question of bilingual studies. For those whose families speak only Spanish, we provide an inconsistent and not terribly successful process of remediation. Whether we adopt "transitional instruction" (learning in Spanish, moving into English) or, as certain zealots would prefer, we settle for the cold-turkey approach that is described as "total (instantaneous) immersion," the process is remedial in nature and cannot escape the stigma which is present in all systems of instruction that are built on separate tracks of early learning. For many of the most successful English-speaking students, on the other hand, foreign language study is a sign of excellence, preeminence, and academic promise.

A less divided pedagogy would address both challenges as one. Learning from peers, within the classroom and beginning in the very earliest years, has been an old and honored method of bilingual education in a number of developed nations. Switzerland is the most obvious example. Teachers speak to children, and conduct their lessons, in two languages. (Depending on the part of Switzerland we visit, we will see whole classes reading, writing, and conversing in both French and German or French and Italian.) Many wealthy North Americans have sent their children to expensive private schools in Switzerland precisely to enable them to grow up with a comfortable fluency in several languages. The parents of those children, diplomatic persons for example, often toil for years in Berlitz classes or with private tutors to achieve a fraction of the competence their youngsters have achieved through easy interaction with their classmates.

Where in the United States would programs of this sort be possible? In view of the fact that nearly 20 million Spanish-speaking people now are residents of almost every state and city in the nation, it is difficult to think of many sections, other than some isolated rural and suburban neighborhoods in Northern states, where totally bilingual education could not be regarded as conceivable. If we speak instead of where it would be "feasible" and where it might be rendered virtually inevitable, we might start by thinking of the Sunbelt states (Florida, Texas, Arizona, California, and New Mexico) and might then consider all those urban areas (New York, Boston, Philadelphia, Chicago, for example) in which as many as one quarter of all students are from Spanish-speaking homes.

Teachers, of course, could hardly be expected to develop the bilingual skills to do the job alone. Until another and a very different generation of instructors has been educated for employment in the public schools, it would be essential to combine Hispanic teachers (and perhaps Hispanic parent aides) in a coordinated effort with the monolingual English-speaking teachers. This raises at once all sorts of obstacles, many of which are sure to surface from the same uneasy personnel who are so easily intimidated by the loss of any real or fantasized hegemony on part of the "professional instructor." I am not speaking, then, of an idea which is politically realistic at the present time. I am thinking of an ultimate objective for a nation which, within the next ten years, will find that some of its most volatile and threatening political dilemmas will involve the rising aspirations and the growing animosity of many of its Spanish-speaking neighbors.

Although I speak of this as an ideal, not as a practical reality to be achieved within the years immediately ahead, this does not mean that schools like this do not exist already. One example is the Oyster Elementary School in Washington, D.C. Sixty percent of the children in this school are from Hispanic families; most of the rest are native English speakers and a large proportion of these children come from very wealthy homes.

"The goal at Oyster," according to a journalist who spent some days within the school last year, "is to create a bilingual child . . . At Oyster, all subjects are in English and [in] Spanish." Every child must acquire fluency in both.

The school is patterned on a European school. "In Europe," according to the principal, "dual-language learning is considered a real asset; people strive to put their children [into] schools where they can learn a second language."

We can guess one probable objection: "Won't this lower everyone's proficiency in English? Won't the children end up losing out on test scores? Isn't that the stuff that really counts?"

Oyster Elementary School is able to boast test scores far above the national norm in academic subjects—two years above the national norm at third grade level and, still more impressive when we think about the ruined kids of Cleveland, as high as three or four grades over the norm at sixth grade level.

"A program like Oyster's," the reporter notes, "serves the needs of both the immigrant and the native American student. All children enter school speaking one language . . . [They] graduate speaking two."

Many of us who studied foreign languages in high school know very well the disappointment of arriving in a European city and discovering that all of our semesters of painstaking language study will not get us to the nearest bathroom or enable us to order lunch or dinner. We also know the shock of meeting African and Dutch and Swiss and Belgian students who are fluent and effective in at least three languages; one of those three is usually our own.

I have spoken above of global literacy. I had in mind a competence that went beyond linguistics. But language is one of the elemental gateways to the other forms of international communication. In the debates surrounding adult education, the point has been made that foreign-speaking students ought to have the prior opportunity to gain a literate effectiveness, if they prefer, within the language that they speak. This is a position that I share. But the dispute would cease to hold so much intensity—and, indeed, would cease to have much meaning—if, at some point in the future, almost all our children should be speakers of two languages.

Bilingual education for all citizens appears a very distant dream. The urgent need today is to provide for those who are not literate in any language. Those who wish should certainly be given opportunity to learn to read the language which they find it natural to speak. The tide of the times, as we know well, is running in the opposite direction.

One politician recently proposed a constitutional amendment that would designate the English language as "official language" of the U.S.A. Walter Huddleston, Democratic senator from Kentucky, has termed this strange proposal "ELA"—the "English Language Amendment." Such an amendment would allow the government to starve out most bilingual education. It would also free the government and public-service corporations from the obligation to print foreign-language versions of essential documents—like bills and ballots.

There is little chance that this amendment will go much beyond the stage of rhetoric. The fact that it could even be suggested does remind us just how far America remains from anything like global vision in this decade. The fortress we have built ourselves is likely to become a bit more lonely.

NOTES

page

employers to train them for the jobs that will open up in the next few years."

5   Juvenile illiterates before the courts: "Eighty percent of the new criminals who pass my desk would not be here if they had graduated from high school and could read and write." (Florida Judge Charles Phillips, cited by Laubach Literacy International, 1982)

United States, forty-ninth among 158 members of the United Nations: Washington *Post,* November 25, 1982; *Foundation News,* January/February 1983.

Prince George's County: Washington *Post,* November 26, 1982.

A lead editorial in the Boston *Sunday Globe,* March 11, 1984, estimates that 40 percent of the city's adult population is functionally illiterate. An op-ed article in the New York *Times,* August 19, 1982, estimates that 800,000 adults in the New York City area are illiterate. Unless New York is three times better educated than the rest of the U.S., this estimate should be approximately 2 million people. For detailed information on literacy needs and programs in the Boston area, contact Tomas Kalmar, Adult Literacy Resource Center, Roxbury Community College, Boston, Massachusetts.

San Antonio: *The Status of Illiteracy in San Antonio,* by José A. Cardena et al., United San Antonio Literacy Committee, August 1983. Author's interviews with Marguerita Huantes, United San Antonio Literacy Committee, and with Carolina Rodriguez, Multilingual Education, Research and Training, San Antonio, March 1984.

Utah: "Adult Literacy in Utah," by Garth L. Mangum, paper prepared for National Institute of Education, November 1, 1983.

Present levels of federal funding and President's request for their reduction: author's interview with Gary Eyre, Executive Director of American Association for Adult and Continuing Education, December 14, 1983.

Executive Director of National Advisory Council on Adult Education, estimate of $5 billion needed to address the problem: "Illiterate? Who, Us?" by Rosa Williams, *Foundation News,* January/February 1983.

Former President Carter: *Addresses of Jimmy Carter,* Department of Archives and History, Atlanta, 1975.

6   *Report of the National Commission on Excellence in Education,* U.S. Government Printing Office, Washington, D.C., April 26, 1983.

2. MATTERS OF EQUIVOCATION: DANGERS OF THE NUMBERS GAME

7   Epigraph: See notes to Chapter 4.

page

Classic methods of equivocation: "Many educational effectiveness studies ask the question, How can we minimize resources and maximize outcomes? Or, more bluntly, How do we make bricks without straw? This leaves schools in the position of 'making the best of a bad situation' while ignoring, or considering as not subject to discussion, the questions, Why are we in such a bad situation? Such an emphasis removes the impetus for social change and guarantees the maintenance of the status quo; optimum programs . . . are abandoned in favor of discussion of which of the available limited options should be selected." ("On Being Suspicious of Technical Solutions to Political Questions," by Mara Sapon-Shevin, in *Curriculum Inquiry*, vol. 14, no. 1, Spring 1984)

8   U.S. Department of Education, first estimate: Far West Laboratory for Educational Research and Development, San Francisco, September 1983.

Office of Vocational and Adult Education, second estimate: U.S. Department of Education, Washington, D.C., June 1983.

White House, third estimate: press release, September 7, 1983.

National Institute of Education, fourth estimate: Dr. Manuel J. Justiz, U.S. Department of Education, Washington, D.C., January 18, 1984; *Newsweek*, July 30, 1984.

U.S. Bureau of the Census, fifth estimate: "Literacy: Current Problems and Current Research," in *Fifth Report of the National Council on Educational Research*, National Institute of Education, Washington, D.C., 1979.

8ff.   *Adult Illiteracy in The United States: A Report to the Ford Foundation*, by Carman St. John Hunter and David Harman, McGraw-Hill, New York, 1979.

Adult Performance Level: cited above.

U.S. Office of Education: cited by Hunter and Harman, above.

9   Carman Hunter, updated estimate: interview with author, December 1983.

Jeanne Chall: *New Views on Developing Basic Skills with Adults*, paper prepared for National Conference on Adult Literacy, Washington, D.C., January 19–20, 1984.

Update by Texas APL: "Selected APL Survey Results," by Jim Cates and Susan White, University of Texas, 1982; updated again in interview with author, March 1984.

10   Projected U.S. population over seventeen years old (1984): 173,829,000 persons, U.S. Bureau of the Census, 1984.

page

Concurrence of Hunter with author's estimates: interview cited above.

Concurrence of APL directors: author's interviews with Jim Cates and Susan White, University of Texas APL, May 1984.

Readability estimates: *U.S. News & World Report*, May 17, 1982. See also "Reducing Functional Illiteracy," Contact Literacy Center, Lincoln, Nebraska, June 1983; and Karen Norton, Laubach Literacy International, 1982. Some of these estimates are low. I have adjusted them in keeping with the views of Michael Fox and others. (See note for p. 32.) Food stamp notices, according to Jeanne Chall, are written at a university level.

11   Jeanne Chall: cited above.

12   *The Other America* (updated edition), by Michael Harrington, Macmillan, New York, 1969.

3. THE PRICE WE PAY

13   Epigraph: New York *Times*, August 19, 1982.

$237 billion: "The Costs to the Nation of Inadequate Education," Report of the Senate Select Committee on Equal Educational Opportunity, Ninety-second Congress, Second Session, U.S. Government Printing Office, Washington, D.C., February 1972.

Costs for welfare, unemployment, etc.: Senator George McGovern, September 8, 1978. See *Congressional Record*, Proceedings and Debates of Ninety-fifth Congress, Second Session, vol. 124, no. 139, Washington, D.C. See also Nancy Eggert (LVA), testimony before House Subcommittee on Post-Secondary Education, September 16, 1982.

Prison population, costs, and literacy levels: "The Social and Economic Impact of Illiteracy in Georgia," Center for Educational Research, Georgia State University, 1970; fact sheet of Laubach Literacy International, 1979; "Report to the Nation on Crime and Justice," U.S. Department of Justice, October 1983; Leo Delaney, Boston Employment Resource Center, interview, August 1984; "Literacy Training in Penal Institutions" (unpublished paper), by Patricia Gold, John Hopkins University, November 1983; interview with Dr. Gold, September 1984.

13,   Sixty percent of prison inmates cannot read above the grade school level:
14   Renée Lerche, The Network, Andover, Massachusetts, interview, August 1984; and Senator Paul Simon (cited above). According to Patricia Gold, 61 percent of prison inmates have less than high school completion. Dr. Gold estimates that approximately the same percentage cannot read above the fourth or fifth grade level. The Washington *Post*, November 3, 1981, reports that "half the inmates at Lorton Reformatory read below the fourth

page

grade level." In a separate article (November 25, 1982), the Washington *Post* suggests that up to 80 percent of prison inmates are nonreaders.

14   Difficulties in finding qualified personnel, problems of insurance industry: *Wall Street Journal,* October 16, 1978, and January 22, 1981.

New York insurance firms: *Functional Literacy and the Workplace,* American Council of Life Insurance, Washington, D.C., 1983. In the same article, Council President Richard S. Schweiker is quoted: "The problem of literacy is of direct concern to us . . . We are a labor-intensive service business and we need well-prepared, competent workers. The importance of effective development of our human capital cannot be minimized . . . We are natural partners in the search for a solution."

16   Forty-five percent do not read newspapers: *U.S. News & World Report,* May 17, 1982. The same article reports that only 40 percent of persons in their twenties read newspapers. "Editors say this was a big factor in the recent closings of major newspapers in Minneapolis, Washington, D.C., and Philadelphia."

Readability levels, newspapers and journals: Publishers offer widely differing estimates. Mine are based on those of Michael Fox, Jon Deveaux, and others who make use of magazines and papers in instruction. Jeanne Chall (cited above) observes that twelfth grade reading levels are essential to read the New York *Times* or *Time* with critical and analytic understanding. The Washington *Post* (November 26, 1982) points out that "most newspapers require twelfth grade competency . . ." See also: *Illiteracy: A Strong Whereas and a Weak Wherefor,* Adult and Continuing Education Today, 1983.

17   Decline in hardcover book sales: Alexander Burke, executive vice president, McGraw-Hill Book Company, in *Publishers Weekly,* September 25, 1978. More recent figures: "The 1983 Consumer Research Study on Reading and Book Purchasing," Book Industry Study Group, Washington, D.C., April 4, 1984.

United States twenty-fourth in books produced per capita: Alexander Burke, cited above.

17   Legal citations: "Illiterate Americans and Nineteenth-Century Courts," by
18   Edward Stevens, essay included in *Literacy in Historical Perspective,* edited by Daniel P. Resnick, Library of Congress, Washington, D.C., 1983.

My thanks to Professors Morton J. Horwitz and Duncan Kennedy of Harvard Law School, and to Judy Hawes of the National Center for State Courts, for my understanding of this issue.

18   Housing contracts in Tennessee: interview with Helen Mann, Chattanooga Area Literacy Movement, August 1984.

page

Naval recruits, $250,000 damage: Senator George McGovern, cited above. See also: "Illiteracy Among Recruits Threatens to Sink U.S. Navy," in Palo Alto *Times*, June 23, 1977. One quarter of naval recruits read below "the minimum level [required] to understand safety instructions . . ." Boston *Globe*, May 1, 1983.

Comic books employed by military: *Foundation News*, cited above.

19   Tensions at Harvard Law School: author's interviews with faculty and students, December 1982.

20   Eastern Airlines: "The O-Ring Factor," by Ellen Goodman, Boston *Globe*, May 10, 1983.

Three-Mile Island: New York *Times*, March 29 and 30, 1979.

4. THE HUMAN COST OF AN ILLITERATE SOCIETY

22   Socrates on literacy and morality: cited in "Readings on Literacy," by Tela Zasloff, in *Literacy in Historical Perspective*, cited above.

22,
23   James Madison: letter to W. T. Barry, August 4, 1822, in *The Complete Madison*, edited by Paul Padover, Harper & Brothers, New York, 1953.

25   "I couldn't understand the bills . . ." Conversation reported to author during interviews with literacy workers, Washington, D.C., April 1984.

27-
29   All quotations not taken from author's interviews are drawn from two sources:
(1) *Foresight*, vol. 1, no. 3, Southern Growth Policies Board, Research Triangle Park, North Carolina, September 1983.
(2) *The Adult Illiterate Speaks Out*, by Anne Eberle and Sandra Robinson, National Institute of Education, Washington, D.C., September 1980.
The second document, one of the most moving and insightful I have seen, derives from the experience of people who have been involved in Vermont Adult Basic Education. Despite my reservations in regard to many of the techniques employed by ABE, this remarkable paper is a tribute to the capability of some extraordinary literacy workers to listen closely to the needs of those they serve. Many of the viewpoints I have stated in this chapter were provoked by my initial reading of this data several years ago. The authors draw some of these words from interviews conducted by other authors. Passages have been condensed and edited for clarity.

5. THE DISENFRANCHISED: SILENT AND UNSEEN

30,
31   Stigma attached to the nonreader: "Not being able to read is 20th century leprosy, is what it is . . . Maybe you won't understand that. Let me ex-

plain it to you. Before you know it, you're being treated as a kid, as half what you used to be treated. That's the major reason why I'm staying as Mr. X." (Interview with an anonymous man, in *The Adult Illiterate Speaks Out*, cited above.)

32   "You have to be careful . . ." *The Adult Illiterate Speaks Out*," cited above.

"Sooner or later, the strategies run out . . ." *The Adult Illiterate Speaks Out.*

140,000 illiterates turned away for lack of funds: *The Ladder*, September/ October 1982. *The Ladder* is the newsletter of a community-based literacy group, "PLAN," directed by Michael Fox. The newsletter is edited by Pat Gatlin. Fox has recently begun a project, "Operation Wordwatch," to assess the readability of public documents and other printed items, and to insist that all materials essential to American consumers be rewritten at a level they can understand. For information on this project or for a subscription to *The Ladder*, write: Push Literacy Action Now, 2311 Eighteenth Street N.W., Washington, D.C. 20009.

33   "Victims exist, but not constituencies . . ." Ernest Boyer, president of the Carnegie Foundation for the Advancement of Teaching, makes this comment: "When I testified on [Capitol] Hill for all the programs, the ABE one brought a big yawn. Most of the programs launched are backed by articulate, strong, organized public-interest groups . . . These people don't have a voice." (Washington *Post*, November 25, 1982)

The National Assault on Illiteracy is a network of over 80 black-run groups throughout the nation. Its national chairman Ozell Sutton and administrative coordinator Meille Smith report that 90 percent of their support comes from black-owned publications associated with Black Media, Incorporated. The organization publishes *The Advancer*, a community-oriented newspaper written at a fourth or fifth grade level. For copies of the paper, and for reprints of a powerful article by its national vice-chairperson, Carrie Haynes, write: Assault on Literacy, 507 Fifth Avenue (Suite 1101), New York, New York 10017.

This organization has been so totally ignored by the white press that virtually no literacy groups run by white people have been aware of its existence. Information provided here was obtained only with great difficulty and received only as this manuscript went to press. For this, I offer my sincere apologies.

36   For discussion of the linguistic and historical issues raised by the speech patterns of my pupils, see *Black English*, by J. L. Dillard, Vintage Books, New York, 1973; *Minority Education and Caste*, by John U. Ogbu, Academic Press, New York, 1978; and "Literacy and Schooling in Subordinate

page

Cultures," by John U. Ogbu, in *Literacy in Historical Perspective*, cited above.

37ff.   Miscalculations of the U.S. census: See "Education of the American Population," by John K. Folger and Charles B. Nam, U.S. Department of Commerce, Bureau of the Census, Washington, D.C., 1960; "American Education: The ABCs of Failure," special supplement to the Dallas *Times Herald*,
December 11–21, 1983; "Plain Talk on the Non-census," by Michael Fox,
in *The Ladder*, May/June 1982.

Detailed information on methods used in 1970 and 1980 census tabulations:
interviews with Dr. Paul M. Siegel, Chief of Education and Social Stratification Branch, Population Division, U.S. Bureau of the Census, January 19,
1984, and with Roslyn Bruno, assistant to Dr. Siegel, March 19, 1984.
Additional data provided by Greg Weyland, Current Population Surveys/
Demographic Survey Division, U.S. Bureau of the Census, and by Richard
Ning, Information Services Department, Boston Regional Office, U.S. Bureau of the Census, August 1984. See also: "Statistical Abstract of the
United States, 1984 (104th edition)," U.S. Bureau of the Census, U.S.
Department of Commerce, Washington, D.C., 1983. Any effort to extract
clear and consistent information from the Bureau of the Census is doomed
to be an arduous and frustrating task. Despite the full cooperation of all
persons I have named, every explanation of the methods used in order to
arrive at final figures has in some respect conflicted with all others. In
twenty years of research, I have never found a comparable morass of tangled
and, at times, incomprehensible statistics. If it is this difficult to get at three
or four essential facts, how can those who handle and assemble such material feel any confidence at all that they are in possession of an accurate
impression of the nation they describe? I have said that any nation that
cannot perceive itself is subject to the dangers that we see in classic tragedy.
In this instance, comedy and tragedy are mercilessly intertwined. I am
convinced of the good will of those I have consulted, but I do not envy
them their thankless task.

In its *1983 Book of the Year*, the Encyclopedia Britannica reports that the
United States has a near 100 percent literacy rate. The source for this figure
is UNESCO. UNESCO's source: the 1970 U.S. census.

38   Years of school attendance and real skills: According to Hunter and
Harman, 30 states insist on only eighth grade competence for the receipt of
a twelfth grade diploma (Hunter and Harman, cited above). Jeanne Chall
(cited above) reports that studies of eight states, in the latter 1970s, indicate
that "minimum competency" tests for grade eleven revealed an average of
seventh/eighth grade competence as adequate to pass. A gap of three to
four years between grade-completion numbers and achieved proficiency
seems standard.

page
39,   Michael Harrington is quoted from *The Other America*, cited above.
40

6. What Is Now Being Done?

41   Epigraph: *The Two Cultures and a Second Look*, cited above.

41,   Two to three million persons reached by Adult Basic Education and U.S.
42   military programs: Washington *Post*, November 27, 1982; "Adult Educa-
             tion—Helping Adults Make It," Adult Education Services, U.S. Depart-
             ment of Education, Washington, D.C., June 1983; "Literacy in the Com-
             munity College," by John Grede, in *Journal of Studies in Technical Careers*,
             Southern Illinois University at Carbondale, vol. 5, no. 4, Fall 1983; "Adult
             Illiteracy in the United States," a brief statement by Carman St. John
             Hunter, in *NAPCAE Exchange*, Summer 1980; "Adult Education Exit and
             Follow-up Assessment Guide," by H. Jack Pfeiffer, Springfield Public
             Schools, Springfield, Illinois, 1982; "Literacy and Human Resources Devel-
             opment at Work: Investing in the Education of Adults to Improve the
             Educability of Children," by Thomas Sticht, Human Resources Research
             Organization, Alexandria, Virginia, February 1983; *Last Gamble on Educa-
             tion*, by Jack Mezirow et al., Adult Education Association of the U.S.A.,
             Washington, D.C., 1975.

             A relevant excerpt from John Grede (cited above): "A 1975 report on U.S.
             programs to improve adult literacy revealed an incredible gap between the
             number of persons who might be seen as needing . . . assistance and those
             who were actually receiving it . . . Programs in adult basic education . . .
             reached fewer than two million of the 60 million target group. Not only was
             the number reached extremely small but some saw adult basic education
             (ABE) as essentially a 'creaming' operation where enrollees were not really
             representative of the hard-to-reach . . ."

             Excerpt from Thomas Sticht (cited above): "Such programs [i.e., ABE] are
             totally inadequate to improve adult competencies enough to offer much by
             way of transfer to the children [of illiterates] or, for that matter, to do much
             for the future life of the adults who participate . . . Most adult basic
             education programs attract and hold adult clients for only about 50 to 100
             hours . . . They typically make only about one to two grade-levels of im-
             provement . . . Even that much gain is suspect in terms of subsequent
             retention of skill."

             Excerpt from Washington *Post* (cited above): " 'On days when I'm de-
             pressed I say we're not even keeping up' with the influx of nonreaders, said
             Paul Delker, director of the federal Adult Basic Education program that
             teaches some reading to 2.2 million adults each year."

             Excerpt from the same article: "The nuclear vigil has required expanded
             remedial reading and math courses for a record number of [military] recruits

page

who read just barely above the fifth-grade level. The armed forces had 220,000 people in remedial math and reading courses last year, focusing on the words and computation needed in the nuclear era."

Excerpt from Mezirow (cited above): "In a very real sense, ABE programs are 'creaming' operations. The least literate and most alienated tend to be excluded . . . ABE cannot pretend to have developed an organizational structure or methods and materials relevant for any but a limited segment of its target population. To reach hard-core illiterates and angry young dropouts . . . will require effective coordination of health, employment and other social services, and a financial commitment by government of a magnitude unknown in Title III [funding vehicle for ABE.]"

Additional data on ABE, and on government funding for its programs, was provided to the author by Gary Eyre, former executive director of the National Advisory Council on Adult Education and presently executive director of AAACE, in interview cited above.

Adult Basic Education programs vary significantly from one state or city to the next. Federal funding is supplemented by state and local contributions, but local contributions are notoriously uneven (Hunter and Harman, cited above). The programs in New Hampshire and Vermont appear to be a great deal closer to the grass roots than some others. This, in part, may be a consequence of rural isolation, with a consequent reduction in top-down control. Funding in these states, however, is as limited as elsewhere.

One understated comment on the limited success of ABE: "Clark (1980) . . . reported that 24 million illiterates have not completed the eighth grade. The fact that 23 million refused to attend ABE programs may indicate that ABE is not meeting their needs . . ." ("Adult Basic Education: Six Years After . . . ," by Jimmy D. Lindsey and Leasa T. Jarman, in *Journal of Reading*, vol. 27, no. 7, April 1984).

In 1983, ABE reported 300,000 functional illiterates in Mississippi. Total numbers served by ABE were 9,000. (Contact Literacy Center, October 14, 1983)

Officially, the Army insists upon ninth grade completion, a GED or high school diploma, and ability to pass two written tests. Yet 27 percent of those who are accepted cannot read at seventh grade level (Laubach Literacy International, 1982). Many, as we know, read at even lower levels. See Chapter 9.

41ff.   Numbers, and reasons given, for "separation" from ABE programs: "Memorandum to State Directors of Adult Education," from William M. Moore, Division of Vocational Research and Adult Services, Department of Education, Richmond, Virginia, September 12, 1983; "Adult Education Program Statistics . . . ," Division of Adult Education Services, Office of Voca-

page

tional and Adult Education, U.S. Department of Education, Washington, D.C., June 1, 1983.

Numbers served by Laubach Literacy International and LVA: Washington *Post,* November 26, 1982. According to Peter Waite, executive director of Laubach, dropout rates in Laubach programs range from 30 to 40 percent. Those figures, he told the Washington *Post,* are typical for presently existing programs. "We have not had a serious impact on the problem," Waite reported in an earlier interview, Washington *Post,* December 10, 1982.

Estimate of about 200,000 semiliterate or illiterate adults in Boston: interview with Seth Racusen, Neighborhood Development and Employment Agency, Boston, October 5, 1984.

42   California figures: memo from Gary E. Strong, California State Librarian, Sacramento, September 2, 1983; author's conversations with Mr. Strong, December 1983 and June 1984. The California Literacy Campaign, with strong community emphasis, is a model of effective local effort. Program Coordinator Carmela Ruby and some gifted colleagues demonstrate what might be done someday with major national commitment.

"Those they serve, moreover, are employable already . . ." Polaroid, in Waltham, Massachusetts, offers training to 700 members of its work force yearly. According to a recent documentary, Polaroid "takes a good employee and makes him better" (Westinghouse Television, Special Report, July 27, 1984).

Only 1 percent of corporate training funds assigned to basic skill instruction: Jorie Mark (American Association for Adult and Continuing Education), quoted in *The Written Word,* Contact Literacy Center, May 1983.

44   Chattanooga Area Literacy Movement, problems with "the ghetto area prospects," methods of recruitment: *The Written Word,* November 1983.

46   "A nonexistent feast": CALM reports that, in the past year, it has changed recruitment methods and has found a strong response. This time, they are faced with the more common problem: They are turning applicants away. (Interview with Helen Mann, Chattanooga Area Literacy Movement, cited above.)

47   "WANTED" poster: reproduced in *The Written Word,* November 1983.

48   "They have no inclination to make use of angry language . . ." An exception to the rule is Michael Fox. In *The Ladder,* January/February 1983, he speaks of issues seldom mentioned by the largest groups: "We cannot be afraid of the word ADVOCACY . . . Without it we are limited, treating only the victims rather than also tackling the social, educational, and political circumstances that do the victimizing . . . We are in . . . a national

crisis and we must work at more than an individual level. The history of other crises shows us that."

Precedence of research interests: "Current research on literacy is experiencing major transitions. Research on the extent of illiteracy is largely a matter of deeper analysis of existing data, recognizing that more powerful notions of literacy are needed *before advances can be made in measurement or teaching* [my emphasis]. Meanwhile, new approaches to exploring the nature of literacy are quickly moving this research forward and are stimulating a good deal of interest from disciplines not previously involved . . ." ("Literacy: Current Problems and Current Research," in *Fifth Report of the National Council on Educational Research,* cited above).

49,
50

Coalition led by booksellers: See note for p. 51.

50,
51

The federal Adult Literacy Initiative: "Fact Sheet, Adult Literacy Initiative," Office of Press Secretary, The White House, Washington, D.C., September 7, 1983; *Education Daily,* September 8, 1983; press release of U.S. Department of Education, Washington, D.C., October 24, 1983; memorandum, Adult Literacy Initiative, Office of the Under Secretary, U.S. Department of Education, August 3, 1984; interview with Joe Casello, Adult Literacy Initiative, August 1984.

Federal initiative and its implementation assessed by community-based organizers: "Identifying Target Populations for Adult Literacy Instruction," unpublished paper by Jon P. Deveaux, Bronx Educational Services, Bronx, New York, May 18, 1984; "Plain Talk on Mediocre Efforts," by Michael Fox, *The Ladder,* January/February 1984.

For a powerful assessment of the failings of the federal initiative, see: "Open Letter to Michael Fox" (dated April 12, 1984) by Jim Cates, Director, Adult Performance Level Project, University of Texas at Austin.

51

"Right to Read," labeled failure by its own director: Gilbert B. Schiffman, quoted in Washington *Post,* November 25, 1982.

51,
52

Private initiative: "Coalition for Literacy," role of B. Dalton Booksellers and other major organizations, described in "Fact Sheet," Contact Literacy Center, November 1, 1983.

B. Dalton has allocated $3 million over five years. The primary goals, apart from helping to advance public awareness, have been direct support of community-based centers and an increase in the number of such centers served from 105 to 300. A literacy specialist, Jean Hammink, has been hired by B. Dalton to provide on-site assistance to the local groups. One of many groups served by B. Dalton is PLAN, the Washington, D.C., program described above.

7. THE PEDAGOGIC TIME BOMB: THE CHILDREN OF NONREADERS

57   Epigraph: *U.S. News & World Report,* May 17, 1982.

57ff.   Historical trends: See Carman St. John Hunter in *NAPCAE Exchange,* cited above; *Literacy in Historical Perspective,* cited above; interviews with Jim Cates, Texas APL, cited above; Jeanne Chall, cited above.

58   Dorothy Shields: *U.S. News & World Report,* May 17, 1982.

59   Report of National Commission on Excellence in Education, cited above.

            The tendency to place responsibility for preschool reading on the parent was echoed in a number of "public service" advertisements placed by some major corporations in newspapers and magazines. See, for example: "You are your child's first teacher . . . Read to your child, beginning at infancy. Make it a special time of warmth and sharing . . . Waldenbooks and *Newsweek* want to help you . . ." (special insert in *Newsweek,* December 20, 1983). A similar statement, printed in the New York *Times* and several magazines in May of 1983, was placed by Pratt and Whitney: "Work with your youngsters tonight and every night . . . If your children are getting a poor education, don't blame someone else. Proper education is the responsibility of the parent. They're not the school's kids. *They're yours"* (*The Reader,* newsletter of LVA, vol. 5, no. 2, May 1983).

60   Deficit-thinking: See, for example, *Blaming the Victim,* by William Ryan, Pantheon Books, New York, 1971.

            Thomas Sticht: quoted in Washington *Post,* November 26, 1982. Sticht's views are expanded in "Literacy and Human Resources Development at Work," cited above.

            "Our severest problems . . ." See *Revolution in Learning,* by Maya Pines, Harper and Row, New York, 1967.

61   "It is never too late . . ." Theodore Sizer, in correspondence with the author, December 30, 1980.

            Thomas Sticht, on impact of parent literacy program on IQ and school performance of children: "Literacy and Human Resources Development at Work," cited above.

62   Charles B. Schultz, Professor of Education, Trinity College, Hartford: letter to the author, June 5, 1984.

            Paulo Freire: in conversation with the author, April 1981.

63ff.   Reading scores and dropout rates for Cleveland public schools: author's interviews with Cleveland school officials and Court Monitor Leonard Stevens, 1980. Note that scores supplied here are not based on longitudinal studies. No such studies had been carried out in Cleveland at the time of my research.

64   "Black English," peer pressures, etc.: J. L. Dillard, cited above.

65   "The early scores mean very little . . ." For other opinions, see: "Literacy: Trends and Explanations," by Jeanne S. Chall, in *Educational Researcher*, vol. 12, no. 9, November 1983; also *High School*, by Ernest L. Boyer, Harper and Row, New York, 1983.

An additional point regarding drop in reading scores: Reading as an organized form of class activity—involving phonics, step-by-step progressions, and consecutive skills—is not regularly taught after fourth grade. Although there is a subject known as "reading" in the requisite curriculum right through the elementary years, children who didn't get the point—who learned to memorize "the way words look and sound" but didn't learn how to create and to decode more complicated words and did not gain the competence to figure out what sounds imply—are in the same position as a college student taking third-year chemistry who never really got the point of valence. Reading instruction after fourth grade is primarily remedial. As we have seen, the stigma attached to children who require this instruction tends to discourage them from confessing what they do not understand.

"Since grade school my teacher would say you need to leard to spell. And yet they never been able to teach me. So they'll say maybe you'l leard next year . . . So as the years gone by the more one has to hide once problem . . ." (letter to the author, 1983).

"A far more likely candidate for later failure." My own experience seems to be reinforced by the increasing emphasis on the intergenerational factor expressed by major black organizations: " 'Black leaders are concerned about a lost generation of young people,' according to Harvard economist Richard Freeman. John Jacob, president of the National Urban League, observes that half of all black children 'have a 50 percent chance of growing up underprivileged, undereducated and underemployed' " *(U.S. News & World Report,* March 20, 1984).

66   "The pedagogic slag heap grows a little higher . . ." Gil Schiffman, of Johns Hopkins University, predicts: "We're going to get a larger and larger number of people like this . . . It may get to the point where things just blow up . . ." (Washington *Post,* November 27, 1982). Michael Fox calculates that about 5,500 illiterate adults are added to the population every day: 2.3 million added every year *(The Ladder,* May/June 1983).

67   Eight out of ten low-income students do not complete their college years: This figure is conservative. Estimates from Northeastern University in Boston give us some sense of the dropout rates. Ninety-five percent of nonwhite freshmen who enrolled in 1976 were not graduated with their class in 1981.

page

Although some of these students may have graduated later, it appears that the majority did not. According to the Boston *Globe*, "though blacks make up almost eight percent of each entering class, the total student population of Northeastern University is only three percent black." Jan Robinson, vice-chancellor for student affairs at the Massachusetts Board of Regents, "stressed that attrition is a national problem, principally among those students, black or white, who come from poor urban backgrounds" (Boston *Globe*, January 13, 1983).

"These poverty kids are bigger problems than we bargained for . . ." I have borrowed from an excellent and angry recapitulation of this trend, offered by Carl Rowan, Chicago *Sun-Times*, May 4, 1983: " 'I believe that parents, not government, have the primary responsibility for the education of their children,' President Reagan says . . . This is a sentiment that millions of Americans will embrace, especially middle-class families where both parents are reasonably educated and living with the children, and daddy has a job. But it has almost no relationship to the world of impoverished, half-parentless children . . . Those children's poverty may include the reality of a teenage mother who never finished high school, or a 40-year-old minority parent who is functionally illiterate." The reaction of the average citizen, Rowan writes, is this: "These poverty children are bigger problems than I bargained for. Let's declare them hopeless and forget them."

67   Smith College transfers student aid criteria to academic merit: "Breaking a 20-year tradition of awarding scholarships solely on the basis of financial need, officials at Smith and Mount Holyoke colleges have discussed plans to offer student aid not based on need in order to attract top students . . . The merit-scholarship programs being instituted at Smith and Mount Holyoke apparently are in response to the steady decline in the numbers of college-age students and the growing need to compete for the best and brightest" (Boston *Sunday Globe*, April 17, 1983).
                   College policies seem to be in line with the desires of the White House. "President Reagan is repeating a bid he made last year to halve the amount spent on programs designed to encourage minority and disadvantaged students to enroll in college. Congress appropriated $164.7 million last year; the President is asking for only $82.3 million . . ." *(Chronicle of Higher Education*, February 8, 1984).

68   President Reagan's response to National Commission: New York *Times*, May 10, 1983; *Time* Magazine, May 9, 1983; Boston *Globe*, May 22, 1983.

                   George Will's comments on "peripheral" issues such as equality and social justice: Boston *Sunday Globe*, May 1, 1983.

                   Florida court decision: New York *Times*, May 5, 1983; "Nightline," ABC News, May 5, 1983 (for transcript: Box 234, Ansonia Station, New York, New York 10023).

68,   Florida junior high school students prompted to drop out: Steven Hanlon, a
69   lawyer representing Florida students, stated that "tens of thousands of those students have dropped out of school . . ." ("Nightline," cited above).

page

"What provision is the nation making for the rest?" An eloquent statement
of this question and its implications is posed by Mary Futrell, president of
the National Education Association, quoted in *In These Times*, March 21–
27, 1984.

69   "The time is over . . ." Ralph Turlington, Florida Commissioner of Education, Boston *Globe*, April 27, 1983. Commissioner Turlington was speaking in this instance of the diplomas granted to prospective teachers. But the
context of his statement, and his simultaneous insistence on denial of diplomas to the seniors in his own home state, make it clear that he applies the
same tough standards to the students in the public schools.

"A stiffening of terminal demands . . ." Ira Jay Winn, California State
University, Northbridge, speaks of the tougher post-hoc standards in these
words: "In trying to force better performance in high schools by upping the
college ante, the University of California is acting like the lifeguard who
holds a life preserver three feet over the head of a drowning man and urges
him to jump for it. It makes great theater—for everyone, that is, except the
victim." The university regents, he writes, "claim that theirs is a golden
bugle . . . Having blown at the wind, they can shake hands and go back to
business as usual" *(Chronicle of Higher Education*, March 2, 1983).

Similar language is used by John H. Lawson, Massachusetts Commissioner
of Education: "If a kid can't clear four feet, it doesn't do much good to raise
the bar to four feet, six inches . . . Higher standards are the result of
reform, not the cause" (Boston *Globe*, May 10, 1983).

69   Answers of Florida students to TV reporter: "Nightline," cited above.

8. BREAKING THE CYCLE: THE MANDATE FOR A NATIONAL RESPONSE

72   Epigraph: *The Other America*, cited above.

White House requests 25 percent reduction in federal funds for education:
Secretary of Education Terrel Bell, quoted in *U.S. News & World Report*,
June 8, 1981.

73   Nearly one fourth of Boston teachers fired: This figure applies to tenured
teachers only. Technically, they were "laid off"—or "excessed" in the local
jargon. (Interviews with Joan Buckley, Massachusetts Federation of Teachers; Irene Sege, Boston *Globe*, Ian Forman, press spokesperson, Boston
Public Schools, September 1984.)

Variations in per-pupil expenditures, Massachusetts: Boston *Sunday Globe*,
May 20, 1984.

"Christopher Jencks in 1972 estimated that the children of the wealthy have twice as many dollars invested in their schooling as the children of the poor . . . There is no reason to believe the gap has narrowed . . . For example, in one Midwestern metropolitan area typical of the country as a whole, in 1981–1982 the teacher-student ratio in inner city high schools was 1:175; in the wealthier suburbs, 1:100; and in the independent country day schools, largely serving an affluent clientele, 1:60" *(Horace's Compromise,* by Theodore Sizer, Houghton Mifflin, Boston, 1983).

73   Computer software in the classrooms: *Wall Street Journal,* May 26, 1983.

74   LVA "barely holding even": *USA Today,* September 28, 1982.

Librarians in financial trouble: "According to a November, 1983 news report delivered by a spokesperson for the American Library Association, the Detroit Public Library System is experiencing extreme financial difficulties, and as a result over a dozen branch libraries are likely to be closed . . . The problem in Detroit is not unusual; many large cities suffering from the recent recession are in similar trouble, including libraries in Chicago, Philadelphia and New York. Libraries in these cities have already closed branches and/or cut back on staff . . ." *(The Written Word,* April 1984).

In face of difficulties, several major libraries have been able to achieve a good deal on extremely modest funds. Notable among these are the Enoch Pratt in Baltimore, the Brooklyn and the Philadelphia libraries, and the Los Angeles County Library. None can make a serious impact without federal funds.

Commitment by McGraw-Hill: See note for p. 197.

76   "Uniformity of content . . ." Uniformity is heightened by state-wide adoption practices. The State of Texas orders all textbooks through a single State Textbook Committee. Because the Texas market is so large, publishers will seldom print editions that are not initially approved in Texas. For details on the impact of the Texas market on the national arena, see: "The Dumbing of America," by Nat Hentoff, *The Progressive,* February 1984. For additional data on the power of the Texas schools to demand modifications in textbooks which will then be sold, unaltered, in all other states, see: Boston *Sunday Globe,* March 4, 1984.

76,   "What argument can still be made that education is 'a local matter?' "
77   Michael Fox writes of this issue in his own non-neutral way: "I think it is time for the President of the United States to declare that adult illiteracy is a national security problem. He should say that in the interest of saving the United States from crime, internal subversion, unemployment and poverty, all adults, 21 years and older, must be able to read at or above the eighth grade level . . . A literate America by 1990 is the target . . . To get there nothing less than national mobilization is necessary" *(The Ladder,* July/August 1983).

page

Jim Cates of the Texas APL states this in his own impassioned terms: "The problem is such that it will not be solved by committees, nor by conventions of persons whose main resource is good intent. Neither will it be solved by Federal hype or the pretense that the problem will go away if we gather collectively in the town square and think good thoughts. The problem of illiteracy is national and, as with other national funding needs, any productive solution must be federally inspired and funded . . . Left to their own devices, the local public educational systems are now contributing approximately one million incompetents annually to the national pool of functional illiterates. Once able to function at least marginally in a simpler time, additional legions of our population are being left behind by technological advance . . . We are hampered by a 'barn-raising' mentality that likens major problems to the simplistic gathering of a band of hardy pioneers coming to the assistance of a frontier neighbor in distress. The increasing sophistication of this society now requires leadership able to see beyond the first line of trees at the edge of the clearing and into the forest of national need. We hear much these days of the coming battle with our international neighbors . . . yet we ignore the consequences of having half our adult population face that battle armed with a pea-shooter. It is not difficult these days to believe that the promise of America may be hereinafter dispensed selectively . . . There is, I suppose, one reward for those who support the status quo. After another decade, who will know the difference?" (Open letter, cited above.)

The view of those who do support the status quo is reflected in these words from *Newsweek*, September 14, 1981: "It is no secret that Ronald Reagan means to do away with the Department of Education. It's just as clear that Secretary of Education Terrel H. Bell supports that goal; last month he sent Reagan a 91-page memorandum recommending that the President reverse a 25-year trend by expelling Washington from the nation's schools. This week a new national journal on elementary and secondary education, called *Education Week*, is publishing excerpts from that well-guarded memo. In it, Bell says bluntly that 'the Federal Government does not have responsibility for education.' "

79   "An unfriendly foreign power . . . act of war." The military metaphor soon became contagious. In a lead editorial two weeks after the Report of the National Commission was released, the Boston *Globe* praised the Massachusetts Board of Regents for having stiffened entrance standards in the state's public four-year colleges. The Regents' move, according to the *Globe*, is "somewhat in the nature of a preemptive first strike . . ." If a liberal newspaper in a city with pronounced antinuclear sympathies could use this terminology without embarrassment, we may imagine the phrasing used—and the climate fostered—in some of the more reactionary sections of the nation.

9. SUMMER 1983

80   Epigraph: See note for p. 80.

80,   "The world is words," Ellen once said to me. "It's like—how do you live if
81   you can't see? My mother only went to fifth grade. How do you explain
          certain things? She knew about cooking ham hocks, southern foods . . .
          Then she went to work for a wealthy family. You would say *gourmet* . . .
          Fancy cooking. She didn't know nothing but you show her a picture. You
          don't give her no instructions 'cause then she's confused." Reminiscing on
          her childhood, she said: "This woman—she was 80 years old. She couldn't
          read. But you give her a Bible. She could *read* it!"

          This story was recorded during August 1983. Since that time, Ellen has
          been spurred by her own courage and ambition to pursue aggressive pro-
          grams of instruction, some of it essentially self-education; but she has also
          enrolled in classes in a setting which has given her strong motivation to
          succeed. One day before very long, she may be writing her own stories and
          producing finished works for publication without mediation from her
          friends.

          Identifying details of Ellen's life and of her children's situation have been
          altered to protect their anonymity.

          "A scar on his forefinger . . ." This is a common souvenir of public educa-
          tion for the children who attended school in Boston in the 1960s. Many
          young adults in Boston's black community still bear those scars today. (See
          Death at an Early Age, by Jonathan Kozol, Houghton Mifflin, Boston,
          1967.)

81,   Requirements for entrance to the military: See notes for Chapter 15. What-
82   ever the formal standards, it is widely known that actual criteria for military
          service are pragmatically adjusted to absorb the needed number of recruits
          in any given year.

          Thomas Sticht: "Strategies for Adult Literacy Development" (unpublished
          paper), Applied Behavioral and Cognitive Sciences, Inc., San Diego, Janu-
          ary 10, 1984. Note that Sticht is not speaking here exclusively of literacy
          training in the military, but of literacy work conducted in several institu-
          tional settings: military, business, industry, etc. Nonetheless, his choice of
          wording ("missions") and his long identification with the military sector
          indicate that military programs are, if not his exclusive focus, unquestion-
          ably foremost in his thoughts. (One would seldom speak of "missions" in
          discussion of a literacy plan devised for Polaroid or Citibank.)

          Sticht has developed his views on literacy in the military in a number of
          publications. One of special interest is "Basic Skills in Defense," published
          by Human Resources Research Organization, Alexandria, Virginia, June
          1982. Although I differ sharply with some of his views, I do not wish my

page

criticism of the military programs in this chapter to be mistaken for a criticism of Sticht's positions. He is consistently more open, less constricted in his focus, and—above all—far less jingoistic than the mainstream organizers of the military's efforts. His open admiration for the literacy campaign in Nicaragua (cf. Chapter 10) would not, I suspect, be voiced by many of his colleagues.

82-
84

"Literacy Instruction in the Military," by Thomas M. Duffy, Communications Design Center, Carnegie Mellon University, November 16, 1983.

This remarkable document merits close examination. Much of the most frightening material has not been included in my brief summation. Duffy tells us, for example, that the Army recently developed a "portable" literacy program which can be carried by the soldier in a briefcase. Two of its initial exercises are described as "Picture Battle" and "Word War." Both are taught by a voice-synthesized speech duplicator which speaks to the soldier from a hand-held computer. The "Hand-held Tutor" (Duffy's term) is now being tested at Fort Stewart, Georgia.

In fairness to the Army, it should be added that the paper uses the expression "whole man focus" in description of the Army's job instruction. How much of "the whole" (or what sort of "a whole") the Army has in mind is not made clear.

84

C. P. Snow: *The Two Cultures and a Second Look,* cited above.

10. THE MYTH OF IMPOTENCE

89

Epigraph: Woodrow Wilson is quoted from "The Meaning of a Liberal Education" (an address to the New York City High School Teachers Association, January 9, 1909), *The Papers of Woodrow Wilson,* vol. 18, edited by Arthur S. Link et al., Princeton University Press, Princeton, 1974.

90

Two to four percent of all illiterate adults now being reached: Hunter and Harman, cited above.

91

Robert Frost: "The Gift Outright," *The Poetry of Robert Frost,* Holt, Rinehart & Winston, New York, 1969.

92

Infant death rate twice that of the middle class American: "Today, a black infant is twice as likely as a white infant to die before his or her first birthday. The most recent national infant mortality data broken down by race show that in 1981, 20 black babies per 1,000 died in their first year, as opposed to 10.5 white babies per 1,000. Had the black rate been the same as the white, 5,584 of the 11,756 black infants who died that year would have lived . . ." *(The Nation,* June 9, 1984). See also Boston *Globe,* June 3, 1984.

93   Sir William Berkeley: See *Virginia 1705–1786: Democracy or Aristocracy?* by Robert E. and B. Katherine Brown, Michigan State University Press, East Lansing, 1964. Berkeley, who lived from 1606 to 1677, was an almost exact contemporary of John Milton. Milton's passionate attacks upon oppressive policies of the Church of England, as well as his defense of the free press, receive an eloquent expression in *Areopagitica*. His ringing words stand in fascinating contrast to the fears of William Berkeley. For additional discussion of religious conflicts which underlay the fear of literacy, see notes to Chapter 12.

Similar fears were expressed in 1793 when Tom Paine's *The Rights of Man* —already having sold 200,000 copies—was banned in England as "seditious libel." Paine himself was driven into exile. Despite supression, the book had sold over a million copies by the time Paine died in 1809. The fear of "over-education" of the masses on the part of Tories finds expression in the words of Patrick Colquoquin, a London magistrate, in 1806: "The prosperity of every state depends on the good habits, and the religious and moral instruction of the labouring people . . . It is not, however, proposed by this institution, that the children of the poor should be educated in a manner to elevate their minds above the rank they are destined to fill in society . . ." The president of the Royal Society, in 1807, offered similar admonitions: "It [education of the working class] would teach them to despise their lot in life . . . , would render them fractious and refractory . . . , would enable them to read seditious pamphlets . . . , would render them insolent to their superiors . . . [In a few years] the Legislature would find it necessary to direct the strong arm of power against them." ("How Illiteracy Became a Problem," by James Donald, in *Boston University Journal of Education*, vol. 165, no. 1, Winter 1983).

95   Cuban literacy campaign: "Methods and Means Utilized in Cuba to Eliminate Illiteracy," Cuban National Commission for UNESCO, Havana, 1965.

95-   Paulo Freire's work in northeastern Brazil: interview with Freire, August 11,
96   1984. See also: *Pedagogy of the Oppressed*, by Paulo Freire, Continuum, New York, 1981; "Cultural Action for Freedom," by Paulo Freire, *Harvard Educational Review*, Cambridge, 1970; and *Pedagogy in Process*, Continuum, New York, 1978. Especially relevant: "The People Speak Their Word," by Paulo Freire, in *Harvard Educational Review*, vol. 51, no. 1, February 1981. For related insights in a North American setting, see *Theory and Resistance in Education*, by Henry A. Giroux, Bergin & Garvey Publishers, South Hadley, Massachusetts, 1983.

97   Thomas Sticht: interview with author, December 1983.

100   "Over-education" leads to "greater discontentment . . ." Warren C. Robinson, Pennsylvania State University (on leave), in *Policy Review*, The Heritage Foundation, Fall 1983.

11. UNEARTHING SEEDS OF FIRE: A PLAN TO MOBILIZE ILLITERATE AMERICA

102   Epigraph: *The Other America,* cited above.

103   "How do you reach them?" Author's interviews, Cleveland, Ohio, September to December 1980.

104   Inetta Bush, an adult learner in Washington, D.C., gives this answer: "We are your best recruiters. We can do your asking for you; we can do your talking for you" *(The Ladder,* May/June 1983).

104   "Certain meanings in their eyes . . ." Another example of the meanings that illiterates may read within the eyes of a prospective tutor or recruiter is reported in *The Ladder,* November/December 1983: "So I called up, what the heck, and set up an appointment. Before I knew it, I was walking around the block a few times getting my nerve up to go into the place. I finally made it through the door . . . They sent me to . . . the intake worker. She gave me that look that says, 'We know you have a problem.' Well, that's true, but I kept thinking while she was asking me a lot of questions that she has a problem too."

The Association for Community Based Education makes this point in discussion of recruitment: "Of the many approaches mentioned, certainly the most time- and labor-intensive is the door-to-door approach . . . However, the process has value beyond recruitment: It provides valuable data regarding community and participant needs which can be useful in the ongoing work . . ." The same report observes: "None of the groups surveyed reported having problems of recruitment. In fact for many programs, the problem is the opposite—having to turn people away, or place them on a waiting list, because the program is already stretched as far as it could be" *(Adult Literacy: Study of Community Based Literacy Programs,* 1983, a publication of the Association for Community Based Education, 1806 Vernon Street, N.W., Washington, D.C. 20009).

105   *Wall Street Journal,* January 17, 1984.

106   Methods of recruitment: See "Literacy Training in the South Bronx," a description of Bronx Educational Services, in *American Educator,* November 1983.

One common term employed by literacy experts in discussion of the agencies that offer services to the nonreader is especially revealing. The standard designation for these agencies is "providers." The term, which appears in virtually every grant proposal I have seen, suggests an age in which the rich were urged by priest or pastor to "provide" (or "make provision") for the poor. Few terms, so innocent in use and so familiar, could afford us better warning of the dangers of an attitude which can no longer be allowed to permeate our work.

page
107ff.   Quotations from Cleveland organizers and illiterates: author's interviews, cited above.

111   Ernest Boyer: *High School*, cited above. Also see: interview with Boyer in Boston *Globe*, September 15, 1983.

111   "Two-way tutoring . . ." One school where this has been done to good effect: South Boston High, Boston, Massachusetts. Headmaster Jerome Winegar is one of many high school principals who give their strong support to this approach.

112   Teachers and students in a literacy team: This is not my own idea. One high school English teacher whom I met four years ago in Indiana has been doing precisely this, with students in his twelfth grade classes. Dozens of others, whom I have not met, are now participating in these school-based "literacy teams" as a part of the routine course of study in their public schools.

114   "In Memory of Sigmund Freud," *Selected Poetry of W. H. Auden*, Vintage Books, New York, 1971.

Yves Dejean, Bank Street College of Education, New York: letter to the author, December 19, 1983.

115   Precedent for "buddy system": author's interview in Cleveland.

"I had a fellow in here . . ." *The Adult Illiterate Speaks Out*, cited above.

116   "Fernando . . ." Names and circumstances are, as always in these instances, disguised.

118   The primacy of the community: For information on community-based literacy action, contact Chris Zachariadis, Association for Community Based Education, cited above.

"A mutuality of learning . . ." The newsletter of Project Literacy, in San Francisco, describes its "learning circle" in these words: "We strive to create a lively and democratic form, a process that will develop trust, mutual respect and allow for a critical communication to develop among participants . . . A diverse group, spanning 25 years in age and including Black, Latin, Asian and white activists, educators, community workers, students, parents and grandparents, our initial stages have included a good deal of 'story-telling' as we seek to construct a way to hear and speak to one another." For information and newsletter, write: Project Literacy, Suite 200-1, 2940 Sixteenth Street, San Francisco, California 94103.

"Let me tell you where to hold these classes . . ." Author's interview in Cleveland.

page
119   "The ideal place . . ." Mike Fox, director of PLAN in Washington, D.C.,
            strongly disagrees. In his experience, the fears of self-identification in the
            neighborhood constitute a strong deterrent. Fox prefers a downtown center.
            Anything that Mike Fox did—in the neighborhood or far outside—would
            be successful, I suspect, because of his amazing energy and ingenuity. This
            case, in my belief, is an exception.

            The Association for Community Based Education seems to support my
            view: "An important factor in recruitment success seems to be the pro-
            gram's setting. Having programs in a familiar, nearby location, attended by
            and often staffed by people from the community, is an incentive in itself"
            (Adult Literacy: Study of Community Based Literacy Programs, cited
            above).

120,   *Unearthing Seeds of Fire*, by Frank Adams with Myles Horton, John F.
121   Blair Publisher, Winston-Salem, 1975.

121c   "The Moral Equivalent of War," in *Memories and Studies*, by William
            James, Greenwood Press, New York, 1968.

122d   The military role in CCC: *The Civilian Conservation Corps, 1933–1942: A
            New Deal Case Study*, by John A. Salmond, Duke University Press, Dur-
            ham, 1967.

122e   WPA, literacy, funding, and results: *The WPA and Federal Relief Policy*, by
            Donald S. Howard, Russell Sage Foundation, New York, 1943.

123f   Illinois Senator Paul Simon: His lecture is reprinted in *Functional Literacy
            and the Workplace*, cited above.

124h $26 billion for the MX missile: *Mother Jones*, August/September 1984. For
            $15 billion already approved, see: *Newsweek*, June 6, 1983.

125i   "The last thing an Establishment would do . . ." *Toward a Literate Soci-
            ety, The Report of the Committee on Reading of the National Academy of
            Education*, by John B. Carroll and Jeanne S. Chall, McGraw-Hill, New
            York, 1975.
                The same volume includes a valuable paper on "The Political Implica-
            tions of a National Reading Effort," by Natalie Saxe and Richard de Lore.
            The authors consider two approaches to a national awakening: one directly
            geared to the eradication of illiteracy, the other with a broader goal of better
            reading skills for all Americans. The latter, they believe, "might find a
            broader ready-made constituency of self-interest," since it would appeal to
            citizens of all economic classes. "But if a program has a broad constituency,
            there is likelihood that the advantaged will benefit more than the disadvan-
            taged: Inequality, if anything, will be increased . . . Even the best-inten-
            tioned reforms have a habit of simply consolidating the power of those who
            already have the power to institute the reforms: 'Helping' turns into a
            paternalism that either leaves the status quo unchanged or makes things

worse. Put in other terms, if illiteracy constitutes, among other things, a condition of powerlessness, one must examine closely the distribution of power and the implicit power relations within a program to combat it."

126   Dallas H. Wilson: quoted in *Pass It On*, newsletter of the Waccamaw Economic Opportunity Council, Inc., Conway, South Carolina, vol. 3, no. 2, June 1983.

127ff.   Words and details reconstructed from author's on-site visits and/or interviews with literacy workers and illiterate students, as well as from materials made available by the directors of these programs, 1983 and 1984. Documents employed in the construction of this composite include materials first published in *American Bookseller*, November 1983, and *Yale Alumni Magazine and Journal*, April 1984.

12. ORAL HISTORY: THE PEOPLE SPEAK THEIR WORD

132   Epigraph: *An Emerson Treasury*, edited by J. Pennells, Siegle, Hill and Company, London, 1977.

Materials developed by LVA: For information, contact Cambridge Publishers, The Adult Education Company, 888 Seventh Avenue, New York, New York 10106. See, especially, *What Is a Crime?*, *These Are Your Neighbors*, and *Memories of East Utica* (two volumes). Other LVA materials: Write Literacy Volunteers of America, 404 Oak Street, Syracuse, New York 13203.

See also: *Books for New Adult Readers*, published by Project: LEARN, an affiliate of Laubach Literacy Action, August 1982. For copies, send $5.00 to Project: LEARN, 2238 Euclid Avenue, Cleveland, Ohio 44118.

Many Laubach affiliates, as well as certain local ABEs, make use of oral history. Laubach is a flexible operation. While its official publications are traditional, some of its affiliates are eclectic and a number of its local leaders draw consistently on input from their students.

133   "Jack gets a job, etc." Stereotypes reported to the author by program directors. They are not directly cited from the sources.

135ff.   "Activated" words: I have drawn again upon the words of Yves Dejean (letter to the author, April 22, 1984).

136,   Author's interviews in Cleveland, cited above.
137

138   Reactions of Theodore Sizer, David Elkind, and Jeanne Chall: author's interviews and correspondence, 1980.

139 "To resurrect the continuity of time . . ." The Madison Literacy Council produces a "Student Literacy Newsletter" composed exclusively of stories told by learners, many drawing on their private histories. The council also produces a handbook, "How to Produce a Student Newsletter, Written by and for Beginning Adult Readers." Write to Madison Literacy Council, 406 East Wilson, Madison, Wisconsin 53703.

  In Lynn, Massachusetts, students from local high schools carried out an oral history/photography project in 1980. The project began with students hearing and recording history as told to them by older citizens. The book, entitled *Voices of a Generation*, is privately printed. One excerpt: "People who have lived the history of their community, frequently lack a social context of open dialogue with younger generations about their pasts. Often fearful and poverty-stricken, the elderly are usually isolated in nursing homes, projects or boarding houses. As a result, a sense of continuity between generations is lost, whole languages are forgotten and past traditions become occasions for secret suffering . . . We reach back to recapture that past, so that future generations will not forget . . ."

140 Literacy movements flowing from the Lutheran and English reformations: "Spreading the Word," by Daniel P. Resnick, in *Literacy in Historical Perspective*, cited above. According to Resnick, the growth of literacy flowing from the influence of Martin Luther reached a remarkable culmination in Scandinavia. In Sweden, between 1645 and 1714, basic literacy in males soared from 50 to 98 percent. See also: "Adult Illiteracy in the United States," essay by Carman Hunter, cited above.

  For discussion of the biblical tradition, and for much of the substance of this and the following pages, I am indebted to Charlesetta Alston, director of the San Francisco Adult Literacy Center. For further information on this woman and her work, write San Francisco Adult Literacy Center, Inc., P.O. Box 15508, San Francisco, California 94115.

141 It may be coincidence but, if it is, then there is also a degree of poetry at stake in the pre-eminence of Lutheran church people in some of the most effective literacy efforts in this nation. Martha Lane, of Lutheran Church Women, discounts the likelihood of any conscious motivation of this sort. Historical reverberations nonetheless are difficult to dismiss. Apart from producing valuable reports on local efforts, the organization has directly funded, among other projects, the work of PLAN in Washington, D.C. For an excellent summary of their work, assembled by Mark F. Wurzbacher, write to Martha Lane, Lutheran Church Women, 2900 Queen Lane, Philadelphia, Pennsylvania 19129.

141 The trivialization of reading matter in Great Britain: *The Uses of Literacy*, by Richard Hoggart, Beacon Press, Boston, 1961.

142 Impact of Calvin and the Puritan reformers: See Daniel P. Resnick, cited above. I am especially grateful to Truman Nelson for discussions of the Puritan tradition in New England. It is notable that one of the most memo-

rable early acts of the New England colonies was the promulgation of a drive for universal literacy. Even as dissenters splintered off into diverse religious groups in Massachusetts, the high esteem attached to education led to the establishment of Harvard College (1636) and to some of the first schools in the new colonies. William Berkeley meanwhile, an adherent of the Church of England (which, by that time, had reverted to more circumspect positions) shared the fears of English bishops that mass education would deprive them of their property and power. The contrast between Massachusetts and Virginia in the 1600s demonstrates one consequence of this divergence.

142   "If and when they do . . ." There are some ways of paying special tribute to those works of oral history, as well as poetry and private testament of other kinds, produced by newly literate adults. American PEN recently announced annual awards for writing done by prison inmates. The competition elicited over 1,000 entries from incarcerated authors. A similar award might someday be established for the work of newly literate adults. Authors such as "Ellen," quoted earlier (in Chapter 9), might find an incentive in the knowledge that such honors are accessible. Although I have cautioned against a false inflation of the literary work of newly literate adults, there is of course a vast amount of work by such adults which calls for no "inflation" to be worthy of esteem.

147   My thanks to Jon Deveaux (Bronx Educational Services), and to friends in Cleveland and in the Boston Community Schools, for many of the ingredients and some of the language that has been employed in this pastiche.

        $120 billion yearly to support our military men in Western Europe: Boston *Globe*, May 22, 1984.

        According to Thomas E. Cooper, Assistant Secretary of the Air Force, $700 million in spare parts—much of it still usable—was junked by Air Force officers in 1983 alone. Similar items were subsequently repurchased at a much higher cost. This one-year waste—what Cooper calls "a horror story" —would have been enough to fund 10,000 Family Learning Centers.

        13. Cause for Celebration (When the People Speak, the Nation Sometimes Has a Chance to Hear)

148   Curmie Price: interview with author, Cleveland, 1980.

149ff. Quotations from author's interviews in Cleveland, cited above.

149   "RIF" stands for Reading Is Fundamental. For information, write RIF, Department P, Suite 500, 600 Maryland Avenue, S.W., Washington, D.C. 20560.

150   "Ordinary trade books . . ." Other books which might well supplement the ordinary trade books I have designated here are those published by

page

Cambridge Publishers exclusively for newly literate adults (address cited above).

150,
151

The one-way library: This idea was first developed, to my knowledge, at the Storefront Learning Center in Boston's South End neighborhood in 1969 and 1970. The Center, like the block in which it once existed, has since been demolished and replaced by upper-income housing.

"The largest numbers of requests . . ." My own dogmatic preconceptions on this matter were sharply undercut by the response of many nonwhite young adults. One eighteen-year-old student whom I taught some years ago in Upward Bound looked at me with cautious humor when I first laid out my own idea of "relevant" materials. "Mr. Kozol," he asked, "do we have to study Malcolm X again?" Asked for his own preference, he selected Elie Wiesel's *Night,* as well as Dickens, Hemingway, and Shakespeare.

152

Millions of books are shredded yearly: Bantam Books alone, according to its own officials, shreds over one million copies yearly. Publishers have told me that "the shredder" is their choice of last resort. Several indicate that it would cost them less to give these books away.

14. TECHNOLOGICAL OBSESSION

157

Epigraph: pamphlet distributed to teachers in a Massachusetts school (origin unknown).

159

Bertolt Brecht: "In Praise of Learning," included in *The Politics of Literacy,* edited by Martin Hoyles, Writers and Readers Publishing Cooperative, London, 1977.

161

Computers in the classroom: IBM, in 1984, sold nearly 800 computers to the Boston Public Schools. According to the Boston *Globe,* "IBM is not just providing hardware . . . The company in effect will become the educator . . ." IBM already has launched a national program using its computers "to teach children how to write everything they know and to read everything they can write" (Boston *Globe,* August 1, 1984).

Aristotle's observation and discussion by W. J. Bate: "The Crisis in English Studies," in *Harvard Magazine,* vol. 85, no. 1, September–December 1982.

162

British use of television as adjunct to personal instruction: *Adult Literacy and Broadcasting: The BBC's Experience,* by David Hargreaves, Nichols Publishing Company, New York, 1980.

Some powerful statements on the dangers and the uses of technology are included in an essay by John Sawyer, president of the Andrew W. Mellon Foundation, adapted from an address delivered in New York City, April 1, 1982. See: "Thoughts on Humanistic Scholarship and Teaching in the

1980's and 1990's," by John E. Sawyer, in *Newsletter*, The American Council of Learned Societies, New York, vol. 33, no. 1 and no. 2, Winter/Spring 1982.

One hopeful sign of the survival of a humanistic emphasis in face of technological and careerist trends: "New Humanities School to Sail Against the Trend," by Fred M. Hechinger, New York *Times*, May 3, 1983.

15. The Obligation of the Universities

163   Epigraph: Richard Sennett, in *The Atlantic*, April 1984.

167   Departmental localism: "Units are no longer homogeneous entities informed by a common curriculum and common purposes. They are composed of diverse and autonomous faculties, which are themselves increasingly heterogeneous mixtures of independent and often unrelated departments. (Even the departments are frequently divided—into subdisciplines and semi-autonomous fiefs constituted by researchers directing large, externally funded projects.)" From "The Liberal Arts' Noble Vision, Employment-Related Education, and the Free-Market Curriculum," by Frederick Krantz, Concordia University, Montreal, in *Chronicle of Higher Education*, January 11, 1984.

168   *Constraint and Variety in American Education*, by David Riesman, University of Nebraska Press, Lincoln, 1956.

        Walter Jackson Bate's essay in *Harvard Magazine* is cited above.

        "Mending Wall," in *The Poetry of Robert Frost*, cited above.

169ff. *In Bluebeard's Castle*, by George Steiner, Yale University Press, New Haven, 1971.

170   *Matthew Arnold's Poems*, Oxford University Press, Oxford, 1913.

        The Renaissance, by Walter Pater, edited by Donald L. Hill, University of California Press, Berkeley, 1980.

171   *The Idea of a University*, by John Henry Newman, University of Notre Dame Press, Notre Dame, 1982.

172   Rockefeller study: *The Humanities in American Life, Report of the Commission on the Humanities* (chaired by Richard Lyman), edited by Gaines Post, University of California Press, Berkeley, 1980:

        "Classic, classical, and class . . ." The first writer to apply the term *classicus* ("first-class") to literature, Aulus Gellius, betrayed his social bias by adding the specific clarification *non proletarius*. I am grateful to Harry

Levin for having noted this. The "casual elisions" of which I spoke are not perhaps so casual after all.

16. Beyond Utility: Literacy Redefined

174   Epigraph: *Riders on the Earth,* by Archibald MacLeish, Houghton Mifflin, Boston, 1978.

Charles Muscatine: in conversation, New York City, December 9, 1982.

178   Sorting skills: "Many students believe that they will emerge from school into an electronic world that will require little reading and writing. Nothing could be further from the truth. In a world overloaded with information, both a business and a personal advantage will go to those individuals who can sort the wheat from the chaff, the important from the trivial. A society in which the habits of disciplined reading, analysis, interpretation and discourse are not sufficiently cultivated has much to fear" (National Assessment of Educational Progress, cited in *U.S. News & World Report,* May 17, 1982).

For another outlook on this question, see: "Cultural Literacy," a paper by E. D. Hirsch, presented at National Conference on Adult Literacy, Washington, D.C., January 19–20, 1984.

179   "Where is it . . . Why is it they don't like us?" The U.S. decision to leave UNESCO, announced in December 1983, represents a bitter index of the growing isolation of our government and people. Sissela Bok points to our government's reduced support for Fulbright programs as another symptom of our cultural isolation. Geographical fragmentation, she observes, is heightened by the policies of certain corporations—as well as by the Soviet and U.S. propaganda agencies—which now distribute inexpensive radios in politically contested regions. These radios, she points out, are so designed as to allow reception only of the broadcasts issued by the donor (conversation with Professor Bok, December 1983).

180   *The New Industrial State,* by John Kenneth Galbraith, Signet Books, New York, 1968.

181   *George Orwell, A Life,* by Bernard Crick, Penguin Books, New York, 1981.

182   Functional literacy two-dimensional: *Adult Functional Competency: A Summary,* University of Texas, Austin, 1975.

17. Borders

183   Epigraph: *The Two Cultures and a Second Look,* cited above.

page
183,   *The Tragedy of Hamlet Prince of Denmark,* by William Shakespeare, edited
184   by Edward Hubler, New American Library, New York, 1963.

184   The use of categories: I am indebted to Sissela Bok for discussion of this
           issue. For a fascinating examination of the ethics of concealment and revela-
           tion, see: *Secrets,* by Sissela Bok, Pantheon Books, New York, 1982.

           The inclination to divide and fragmentize our knowledge takes some of its
           origins from the Socratic period. Socrates and Plato, in E. A. Havelock's
           words, "created 'knowledge' as an object and as the proper content of an
           educational system, divided into the areas of ethics, politics, psychology,
           physics, and metaphysics. Man's experience of his society, of himself and of
           his environment was now given separate organized existence in the abstract
           word . . . Europe still lives in their shadow, using their language, ac-
           cepting their dichotomies . . ." (quoted in "Discourses of Power," by
           Adrian T. Bennett, in *Boston University Journal of Education,* vol. 165, no.
           1, Winter 1983). Whatever the "shadow" this has cast upon contemporary
           learning, the recent proliferation of our academic subdivisions—and the
           secretive divisions fostered by the military's impact on much scientific re-
           search—surely bring a heightened fragmentation which can hardly be at-
           tributed to Socrates.

185   *Selected Poetry of W. H. Auden,* cited above.

           Functional literacy: The term, employed by Dr. Norvell Northcutt in the
           early 1970s, is used today with serious reservations by his capable successors
           at the Texas APL. Unhappily, the term seems to have been frozen into
           public discourse.
               For a thoughtful criticism of this term in its persistent usage, see "Liter-
           acy and Minority Language Groups," a paper by Nina Wallerstein, Univer-
           sity of New Mexico, presented to the National Conference on Adult Liter-
           acy, Washington, D.C., January 19–20, 1984.

           According to David Harman, "The U.S. Army was the first to define func-
           tional literacy . . . during World War II . . ." ("Illiteracy: An Over-
           view," in *Harvard Educational Review,* vol. 40, no: 2, May 1970). Harman is
           not quite right. The U.S. Bureau of the Census used this term in 1940 and
           defined it as applying to any adult who had had less than five years of
           school. The earliest use of the term in the United States appears in publica-
           tions of the CCC during the 1930s. It was employed by military organizers
           of the CCC in reference to those adults who had received less than three
           years of schooling. The military origins of this expression seem explicit.
           ("Education of the American Population," by John K. Folger and Charles
           B. Nam, cited above.)

           In discussion of reading programs funded by the federal government, the
           Rockefeller study stated this concern: "However, the legislative language
           and goals . . . point to a narrow and quantitative definition of compensa-
           tory education and basic skills. This definition implicitly excludes the hu-

manities beyond the bare minimum of literacy. Literacy is the foundation for learning . . . , but when the government interprets literacy too narrowly it inadvertently impairs the educational foundation it intends to strengthen." William Berkeley would not have regarded it as inadvertent, but the emphasis is right and the concern is justified.

186   For examination of the concept of "competencies" as "a fixed inventory of skills that can be assessed outside the context of applications," see *The Psychology of Literacy*, by Sylvia Scribner and Michael Cole, Harvard University Press, Cambridge, 1981.

187,   J. Robert Oppenheimer: *Time*, September 29, 1961; *Secrets*, by Sissela Bok,
188   cited above; *American Scientists and Nuclear Weapons Policy*, by Robert Gilpin, Princeton University Press, Princeton, 1962.

188   C. P. Snow spoke of the two cultures in these words: "Persons educated with the greatest intensity can no longer communicate with each other on the plane of their major intellectual concern. This is serious for our creative, intellectual and, above all, our normal life. It is leading us to interpret the past wrongly, to misjudge the present, and to deny our hopes of the future. It is making it difficult or impossible for us to take good actions" *(The Two Cultures and a Second Look*, cited above).

"Too many boundaries . . ." Theodore Sizer, former headmaster of Phillips Andover Academy, has commented on the compartmentalization of subject matter by separate members of the high school faculty: "It will take a heroic leap for each of us to escape the entrapment of this manner of organization and the hold on us of our own disciplines" (Boston *Globe*, November 28, 1983). See also: *Horace's Compromise*, by Theodore Sizer, cited above.

190   *Walden and Civil Disobedience*, by Henry David Thoreau, W. W. Norton, New York, 1966.

"September 1, 1939," in *Selected Poetry of W. H. Auden*, cited above.

The term "schizophrenia" was first employed by Dr. Eugene Bleuler in 1910 in *Psychiatrisch-Neurol. Wochenschr.*, translated into English in *The Lancet*, 1912.

191   *A Portrait of the Artist as a Young Man*, by James Joyce, Penguin Books, Baltimore, 1976.

18. INSCRIPTIONS

193   "Excellence restored . . ." Truth is stranger than prophecy: "At a White House ceremony yesterday, President Ronald Reagan claimed credit for launching a school reform movement he said has ended 20 years of aca-

demic decline . . . The ceremony celebrated what Reagan called the 'electrifying' response across the country to the harsh verdict on U.S. schools rendered last spring by his National Commission on Excellence in Education . . . At the ceremony on the South Lawn, Education Secretary T. H. Bell released a report called 'A Nation Responds' . . ." (Boston *Globe*, May 12, 1984).

197   This initiative was undertaken with a grant from Harold W. McGraw, Jr., chairman of McGraw-Hill. For information, write: Business Council for Effective Literacy, 1221 Avenue of the Americas, New York, New York 10020.

Book Industry Study Group: "The 1983 Consumer Research Study on Reading and Book Purchasing," cited above.

AFTERWORD

205   *Death at an Early Age*, cited above.

President Reagan quoted: New York *Times*, December 9, 1983.

209   Blaming the left for educational decline: "The liberal reformers had a running field as open as it ever gets in the public-policy game, and they blew it. They failed. The state of the schools and the drop in test scores are an unanswerable indictment." (Editorial in the *Wall Street Journal*, cited in *Chronicle of Higher Education*, May 11, 1983).

211   Recent cuts in Title I: In 1982, what had been known as "Title I" was, in effect, translated into "Chapter One." Drastic cuts in Chapter One are not willingly conceded by Department of Education representatives. Officials in the Boston office, USDOE, speak of programs being "severely limited" at worst. Teachers do not hesitate to call it decimation.

212   Theodore Sizer: *Horace's Compromise*, cited above.

Statistics on teacher qualifications: *U.S. News & World Report*, March 14, 1983; Boston *Globe*, August 23, 1983.

Carnegie Foundation for the Advancement of Teaching: Average teacher salaries are summarized in a report prepared by Emily Feistritzer, cited in Boston *Globe*, August 23, 1983.

213   Salaries in Oakland schools: Oakland *Tribune*, February 27, 1983; interview with Diane Thompson, personnel office, Oakland Public Schools, August 1984.

214   Massachusetts certification: *The Humanities in American Life*, cited above.

page
215

Changes in certification and in colleges of education: New Jersey Governor Thomas Kean made suggestions to this effect in 1983. "Besides monetary inducements, he suggested changes in teacher certification rules . . . For example, college graduates who had not taken traditional education courses but who were skilled professionals in certain areas could obtain certification through one-year internships." (New York *Times,* September 11, 1983).

Massachusetts, unfortunately, appears to be moving in the opposite direction. "Promising students," reports the Boston *Globe* (July 21, 1984), "are being discouraged from pursuing teaching careers by new state certification regulations that place unnecessary burdens on liberal arts colleges, representatives of some private colleges say . . . 'They strike right at the heart of the notion that we want broadly educated people as teachers,' Jill Conway, Smith College President, said of the rules . . ." According to the *Globe,* the state's new regulations require prospective teachers "to spend 21 semester hours in education courses" and require that "programs in each discipline receive separate approval from the state." James Case, director of state certification, "scoffed at the charge that . . . the regulations were designed to protect the large teacher education programs at the state colleges and to force liberal arts colleges out of teacher preparation." The regulations, he conceded, "do favor institutions that have a larger commitment to teacher training and not those that give degrees with their left hand." Claiming that liberal arts preparation and the wish to be a teacher are not enough in today's schools, Case stated: "Yes, of course, we want to encourage lots of bright people to teach, but not at the expense of lowering standards." The *Globe* observed that, as a consequence of this decision, "a Harvard student who wants to teach" in Massachusetts has to settle for a job in one of its exclusive private schools. Case himself, ironically, holds degrees from both Princeton and Harvard.

Appendix: BILINGUAL LITERACY

220

"Only two percent . . ." *The Humanities in American Life,* cited above.

221

The National Commission on Excellence in Education observes that "proficiency in a foreign language ordinarily requires from 4 to 6 years of study . . ." It therefore suggests that foreign language study should be started in the elementary schools. Unfortunately, the same administration has been vigorously opposed to efforts that might open up our monolingual culture to bilingual education.

222

Oyster Elementary School: Washington *Times,* April 24, 1984.

223

"English Language Amendment": Dallas *Times Herald,* June 24, 1984.

ACKNOWLEDGMENTS

This book would not have been written if it had not been for Deborah Stone. She began this work with me when I was first examining the Cleveland situation, continued through the many years of growing resolution, and shared with me the virtually unending labor of the final eighteen months. In a decade when so many people Debby's age have chosen the ruthless competition and reactionary values that dismiss the suffering of those whom they are careful not to know, I am very lucky to have found an ally who embodies all the selflessness of a departed decade and who makes the future hopeful with her courage and her love.

Dozens of scholars have given me guidance in this work since its inception. For early advice, I am indebted to Asa Hilliard, Theodore Sizer, David Riesman, Jeanne Chall, David Elkind, Mark Shedd, Gaines Post, John Holt, and Ervin Gaines. For repeated help in locating unpublished documentation and statistics, I am grateful to Carmela Ruby, Art Ellison, Renée Lerche, David Crandall, Carman Hunter, Rhonda Kadavy, Gary Eyre, Thomas Sticht, and especially to Tisha Graham and Jon Deveaux. For detailed criticism and for personal encouragement, I have been helped by Roger Boshes, Truman Nelson, Yves Dejean, Peter Waite, Charlesetta Alston, Marguerita Huantes, Susan White, Marty Williams, and Michael James. I am particularly fortunate to have found in Phil Pochoda and Paul Aron two remarkable and patient editors. I would like to thank them both for their commitment to this book.

For unusually careful commentary on the final version of this book, I am indebted to Harry Levin, Irving Babbitt Professor of Comparative Literature, emeritus, at Harvard; Henri Peyre, Sterling Professor, emeritus, at Yale; Mike Fox, Director of "Push Literacy Action Now" in Washington, D.C.; Charles Schultz, Professor of Education at Trinity College; Jim Sears, Professor of Education at the University of South Carolina; and Jim Cates, Director of the Texas APL.

Early in this project, I was given generous support by Carol Bernstein Ferry, Charles Merrill, the Cleveland Foundation, the Jaffe Foundation, the Stone Charitable Foundation, and the Stop & Shop Foundation. Although my initial plan of work was very different at that time, and although I could not possibly have guessed the journey I would finally take, all of these groups and individuals were patient with the twists and turns that I pursued. Their backing came during a time when sustenance for research of this kind was difficult to find.

Finally I would like to thank those hundreds of illiterate adults who shared with me the fears and hopes with which they live. Only a few of those adults will read these words. Many, I hope, will live to write their own.

Index

A

B

INDEX 265

Democracy, illiteracy and, 23
Department of Defense, 83
Department of Education, 8, 9,
    28, 50
Dickens, Charles, 171, 172
Donne, John, 185
Duffy, Thomas, 82–84
Dulles, Alan, 187

E

Eastern Airlines, 20
Einstein, Albert, 173
Elderly people, as literacy
    tutors, 112–14
Elkind, David, 138, 166
Emerson, Ralph Waldo, 132,
    157, 198
Engels, Friedrich, 140
English Language Amendment,
    223

F

Fast-food chains, 31–32
Ferrer, Raul, 78
Florida State Department of
    Education, 46–47, 68, 69
Ford, Henry, 178
Ford Foundation study, 8
Frank, Hans, 169, 172
Freedom of the Press, 77
Freire, Paulo, 95, 96
Freud, Sigmund, 114
Frost, Robert, 91, 168–69

G

Galbraith, John Kenneth, 180
Gandhi, 101, 177
General Accounting Office, 83
Goebbels, Joseph, 178

H

Haldeman, H. R., 209
Hamlet (Shakespeare), 183–84
Harman, David, 8, 9, 114
Harrington, Michael, 12, 39,
    40, 72, 102
Harvard Law School, 19
Harvard University, 19–20
Head Start, 62n, 102
Health care, illiteracy and, 14,
    25
Heritage Foundation, 100, 154
Hicks, Louise Day, 94
Highlander Folk School, 120–
    21
Hispanics, 115
    bilingual literacy, 219–22
Hitler, Adolf, 178
Hoggart, Richard, 141, 142
Horton, Myles, 120
Howard Johnson's, 31
Howe, Harold, 197
Huddleston, Walter, 223
Humanism, 169–73
Hunt, Howard, 209
Hunter, Carman St. John, 8, 9,
    10, 64, 114